COVENANT & CONVERSATION
A WEEKLY READING OF THE JEWISH BIBLE
DEUTERONOMY: RENEWAL OF THE SINAI COVENANT

Other works by the author

A Letter in the Scroll / Radical Then, Radical Now

Celebrating Life

Ceremony & Celebration

The Dignity of Difference

Faith in the Future

From Optimism to Hope

Future Tense

The Home We Build Together

The Jonathan Sacks Haggada

The Koren Sacks Siddur

The Koren Sacks Maḥzorim

Not in God's Name

The Politics of Hope

To Heal a Fractured World

Rabbi Jonathan Sacks

COVENANT & CONVERSATION

A Weekly Reading of the Jewish Bible

DEUTERONOMY: RENEWAL OF THE SINAI COVENANT

The Goldstein Edition

Maggid Books & The Orthodox Union

Covenant & Conversation
Deuteronomy: Renewal of the Sinai Covenant
First Edition, 2019

Maggid Books
An imprint of Koren Publishers Jerusalem Ltd.

POB 8531, New Milford, CT 06776-8531, USA
& POB 4044, Jerusalem 9104001, Israel
www.maggidbooks.com

© Jonathan Sacks 2019

Cover image:
Detail from *Testament and Death of Moses*,
by Luca Signorelli and Bartolomeo della Gatta

The publication of this book was made possible through
the generous support of *Torah Education in Israel*.

All rights reserved. No part of this publication may be reproduced, stored in a retrieval system or transmitted in any form or by any means, electronic, mechanical, photocopying or otherwise, without the prior permission of the publisher, except in the case of brief quotations embedded in critical articles or reviews.

ISBN 978-1-59264-024-9, *hardcover*

A CIP catalogue record for this title is
available from the British Library

Printed and bound in the United States

כִּֽי־קָר֥וֹב אֵלֶ֛יךָ הַדָּבָ֖ר מְאֹ֑ד בְּפִ֥יךָ וּבִלְבָבְךָ֖ לַעֲשֹׂתֽוֹ׃
(דברים ל, יד)

For this word is very close to you;
it is within your mouth
and your heart to complete it.
(DEUT. 30:14)

With profound gratitude to our parents

GLORIA and ARNOLD GOLDSTEIN
and
MIRA and SAUL KOSCHITZKY

for instilling in your children, grandchildren and great-grandchildren a genuine love of Torah and learning.

And with enormous appreciation to

RABBI LORD JONATHAN SACKS

for inspiring the world with your scholarship.

Tamar and Eric Goldstein
תמוז תשע״ט
July 2019

Contents

Deuteronomy: Covenant Society

With the book of Deuteronomy, the entire biblical project becomes lucid and reaches its culmination. Deuteronomy is the last act of the Jewish people's drama before becoming a nation in its own land, and it forms the context of all that follows. It is the deepest and most remarkable statement of what Judaism is about, and it is no less relevant today than it was then. If anything, it is more so.

Among other things, the book tells us what Judaism is not. It is not a drama about the salvation of the soul and the rescue of humanity from the lingering effects of original sin. Indeed there is nothing in the Hebrew Bible about original sin, nor does the idea accord with its theology, according to which we are punished for our own sins and not for those of distant ancestors like Adam and Eve.[1] At the very most, the Bible talks about visiting the sins of the fathers on the children to the third and fourth generation,[2] not about doing so for hundreds of generations. Deuteronomy is not Christianity.

Nor is it Islam. The term *Islam,* meaning "submission" or "surrender" to the will of God, does not exist as a concept in Judaism at all.

1. Jer. 31:29–30; Ezek. 18:2.
2. For example, Ex. 20:15.

Strikingly in a religion that contains 613 commands, there is no Hebrew word that means obedience. The closest equivalent – *shema* – means not obedience but rather hearing, listening, striving to understand, internalising, and responding in deed. The very tone and texture of Deuteronomy is directed not at blind obedience but at the contrary: it is a sustained attempt to help the people understand why it is that God wants them to behave in the way that He does, not for His sake, but for theirs.

Deuteronomy roots Jewish law less in the arbitrary will of the Creator than in the concrete history of the nation and its collective memory of what it felt like to be slaves, without rights, without rest, without dignity, and without hope. We see in Deuteronomy precisely why the events of the book of Exodus were necessary. The people had to remember what it felt like to live within a society that accorded minorities no rights and that treated much of humanity as a corvée, a conscripted labour force.

Why, though, should religion be involved in society at all? Maimonides tells us that Judaism is directed towards perfection of the body and of the soul. The latter is higher in value, but it cannot be achieved without the former – by which he means perfection of society. For, as he says, "the well-being of the soul can only be obtained after that of the body has been secured." It is absurd to suppose that people can reach spiritual heights if they lack the most basic material necessities. "A person suffering from great hunger, thirst, heat, or cold, cannot grasp an idea even if communicated by others, much less can he arrive at it by his own reasoning." So a good society is a precondition of spirituality. This requires, first, "removing all violence from our midst," and second, "teaching every one of us such good morals as must produce a good social state."[3]

Hence the programme of Deuteronomy, which is fundamentally about the creation of *a good society based on collective responsibility*, or, as the opening phrase of the Preamble to the United States Constitution puts it, forming a group of "We, the people," under the sovereignty of God. The good society is the essential precondition of spiritual individuals, "since man, as is well known, is by nature social."[4]

3. Maimonides, *Guide for the Perplexed*, III:27.
4. Ibid.

Such a society is to be based on justice and *tzedaka*, meaning more than merely procedural justice, but in addition what we would call equity or fairness. Nor is that society to be based on abstract principles alone. Instead it is grounded in collective memory and active recall, in particular through celebrations at the Temple at various points of the year.

Underlying this thesis – that the life of faith requires a society dedicated to goodness as a whole – is the poignant story of Noah in the book of Genesis. Noah is the only person to be called righteous in the entire Hebrew Bible, but in the end Noah saved only his family, not his generation. He kept his own moral standards intact but failed to be an inspiration to others. Individual righteousness is not enough.

Likewise, it was not enough for Abraham and Sarah and their descendants to be a family or clan in the midst of a larger social unit. We see this repeatedly in Genesis. Every time a member of the family has some form of engagement with the wider society, they face danger, most often in the form of sexual assault. This reaches a terrifying denouement in Genesis 34, where Jacob's daughter Dina is abducted and raped by the local prince, Shechem. No one emerges well in this story, which is there to tell us that in the long run, individual piety is unsustainable without collective moral responsibility.

Deuteronomy is in essence a programme for the creation of a moral society in which righteousness is the responsibility of all. The good society was to be, within the limits of the world as it was thirty-three centuries ago, an *inclusive* if not an entirely egalitarian one. Time and again we are told that social joy must embrace the widow, the orphan, the stranger, and the Levite, people without independent status or means. It is to be *one nation under God.*

Freedom and Order: Can They Coexist?

To understand the significance of the Torah's ending we have to go back to the beginning. That was when, in shaping the universe, God created order out of chaos, *tohu vavohu*. Then, in a gesture of love and faith, He created human beings, endowing each with His own image and likeness. This was the most fateful act in creation; gifted with freedom, humans misused it, so that where there was order, now there was chaos.

The breakdown took two different forms. The first was *freedom without order*. First Adam and Eve sin and thereby lose paradise. Then Cain murders Abel and violence enters the human condition. Finally, with the generation of the Flood, "The Lord regretted that He had made human beings on the earth, and was pained to His very core" (Gen. 6:6). Freedom without order equals chaos.

The second form of breakdown is the opposite: *order without freedom*. This seems to be at least one of the themes of the story of the Tower of Babel. How we construe it depends on how we understand its opening sentence, "The whole world had one language and [thus] common speech" (Gen. 11:1). This might be a story about the beginning of human history, when everyone shared a single language and could freely communicate. On this reading, Babel is another story of paradise lost – the fragmentation of humanity into diverse cultures unable to communicate with one another.

However there is another possibility, based on the fact that in Genesis 10, the previous chapter, humanity had already been divided into seventy nations speaking seventy different languages. If Genesis 10 and 11 are in chronological sequence, then the story of Babel is not about some past golden age, but the opposite. Humanity had already developed into different cultures and languages. Babel represents the first empire and thus the first attempt by one culture to impose itself by force on others. That is what empires do: they force the countries they conquer – or at least their administrative elite – to speak the imperial language. That, for example, is why the languages of South America are Spanish and Portuguese. Empires stamp out local cultures, which they see as potential threats to their own hegemony. The Hebrew Bible is a sustained protest against empires and their attempt to impose a human unity on God's created diversity.

If that is so, then the Babel story is a critique of empire which imposes order by denying freedom to the mass of humanity. There is a telling midrash on this that says that while the tower was being built, when a human being fell to his or her death, no one noticed, but when a brick fell, people lamented.[5]

---

5. *Pirkei DeRabbi Eliezer* 24.

Babel aside, Genesis is in any case a sustained critique of empire, and urban life as a whole. We see this in the story of Lot and his two visitors. We see it again in the story of Shechem and Dina. We see it yet another time in the attempted seduction of Joseph by Potiphar's wife. Most fundamentally, we see it in the unfolding story of Exodus in which the greatest empire of the ancient world enslaves an entire nation of Hebrews.

If freedom without order equals chaos, then order without freedom equals slavery. Hence the fundamental question to which the Hebrew Bible is the answer. How can you have order without slavery? How can you have freedom without chaos? *How can you have law-governed liberty?*

To put it more basically still: *How can we create structures of cooperation in a world of conflicting human wills?* Then, and still today, there are three ways in which we can get people to do what we want them to do. The first is to pay them to do so – the market economy. The second is to force them to do so – the world of power and the state. In both of these, individuals remain individuals in pursuit of their own private interests and desires.

There is a third way: to get individuals to come together in a pledge, a bond, of mutual fidelity and collective responsibility. This is no longer a world of separate "I"s in pursuit of self-interest. It is a world of a collective "We," in which we agreed to merge our identity into something larger than us, which defines who we are and which obligates us to a set of undertakings by which we freely choose to be bound. This is the world of *covenant,* and it is what the Torah is about.

The World of Covenant

Covenants are an essentially secular phenomenon. They existed in the form of agreements between states in the ancient Near East. Fundamentally a covenant is a peace treaty. It can exist between states of roughly equivalent power, in which case it is a parity treaty. But it can also exist between states of radically different power, in which case it is called a suzerainty treaty. That is the story of Exodus and Deuteronomy, in which the Jewish people make a covenant with God.

This was revolutionary. Covenants were common in the ancient Near East. But covenants between God and a people were unknown, indeed inconceivable. It was unimaginable that God would seek to constrain His own powers in the name of righteousness and justice. It was unfathomable that a supreme power would make a treaty with any people on earth, let alone the supremely powerless.

The key covenant was made at Mount Sinai, as described in Exodus 19–24. This in principle should have been where the Torah reached its culmination. But it turned out not to be so. Despite the fact that the Jewish people agreed three times to accept the terms on which God was to become their sovereign, it was not yet ready for such responsibility. That is the significance of the story of the Golden Calf.

Bereft of Moses, unsure what had become of him, the Israelites sought an oracle, something to tell them what to do and what to become. They were still in an age of magical thinking in which people do what the gods require and gods produce the outcome the people desire. That is not what the biblical covenant is about. It is about *the acceptance of responsibility*. It is about being guided by the experience of history, not about having responsibility for history taken from the people and assumed by God Himself. Covenant is supremely an *ethic of responsibility*.

That is why there is a long hiatus in the story of the Exodus. The people have to learn to fight their own battles. They must discover that God is a force within, giving them strength, rather than a force outside that fights their battles for them. They must discern the God who is close – within the camp – and not one who is distant, who performs miracles, liberates the Israelites, brings plagues against the Egyptians, sends the people water from a rock and food from heaven, and divides the sea for them. God has to be *in the midst of the camp*, not just at the top of the mountain. That is, in essence, what the biblical story from Exodus 25 to Numbers 10 is about. It tells us that to have the Divine Presence *within the camp*, close, not distant, a special ethic has to apply: the law of holiness. That demands a Sanctuary, with all its associated laws. Above all, there must be no confusion or conflation between the domain of the holy, which is beyond time and mortality, and the secular, the ordinary, the world of mortality, marked as it is by death, disease, disfigurement, and defilement. The holy must be a radical break with the merely human. That is the basis of the laws of sacrifice and sanctity that take up this long diversion, comprising the last third of Exodus, the whole of Leviticus, and the first third of the book of Numbers.

All of this was the consequence of the Israelites seeking not just God-as-King, but also God-as-Presence. The key words here – *Mishkan* (Sanctuary), SH-KH-N, the verb "to dwell within," and the rabbinic Hebrew word *Shekhina*, "Divine Presence" – all have to do with the idea of closeness and intimacy. A *shakhen* is a next-door neighbour. The Israelites sought God in the midst of their collective life, in the town square, as it were. This too is part of what Deuteronomy is about: a society worthy of being a home for the Divine Presence.

What then is the significance of this *Mishneh Torah*, this repeated and renewed covenant, over and above the one made at Mount Sinai and described in Exodus 19 to 24? The short answer is: responsibility.

We have met covenants before. God makes one with Noah. He makes a further one with Abraham, and He makes a third with the Israelites at Sinai. But notice the difference. The covenant with Noah is entirely unilateral. God speaks, issuing certain rules, and nothing more is required from Noah himself. The covenant with Abraham is more demanding in the sense that Abraham himself has to perform an act – namely circumcision – for himself and the male members of his family. The covenant with the Israelites at Sinai is more demanding still in that God insists that Moses indicate the nature of the agreement to the Israelites, and only when they agree, which they do three times (Ex. 19:8; 24:3, 7), does the covenant have force.

But note that all three covenants begin with an act of divine initiative. The fourth, which comprises the whole of the book of Deuteronomy, is undertaken by human initiative. It is Moses who rehearses and recites the whole content and context of the covenant. That is why Deuteronomy is the turning point in Jewish history. It marks the move from divine initiative to human responsibility. Without Deuteronomy, the Israelites would not have made the necessary move to becoming not merely God's subjects but also His partners in the work of redemption.

Covenantal Language

Deuteronomy is a book about covenant and, in fact, the entire book is structured along those lines, as we will discuss below. Here, I want simply to show that Deuteronomy has a distinctive vocabulary, one that is key to the project of the covenant society. These are the distinctive words:

Listen

This, *shema,* is the single most important word of the book; it occurs no less than ninety-two times. I have already indicated that the use of this word rather than any term that means to obey is a clear signal that the Torah expects us to understand why certain things are commanded or forbidden. God is not a tyrant who rules our lives according to His whim. He is, rather, a teacher who expects us to understand as well as keep the rules.

However there is something more at stake here. Let me quote from my own moral tutor, the late Sir Bernard Williams: "The most primitive experiences of shame are connected with sight and being seen, but it has been interestingly suggested that guilt is rooted in hearing, the sound in oneself of the voice of judgement; it is the moral sentiment of the word."[6]

As Williams notes, our first desire on feeling shame is to be invisible. However, "with guilt, it is not like this; I am more dominated by the thought that even if I disappeared, it would come with me." This I believe is the fundamental theme of the story of Adam and Eve and the forbidden fruit. It is not a story, as is so often thought, about sexuality or even sinfulness as such. It is a story about the difference between seeing and hearing. Adam and Eve see something beautiful and want it, and allow their sense of sight to dominate their sense of listening to the divine word.

To use slightly different terminology, sight has to do with other-directedness, whereas hearing has to do with inner-directedness. This tells us that Deuteronomy is inviting the Israelites to follow their own inner voice, the voice of God within, rather than to see how others behave and seek to imitate them. So hearing is the fundamental verb of Deuteronomy.

Love

The next, strikingly, is love. The verb appears fifteen times in Genesis, but always between human beings. It appears twice in Exodus, and twice in

6. Bernard Williams, *Shame and Necessity* (Berkeley: University of California Press, 1994), 89.

Leviticus, in the famous chapter 19, the holiness code, where it speaks of love of the neighbour and of the stranger. In Numbers it does not appear at all. In Deuteronomy, however, it appears no less than twenty-three times, and almost invariably about the relationship between God's love of His people and His people's love for Him. Most famous is the command, "You shall love the Lord your God with all your heart, all your soul, and all your might" (Deut. 6:5). But no less powerfully, other passages speak of God's love for His people.

> The Lord did not set His affection on you and choose you because you were more numerous than other peoples, for you are the fewest of all peoples. But it was because the Lord loved you and kept the oath He swore to your ancestors that He brought you out with a mighty hand and redeemed you from the land of slavery, from the power of Pharaoh, king of Egypt. Know therefore that the Lord your God is God; He is the faithful God, keeping His covenant of love to a thousand generations of those who love Him and keep His commandments. (Deut. 7:7–9)

And again with surpassing beauty:

> To the Lord your God belong the heavens, even the highest heavens, the earth and everything in it. Yet the Lord set His affection on your ancestors and loved them, and He chose you, their descendants, above all the nations – as it is today. Circumcise your hearts, therefore, and do not be stiff-necked any longer. For the Lord your God is God of gods and Lord of lords, the great, mighty, and awe-inspiring God, who shows no favouritism and accepts no bribe. He upholds the cause of the orphan and widow, and loves the stranger, giving them food and clothing. And you are to love those who are strangers, for you yourselves were strangers in Egypt. (Deut. 10:14–19)

There is nothing dull or dry about the religious life as conceived by Deuteronomy. It is a tightly interconnected fabric of love, loyalty, and liberty.

Joy

The root S-M-Ḥ, to rejoice, occurs once in each of Genesis, Exodus, Leviticus, and Numbers, but no less than twelve times in Deuteronomy. The essence of life in the Promised Land is joy and thanksgiving. Indeed, the curses in Deuteronomy 28, unlike their counterparts in Leviticus 26, were prompted not by idolatry or wilful abandonment of the faith but simply "because you did not serve the Lord your God joyfully and gladly in the time of prosperity" (Deut. 28:42). Émile Durkheim called this "collective effervescence," and saw it as essential to the role of religion in bonding a society together as a moral unit.

Remembering, Not Forgetting

Repeatedly, Deuteronomy tells us not to forget, always to remember. Christine Hayes in her book *What's Divine about Divine Law?*[7] points out that there is a dispute throughout Jewish history as to whether the law has its source in divine will or divine wisdom. In Deuteronomy, however, it has its source in something else altogether, namely the shaping experiences of Jewish history, especially in the early years of the people, which we are to carry within us as memory and identity. We know what it feels like to be afflicted; therefore, we must not afflict others.

Handing On of Memory and Identity

We are commanded to talk about the laws of the Torah to our children when we sit in our house, walk on the way, lie down, and rise up. Deuteronomy continues the programme begun in the book of Exodus, and even before that in the comment that God chose Abraham "so that he will instruct his children and his household after him to keep the way of the Lord by doing what is right and just" (Gen. 18: 19). It is not enough to keep the law. We must hand it on across the generations.

A Covenantal Literary Structure

More perhaps than any other book in Torah, Deuteronomy is a highly structured work, blending together genres in a composite form that is

7. Princeton, NJ: Princeton University Press, 2017.

both unique and inspiring. The sages recognised this explicitly. Elsewhere in the Torah some rabbis held that the juxtaposition of passages – *semikhut haparshiyot* – was deliberate, so that we can always uncover a principle or proposition from the mere fact that passage Y occurs immediately after passage X. Others, however, did not, holding that *ein mukdam ume'uḥar baTorah,* meaning, the Torah does not always follow a strict chronological sequence, so there may be no significance to the fact that the passages are in the order they are. Yet everyone agrees that there is precise order and structure in the book of Deuteronomy (Berakhot 21b). But what is that order?

Additionally, the sages originally called this book *Mishneh Torah,* a "second law." Hence the Greek, *Deuteronomy,* which means "second law." But in what sense does the book constitute a second law? Some of the laws Moses states in the book have appeared before; others have not. Is it a repetition of the laws Moses received at Sinai and the Tent of Meeting? Is it something new? What exactly is the meaning of *Mishneh Torah*?

Moreover, the book represents the speeches Moses delivered in the last month of his life to the generation that would cross the Jordan and enter the Promised Land. Why is it included in the Torah at all? If the Torah is a history book, then we should proceed directly from the end of Numbers, the arrival of the Israelites at the banks of the river Jordan, to the book of Joshua, when they crossed the river and began their conquest of the land. If the Torah is a book of law, then Deuteronomy should just be a collection of laws without all the historical reminiscence and prophecy it contains. What kind of book is Deuteronomy and what is its significance to the Torah as a whole?

A number of archaeological discoveries have thrown new light on these questions. They are the engraved records of ancient treaties between neighbouring powers. Among them are the "Stele of the Vultures" commemorating the victory of Eannatum, ruler of Lagash in southern Mesopotamia, over the people of Umma, and the stele of Naram-Sin, king of Kish and Akkad, a treaty with the ruler of Elam. Both date from the third millennium BCE, that is to say, before the time of Abraham.

What the treaties show is the precise form of ancient covenants. They had six parts:

1. They began with a *preamble,* establishing the identity of the person or power initiating the covenant.
2. This was followed by a *historical prologue,* reviewing the history of the relationship between the two parties to the covenant.
3. Then came the provisions of the covenant itself, the *stipulations,* which were often stated in two forms, (a) general principles and (b) detailed provisions.
4. There then followed a provision for the covenant to be *deposited* in a sacred place and *read on a regular basis.*
5. Next came the *sanctions* associated with the covenant, namely the blessings that would follow if it was adhered to, and the curses that would occur if it is broken.
6. Lastly there was a statement of the *witnesses* to the agreement – usually the gods of the nations involved.

It is remarkable to note that this structure is mirrored precisely in the book of Deuteronomy. The entire book is, in fact, structured as an extended covenant, on precisely these lines. This is how it works:

1. Preamble	1:1–1:5	Announces place, time, and person initiating the covenant that follows: Moses on behalf of God.
2. Historical prologue	1:6–4:49	Moses recapitulates the history that has brought the people to where they are, mostly recalling the events described in the book of Numbers.

3. Stipulations	(a) 5:1–11:32 (b) 12:1–26:19	(a) General provisions: Ten Commandments, *Shema*, etc. Recapitulation of events surrounding the making of the covenant at Sinai. (b) Specific provisions: the details of the law, with special reference to how they are to be carried out by the people as a whole in the Land of Israel.
4. Deposition and regular reading	27:1–26; 31:1–30	The law is to be inscribed on stone (stele) at Mount Ebal; the Torah written by Moses will be placed in the Ark, to be read in public by the king at a national assembly held every seven years.
5. Sanctions: the blessings and the curses	28:1–69	Chapter 28 states the blessings and curses; 29–30 the actual covenant renewal, together with a statement that even if the people break the covenant and the curses come to pass, return, *teshuva*, is still possible.
6. Witnesses	30:19–32:1	"Heaven and earth" (Deut. 4:26; 30:19; 31:28; 32:1) serve as witnesses, as does "This song" (31:19).

In other words, apart from Moses' song and blessing of the tribes, with which the book and Moses' life come to an end, the entire book of Deuteronomy is a covenant on a monumental scale.

We now see the extraordinary nature of the book. It has taken an ancient political formula and used it for an entirely new purpose.

The structure of the book is now clear. It follows precisely the structure of an ancient suzerainty treaty between a strong power, God, and a weak one, the Israelites. Politically, such treaties were well known in the ancient world, but religiously this is unique. For it means that God has taken an entire nation to be His "partners in the work of creation" by showing all humanity what it is to construct a society that honours each individual as the image of God.

We now understand what *Mishneh Torah* means. It means that this book is a "copy" of the covenant between God and the people, made at Sinai, renewed on the bank of the Jordan, and renewed again at significant moments of Jewish history. It is the written record of the agreement, just as a *ketubba* is a written record of the obligations undertaken by a husband towards his wife.

We now also understand the place of Deuteronomy in Tanakh as a whole. It is the axis on which all Jewish history turns. Had the generation that left Egypt had the faith and courage to enter the Promised Land, all Jewish history would turn on the revelation at Sinai. In fact, though, the episode of the spies showed that that generation lacked the spirit to do so. Therefore the critical moment came for the next generation, when Moses at the end of his life renewed the covenant with them as the condition of their inheritance of the land. The four previous books of the Torah lead up to this moment, and all the other books of Tanakh are a commentary to it – an account of how it worked out in the course of time.

Deuteronomy is the book of the covenant, the centrepoint of Jewish theology, and the project it defines is unique. For it aims at nothing less than the construction of a society that would moralise its members, inspire others, and serve as a role model of what might be achieved were humanity as a whole to worship the one God who made us all in His image.

Deuteronomy: A Political Theory

No book of the Hebrew Bible so fuses theology, spirituality, morality, and law. And the central emphasis is on society, rather than on the individual and his or her relationship with God. So, for example, in the first account of the Ten Commandments, in the book of Exodus, the reason for keeping Shabbat is because God created the universe in six days and rested on the seventh. In Deuteronomy, however, Shabbat is given a quite different logic, namely, the importance of freedom:

> The seventh day is a sabbath to the Lord your God. On it you shall not do any work, neither you, nor your son or daughter, nor your male or female servant, nor your ox, your donkey, or any of your animals, nor any foreigner residing in your towns, so that your male and female servants may rest, as you do. (Deut. 5:14)

Likewise the festivals: elsewhere they are related to the historic events that brought them into existence, or the sacrifices to be offered on those days. However in Deuteronomy, the festivals are about collective celebration: "You, your sons and daughters, your menservants and maidservants, the Levites in your towns, and the strangers, the fatherless, and the widows living among you" (Deut. 16:11).

Equally remarkable is the very limited space devoted to two of the central institutions of the covenant society. The Temple is not directly referenced at all, neither the building nor its location, despite the strong insistence throughout Deuteronomy that there be a single central Sanctuary. Even more remarkably, the king, linchpin of the political system, is given no special powers of legislation. There is no metaphysical justification for there to be a political head of the nation – unlike those that existed in virtually every other ancient religious document. Uniquely, the king had no legislative role. He, like anyone else, was subject to the law, not its author.

What we have in Deuteronomy, in other words, is a political theory of immense depth and power. Nor was this confined to the biblical period alone. It became the inspiration of the modern movement in the direction of liberal democracy. This was due to the fact that there was not one form of protest against the Roman Catholic Church in the sixteenth century, but two. One, developed by Luther, focused on Paul and the New Testament. The other, developed by Calvin, drew its inspiration from the Hebrew Bible, especially the book of Deuteronomy. That meant that Calvinist regions – such as Geneva, Holland, Scotland, and

England, as well as the Pilgrim Fathers of the United States – developed strong civil societies, whose basic understanding of morality was identical with that of the book of Deuteronomy.

Specifically, these societies emphasised the responsibilities, individual and collective, of each member of the society, and not the overarching responsibility of the head of state or of government.[8] Thus the political philosophy of Deuteronomy has direct and immediate relevance to the issues faced by the contemporary West. As Eric Nelson writes in his *The Hebrew Republic*, the roots of modern politics are indeed biblical rather than Greek – the philosophy that prevailed during the Renaissance.[9]

Deuteronomy tells us that freedom requires engagement by each of us; it cannot be delegated away or outsourced to governments alone. It tells us that we need to preserve our collective memories if we are to safeguard our identity and keep faith with the past for the sake of the future and for generations not yet born. It is a brilliant, beautiful fusion of high religious sentiment and detailed social legislation that has never been surpassed. It was and remains a political classic, reminding us of the fundamental truth that we are in danger of forgetting: that a free society is a moral achievement, and without active citizenship exercised for the common good, we will lose that freedom which is God's greatest gift to us.

---

8. I have set out my account of this political philosophy in three books: *The Politics of Hope* (London: Jonathan Cape, 1997), *The Home We Build Together* (London: Continuum, 2007), and *The Dignity of Difference* (London: Continuum, 2003).
9. Eric Nelson, *The Hebrew Republic: Jewish Sources and the Transformation of European Political Thought* (Cambridge, MA: Harvard University Press, 2010).

Devarim
דברים

As we noted in the introduction, the book of Deuteronomy as a whole is structured on the model of a covenant, and represents Moses' renewal of the Sinai covenant with the next generation, who would enter the Promised Land and there create a covenant-based society. Accordingly, the *parasha* of *Devarim* opens with the first two elements of a covenant document: a preamble identifying the speaker and context (Deut. 1:1–5) and a historical prologue recalling the events that led to the covenant and its renewal (beginning at 1:6).

The preamble identifies time and place: the last weeks of Moses' life, with the people encamped by the banks of the Jordan. Moses recalls his appointment of leaders, the sending of the spies, and the people's failure of nerve that led to the forty-year stay in the wilderness. Moving to more recent episodes, he reminds the people of their victories over Moab and Ammon and the settlement of their land by the tribes of Reuben and Gad and part of Menashe. The *parasha* ends with Moses' description of his appointment of, and encouragement to, Joshua as his successor.

The first of the following essays is about the change in Moses' role in these last weeks of his life, as he becomes the great exemplar of the teacher as hero. The second is about how the name of the book – *Devarim*, "words" – precisely encapsulates its three primary messages. The third focuses on the rabbinic interpretation of a place name and what it tells us about leadership. The fourth is about a key word of Deuteronomy, *tzedek*, and its precise nuance as justice tempered by compassion. The fifth is about the first chapter of Isaiah, read as the *haftara* to our *parasha* and the prelude to the fast of Tisha B'Av.

The Teacher as Hero

Imagine the following scenario. You are 119 years and 11 months old. The end of your life is in sight. Your hopes have received devastating blows. You have been told by God that you will not enter the land to which you have been leading your people for forty years. You have been repeatedly criticised by the people you have led. Your sister and brother, with whom you shared the burdens of leadership, have predeceased you. And you know that neither of your children, Gershom and Eliezer, will succeed you. Your life seems to be coming to a tragic end, your destination unreached, your aspirations unfulfilled. What do you do?

We can imagine a range of responses. You could sink into sadness, reflecting on the might-have-beens had the past taken a different direction. You could continue to plead with God to change His mind and let you cross the Jordan. You could retreat into memories of the good times: when the people sang a song at the Red Sea, when they gave their assent to the covenant at Sinai, when they built the Tabernacle. These would be the normal human reactions. Moses did none of these things – and what he did instead helped change the course of Jewish history.

For a month Moses convened the people on the far side of the Jordan and addressed them. Those addresses form the substance of the book of Deuteronomy. They are extraordinarily wide-ranging, covering a history of the past, a set of prophecies and warnings about the future, laws, narratives, a song, and a set of blessings. Together they constitute the most comprehensive, profound vision of what it is to be a holy people, dedicated to God, constructing a society that would stand as a role model for humanity in how to combine freedom and order, justice and compassion, individual dignity and collective responsibility.

Over and above what Moses *said* in the last month of his life, though, is what Moses *did*. He changed career. He shifted his relationship with the people. No longer Moses the liberator, the lawgiver, the worker of miracles, the intermediary between the Israelites and God, he became the figure known to Jewish memory: *Moshe Rabbenu*, "Moses, our teacher." That is how Deuteronomy begins – "Moses began to expound this Law" (Deut. 1:5) – using a verb, *be'er*, that we have not encountered in this sense in the Torah and which appears only one more time towards the end of the book: "And you shall write very clearly [*ba'er hetev*] all the words of this law on these stones" (27:8). He wanted to explain, expound, make clear. He wanted the people to understand that Judaism is not a religion of mysteries intelligible only to the few. It is – as he would say in his very last speech – an "inheritance of the [entire] congregation of Jacob" (33:4).

Moses became, in the last month of his life, the master educator. In these addresses, he does more than tell the people *what* the law is. He explains to them *why* the law is. There is nothing arbitrary about it. The law is as it is because of the people's experience of slavery and persecution in Egypt, which was their tutorial in why we need freedom and law-governed liberty. Time and again he says: You shall do this because you were once slaves in Egypt. They must *remember* and never *forget* – two verbs that appear repeatedly in the book – where they came from and what it felt like to be exiled, persecuted, and powerless. In Lin-Manuel Miranda's musical *Hamilton*, George Washington tells the young, hot-headed Alexander Hamilton: "Dying is easy, young man; living is harder." In Deuteronomy, Moses keeps telling the Israelites, in effect: Slavery is easy; freedom is harder.

Throughout Deuteronomy, Moses reaches a new level of authority and wisdom. For the first time we hear him speak extensively in his own voice, rather than merely as the transmitter of God's words to him. His grasp of vision and detail is faultless. He wants the people to understand that the laws God has commanded them are for their good, not just God's.

All ancient peoples had gods. All ancient peoples had laws. But their laws were not from a god; they were from the king, pharaoh, or ruler – as in the famous law code of Hammurabi. The gods of the ancient world were seen as a source of power, not justice. Laws were man-made rules for the maintenance of social order. The Israelites were different. Their laws were not made by their kings – monarchy in ancient Israel was unique in endowing the king with no legislative powers. Their laws came directly from God Himself, creator of the universe and liberator of His people. Hence Moses' ringing declaration: "Observe [these laws] carefully, for this will show your wisdom and understanding to the nations, who will hear about all these decrees and say, 'Surely this great nation is a wise and understanding people'" (Deut. 4:6).

At this defining moment of his life, Moses understood that, though he would not be *physically* with the people when they entered the Promised Land, he could still be with them intellectually and emotionally if he gave them the teachings to take with them into the future. Moses became the pioneer of perhaps the single greatest contribution of Judaism to the concept of leadership: the idea of *the teacher as hero*.

Heroes are people who demonstrate courage in the field of battle. What Moses knew was that the most important battles are not military. They are spiritual, moral, cultural. A military victory shifts the pieces on the chessboard of history. A spiritual victory changes lives. A military victory is almost always short-lived. Either the enemy attacks again or a new and more dangerous opponent appears. But spiritual victories can – if their lesson is not forgotten – last forever. Even quite ordinary people, Yiftah, for example, or Samson, can be military heroes. But those who teach people to see, feel, and act differently, who enlarge the moral horizons of humankind, are rare indeed. Of these, Moses was the greatest.

Not only does *he* become the teacher in Deuteronomy. In words engraved on Jewish hearts ever since, he tells the entire people that they must become *a nation of educators*:

> *Make known to your children and your children's children,* how you once stood before the Lord your God at Horeb. (Deut. 4:9–10)

> *Teach [these words] repeatedly to your children,* speaking of them when you sit at home and when you travel on the way, when you lie down and when you rise. (Deut. 6:7)

> *In the future, when your child asks you,* "What is the meaning of the testimonies, decrees, and laws that the Lord our God has commanded you?" tell him, "We were slaves to Pharaoh in Egypt, but the Lord brought us out of Egypt with a mighty hand...." (Deut. 6:20–21)

> *Teach them to your children,* speaking of them when you sit at home and when you travel on the way, when you lie down and when you rise. (Deut. 11:19)

Indeed, the last two commands Moses gave the Israelites were explicitly educational in nature: to gather the entire people together in the seventh year to hear the Torah being read, to remind them of their covenant with God (Deut. 31:12–13), and, "Write down for yourselves this song and teach it to the people of Israel" (31:19), understood as the command that each person must write for himself a scroll of the law.

In Deuteronomy, a new word enters the biblical vocabulary: the verb L-M-D, meaning to learn or teach. The verb does not appear even once in Genesis, Exodus, Leviticus, or Numbers. In Deuteronomy it appears seventeen times.

There was nothing like this concern for universal education elsewhere in the ancient world. Jews became the people whose heroes were teachers, whose citadels were schools, and whose passion was study and the life of the mind.

Moses' end-of-life transformation is one of the most inspiring in all of religious history. In that one act, he redeemed his career from tragedy. He became a leader not for *his* time only but for *all* time. His body did not accompany his people as they entered the land, but his teachings did. His sons did not succeed him, but his disciples did. He may have felt that he had not changed his people in his lifetime, but in the full perspective of history, he changed them more than any leader has ever changed any people, turning them into the people of the book and the nation who built not ziggurats or pyramids but schools and houses of study.

The poet Shelley famously said, "Poets are the unacknowledged legislators of the world."[1] In truth, though, it is not poets but teachers who shape society, handing on the legacy of the past to those who build the future. That insight sustained Judaism for longer than any other civilisation, and it began with Moses in the last month of his life.

1. Percy Bysshe Shelley, "A Defence of Poetry," in *The Selected Poetry and Prose of Shelley*, ed. Harold Bloom (Toronto: New American Library, 1996), 448.

The World We Make with Words

The fifth book of the Torah was originally known to the sages as *Mishneh Torah,* a restatement of the law. Hence the English name Deuteronomy, from the Greek *deuteros nomos,* or "second law." It was called this because in it Moses reviews the history of the Israelites after leaving Egypt and recapitulates the main contents of the law. This is no mere repetition. There are laws Moses mentions in the book that have not been stated before, and others that have been stated before that he does not mention. Even his retelling of certain events differs here from elsewhere. So, for instance, in Numbers it is God who tells Moses to send the spies, whereas in *Parashat Devarim* it is the people who ask for them to be sent.[1]

The differences have to do with time, place, and context. In Deuteronomy, Moses is speaking forty years after the Exodus. The Israelites have arrived at the far side of the Jordan, within sight of the Promised Land. The people themselves have changed. They are no longer the generation born in slavery; they are the generation about to enter and conquer the land. Moses consistently speaks to the nation as a whole,

1. Num. 13:2; Deut. 1:22.

reminding the people of the society they are about to create, the temptations to which they will be exposed, and the faith they must carry with them. The book is not so much a "second" law as a reframing of the law as a whole, a vision of a society under the sovereignty of God and of Israel as an *am kadosh*, a "holy people," a phrase that appears four times in the book but nowhere else in Tanakh.[2]

However, tradition came to know the fifth book, as it did the other four, not by reference to subject matter but by a key word appearing in the first verse. This seems to be random and incidental, but I have argued in the case of the other books that these names convey important insights into their overarching themes. The same is true about the book known to Jewish tradition not as *Mishneh Torah* but as *Devarim*, "words," taken from the opening verse: "These are the *words* Moses spoke to all Israel in the desert, east of the Jordan."

The name "words" seems bland and unspecific. Is not the whole of Torah "words"? Why this book in particular? What is the connection between the title and the contents? What insight does the name yield into the nature of this, the last of the five Mosaic books? I believe the insight is profound, and it points to three dimensions of this magnificent and world-changing work.

The first is about Moses himself. He is a man transformed. Recall his words to God at the burning bush at the very outset of his mission: "Moses said to the Lord, 'O Lord, I have never been a man of words [*ish devarim*], neither in the past nor since You have spoken to Your servant. I am slow of speech and tongue'" (Ex. 4:10). The individual who said "I have never been a man of words" becomes, at the end of his life, the man of words, the most eloquent spokesman of God in all history. The speeches of Deuteronomy reach to the furthermost horizons of the

2. In Exodus 19:6, Israel is summoned to be a *goy kadosh*, a "holy nation," but there is a difference between a nation and a people. *Goy* is related to the word *geviya*, "a body," and is thus a metaphor for a group seen as an integrated body politic. According to Malbim, a *goy* is marked by four characteristics: shared territory, shared language, shared ethnicity, and shared political structure. It would follow that *am* is a more fundamental quality linking people who remain connected with one another even in exile and dispersion. In contemporary terms, Israel is a nation in its land, while Jews, whether in Israel or the Diaspora, are a people.

prophetic imagination. And they are Moses' words. That is the point. In the other four books of the Pentateuch the narrative voice is anonymous – "And it came to pass" – while the commanding voice is the voice of God – "And God spoke these words, saying…" What is unique about Deuteronomy is that it is the reported speech of a human speaker. But how can the words of a human being be divine?

Each time we pray the supreme prayer, the *Amida*, we begin by saying silently a verse from Psalms: "O Lord, open my lips, and my mouth shall declare Your praise" (Ps. 51:17). At the highest point of the encounter with God, we do not speak: we are spoken. We open our mouths but the words we utter do not come *from* us, though they come *through* us. Prayer, like prophecy, is an extinction of the self (known in Jewish mysticism as *bittul hayesh*) in the presence of the One-who-is-all.

For everyone else except Moses this extinction is partial, never complete. Even the greatest of the other prophets retained something of themselves, colouring and giving distinctive character to their prophecies. Of Moses alone – "more humble than any man on the face of the earth" (Num. 12:3) – could it be said that his words, *devarim*, were the words of God. It was precisely because he said "I have never been a man of words" that he became the man of *devarim*, the one whose words were not his own but those of the Divine Presence, the *Shekhina*, speaking through his lips.[3]

The second significance is political. The last book of the Pentateuch is the supreme covenantal document in history. It is the foundational text of covenantal politics.

The late Daniel Elazar, the political scientist who pioneered the academic study of covenantal politics, explains that there are three fundamental types of political structure, differentiated by the way they come into existence.[4] The first is by *conquest*. This produces hierarchical regimes: the conqueror on top, his agents in the middle, and the people underneath. The second is by *organic development*, from families to tribes

3. See Megilla 31b; Maharal, *Tiferet Yisrael*, ch. 22; *Or HaḤayim* to Deut. 1:1; commentary of Rabbi Yaakov Emden to Sanhedrin 99a.
4. See Daniel Elazar, *Covenant and Polity in Biblical Israel: Biblical Foundations and Jewish Expressions* (London: Routledge, 1994), 35–50.

to large national structures. In such societies, elites emerge and political power gravitates into their hands. The third is by *covenant*. Covenant societies "emphasize the deliberate coming together of humans as equals" to establish societies that "reaffirm their fundamental equality and retain their basic rights."[5] The great age of covenantal politics was the seventeenth century, when the Swiss, Dutch, Scots, English Puritans, and American Founding Fathers "conceived of civil society in covenantal terms" and "wrote national covenants to which loyal members of the body politic subscribed."[6]

It is no accident that covenant emerged as the key idea in the seventeenth century, for it was then, under the twin influence of the Reformation and the spread of printing, that Europeans for the first time read the Hebrew Bible for themselves, in their homes and in their own language. Western freedom is biblical freedom.

If conquest represents *the politics of power*, and organic development *the politics of the elite*, covenant is *the politics of the word*. It involves a document, such as the American Declaration of Independence, to which all sides agree to be bound. Indeed, the very existence of nations defined by covenant depends on *devarim*, words.

Covenants involve a highly specialised use of language to which the Oxford philosopher John L. Austin gave the name *performative utterance*.[7] Normally, language is used to describe or express. Occasionally, however, it is used to create – and what it creates are moral relationships, obligations. When I say "I promise to" I do not merely *describe* a promise, I *make* one.

A covenant is a mutually binding promise. At Mount Sinai, Israel became a nation brought into being by a mutually binding pledge between the people and God in which God adopted the people as His own, and the people agreed to be bound by His word. At the climax of the book of Deuteronomy, in chapter 29, Moses renews the covenant with the next generation.

5. Ibid., 38.
6. Ibid., 20.
7. John L. Austin, *How to Do Things with Words* (Oxford: Clarendon Press, 1962).

So the second significance of *devarim*, "words," is that it is the supreme expression of the politics of the word: a society founded on the basis of a covenant, a text, a set of mutual promises, by which God and His people pledge themselves in loyalty to one another.

The third significance is in some ways the most moving. The history of Israel is unique. Other civilisations have come and gone. The people Israel has survived – under circumstances that rendered its survival improbable, seemingly impossible. No other nation has preserved its identity under conditions of exile and dispersion as a minority without power and often without rights. None has so consistently refused assimilation to the dominant culture or conversion to the dominant faith. How did it happen? That it happened because of divine providence I believe with perfect faith. But how exactly?

The answer lies in one of the key texts of Judaism, from the prophet Hosea:

> Return, O Israel, to the Lord your God.
> Your sins have been your downfall!
> Take words [*devarim*] with you
> and return to the Lord. (Hos. 14:2)

The meaning of this verse is that Hosea is speaking about repentance (confession, apology, resolution) as opposed to sacrifices: "Offer words, not animals." Beneath the surface, however, Hosea is saying something more fundamental. Your relationship with God is based on words – the Torah that constitutes the covenant, the marriage contract, between Israel and its sovereign Lord.

A politics based on power comes to an end when a nation is defeated and loses power. A politics based on organic development, on the long experience of a people living together in the same land, is destroyed when the people are uprooted from the land and scattered over the face of the earth. Neither of these two forms of national existence can survive defeat and dispersion. Once lost, they are gone, never to return.

Israel's existence as a nation, however, is not based on power or a land (though it longs for and is promised both) but on words – the words of God to Israel and the acceptance of those words by Israel. *So long as the word exists, Israel exists; and because God is eternal and never revokes His word, Israel will always exist.* Because Israel's very being as a nation is constituted by *devarim,* the "words" of God, there is always the possibility and promise of return. Israel, alone among the nations of the world, survives the loss of power and land because there is something it will never lose: God's word given and received in love. "Take words" – the words of the covenant – "with you and return to the Lord."

Israel survived because it never lost the words that bound it to God and God to it. That was the basis of its survival in exile. Those "words" were never rescinded. Hence Israel never lost the promise of return.

So the decision to call the fifth and final book of the Torah *Devarim* was neither random nor insignificant. It brought together in a single word the three main themes of the book: the uniqueness of Moses as a prophet, the uniqueness of Israel as a nation, and the uniqueness of Jewish history as a narrative of exile and return. The book of *Devarim,* "words," is the supreme expression of the power of the word to link heaven and earth, God and a people, in an unbreakable bond of mutual loyalty.

Today, more than three thousand years later, we are in a position to understand in the full survey of history that words proved more powerful than power and more lasting than land. The word lives and gives life to the people who dedicate their life to the word.

Counsel for the Defence

There are times when, beneath the surface of an apparently simple verse, an intense drama is taking place. So it is with the opening verse of *Parashat Devarim*.

The text seems simple enough. "These are the words Moses spoke to all Israel in the desert east of the Jordan, in the Aravah, opposite Suph, between Paran and Tophel, Laban, Hazeroth and Di Zahav" (Deut. 1:1). The sages, however, sensitive to the slightest nuance, heard something strange and suggestive in these words.

What is Di Zahav? Clearly it is the name of a place. But it has not been mentioned before. How then does it help us locate where the great last speeches of Moses took place, if we have no way of knowing where it was?

Besides which, the name itself is suggestive. *Di Zahav* means "enough gold." Might there not be a subtle reference here to an episode which involved gold – namely, the Golden Calf, the worst sin of the previous generation? On this slender basis, the sages built one of their most daring interpretations:

> Moses spoke audaciously towards Heaven.... The school of R. Yannai learned this from the words "*Di Zahav*." What do these

> words mean? They said in the school of R. Yannai: Thus spoke Moses before the Holy One, Blessed Be He: Sovereign of the universe, the silver and gold which You showered on Israel until they said, Enough, was what caused them to make the calf.... R. Ḥiyya b. Abba said: It is like the case of a man who had a son. He bathed him and anointed him and gave him plenty to eat and drink and hung a purse around his neck and set him down at the door of a house of ill-repute. How could he help sinning? (Berakhot 32a)

Moses, in this dramatic re-reading, has been transformed into counsel for the defence. Yes, he says to God, the people committed a sin. But it was You who gave them the opportunity and the temptation. Without gold, they could not have made the calf. Who told them to ask their Egyptian neighbours for gold? It was You.[1] This was not something they did of their own accord. Therefore You must not blame them. Please, instead, forgive them.

We hear, in this aggadic passage, one of the most striking and humane motifs in rabbinic thought. It is called *limmud zekhut,* the act of judging favourably or arguing the case for the defence. It means placing a positive construction on events, pleading a cause, setting forth the case for mercy or at least mitigation of sentence.

The sages sought to exonerate Israel. Yes, to be sure, judging by appearances, they may have been guilty of waywardness, backsliding, and ingratitude. They may often have failed to live up to the highest ideals of the Torah. Yet consider the difficulties they faced, the dangers they went through, the temptations that surrounded them. Even the making of the Golden Calf, their greatest sin, was in some measure excusable.

Limmud zekhut has a rich history in Aggada and halakha, Jewish thought and law. One of its classic expressions is to be found in Maimonides' *Epistle on Martyrdom,* written around 1165.[2] Spain had been

1. In Ex. 3:22; 11:2; 12:35.
2. Text and commentary can be found in *Epistles of Maimonides: Crisis and Leadership,* ed. Abraham S. Halkin and David Hartman (Philadelphia: Jewish Publication Society, 1993).

invaded by an extremist Muslim sect, the Almohad, which confronted Jews with the choice: convert or die. Maimonides' own family was forced to flee. Some Jews, however, stayed, publicly embracing Islam while secretly remaining Jews – forerunners of the later Marranos, who converted to Christianity.

One of the forced converts wrote to a rabbi to ask whether he was right to continue to practise as many mitzvot as he could in secret. The rabbi wrote back a dismissive reply, saying that now that he had abandoned Judaism, every religious deed he performed was not a merit but a sin. Appalled by this reply, Maimonides wrote the *Epistle*, saying that indeed Jews should leave Spain and go somewhere where they could practise their religion openly – but those who stayed and converted under fear of death should not be regarded as sinners. To the contrary, every mitzva they do is still a good deed. Indeed, in one sense, it is a great deed since "the reward is much greater for a person who fulfils the Law and knows that if he is caught, he and all he has will perish."[3] In the course of the letter, Maimonides cites a host of examples in which the sages say that the greatest of the prophets were criticised by God when they criticised the Jewish people. His conclusion is that "it is not right to alienate, scorn, and hate people who desecrate the Sabbath. It is our duty to befriend them, and encourage them to fulfil the commandments."[4]

It is a note that sounds again during the time of the hasidic movement, most famously in many stories attributed to the great Rabbi Levi Yitzhak of Berditchev (1740–1809). In one such story, possibly apocryphal, it is said that Levi Yitzhak saw a Jew smoking in the street on Shabbat. He said, "My friend, surely you have forgotten that it is Shabbat today." "No," said the other, "I know what day it is." "Then surely you have forgotten that smoking is forbidden on Shabbat." "No, I know it is forbidden." "Then surely, you must have been thinking about something else when you lit the cigarette." "No," the other replied, "I knew what I was doing." At this, Levi Yitzhak turned his eyes upwards to heaven and said, "Sovereign of the universe, who is like Your people Israel? I give this man every chance, and still he cannot tell a lie!"

3. Ibid., 33.
4. Ibid.

The great leaders of Israel were defenders of Israel, people who saw the good within the not-yet-good. Where did they learn it from? From the prophets themselves. Most notable in this regard is a figure not usually associated with good news, namely, Jeremiah. His name is associated with bad tidings, yet it is he who says in the name of God:

> I remember the devotion of your youth,
> How as a bride you loved Me
> And followed Me through the desert,
> Through a land not sown. (Jer. 2:2)

Among the greatest prophecies of hope are the concluding chapters of Isaiah, from which all seven *haftarot* of consolation, read between Tisha B'Av and Rosh HaShana, are taken. In fact, almost every prophet gave voice to hope. The prophets criticised Israel, but always and only out of love. Amos delivered the most paradoxical of all these utterances: "You only have I chosen of all the families of the earth; therefore I will punish you for all your sins" (Amos 3:2). The very suffering of the Jewish people, implied Amos, was a sign of their chosenness, their preciousness in the eyes of God.[5]

Parashat Devarim is always read on the Shabbat before Tisha B'Av, the most tragic date in the Jewish calendar, on which both the First and Second Temples were destroyed and on which many other historic catastrophes occurred.

The *haftara*, the "vision" contained in the first chapter of Isaiah, is one of the most searing indictments in all literature of the corruption of a people. The book of Deuteronomy is itself consistently harsh in its judgement of the Israelites. And Jews suffered. Twice they had seen their holiest site destroyed. The first time, when they were exiled to Babylonia, there was consolation. Jeremiah told them that within seventy years they would return, and so it was. But the second time, at the hands of Rome, no end was in sight. The Bar Kokhba Revolt failed. The Roman emperor Hadrian imposed savage penalties. An extraordinary passage in the Talmud tells us how close Jews came to despair:

5. A point also made by Judah Halevi in *The Kuzari*.

> R. Yishmael b. Elisha said: Since the day that a government has come into power which issues cruel decrees against us and forbids us to enter into the "week of the son" we ought by rights to issue a ruling forbidding Jews to marry and have children, so that the seed of Abraham our father would come to an end of its own accord. (Bava Batra 60b)

Faced with such hopelessness, the Jewish people might have concluded that the mission God had given them was impossible. However hard they tried, it seemed, they fell short. They suffered. It seemed as if their punishment exceeded all bounds.

It was a moment of crisis. What, at such times, is the role of a sage? The sages were not prophets, but they knew they carried the same responsibility: "From the day the Temple was destroyed, prophecy was taken from the prophets and given to the sages" (Bava Batra 12a). They knew that at times of comfort and complacency, the task of the prophet is to warn of impending danger, to detect the first signs of moral drift. But at times of trouble, the role of the prophet is to bring hope.

That is what the sages did. Following the precedent of the prophets but going beyond them, they engaged in being *melamed zekhut* for the Jewish people. They became counsels for the defence. They spoke the good news about Jews: "Even the emptiest of Israel is as full of good deeds as a pomegranate is of seeds" (Sanhedrin 37a); "Let Israel alone: they may not be prophets, but they are the children of prophets" (Pesaḥim 66a); "They are believers, the children of believers" (Shabbat 97a); "A Jew who sins remains a Jew" (Sanhedrin 44a). Throughout the rabbinic and post-rabbinic literature this note sounds time and again – a note of love, generosity of spirit, affection, even admiration, for this people who, though much afflicted, never gave up its faith.

That is what the sages did on *Shabbat Ḥazon*, the Shabbat before Tisha B'Av, the most painful Shabbat of the year. They introduced into the first verse of *Devarim*, the *parasha* always read at this time of the year, a note of defence. It is true that Israel sinned, nowhere more so than when they made the Golden Calf, but even then there was a case to be argued in mitigation. This, they said, is what Moses did. Do not blame them, he said to God. They had gold only because You told them to take it, and without the gold there could have been no Golden Calf. Moses, often the Israelites' greatest critic, here becomes attorney for the defence. Thus the sages introduced a note of hope into what otherwise might have been the Shabbat of despair.

We are a self-critical people. The Hebrew Bible is the most self-critical of all national literatures. We know our failings. There is something admirable about this honesty. But it must never leave us bereft of hope. Jewish leadership, as the sages understood it, is about giving expression to love, respect, even awe for the Jewish people, who – though it has come through an unparalleled history of suffering – still survives, still flourishes, and still bears witness to the living God.

We are not short of critics, internal and external. What we need by way of balance is the voice of those who are *melamed zekhut*, who see our faults but see our virtues also, who know the price we have paid for following God's pillar of fire through the wilderness of time and space, faithful to His call, loyal to His word.

Tzedek: *Justice Tempered by Compassion*

As Moses begins his great closing addresses to the next generation, he turns to a subject that dominates the last of the Mosaic books, namely, justice:

> I instructed your judges at that time as follows: "Listen to your fellow men, and decide justly [*tzedek*] between each man and his brother or a stranger. You shall not be partial in judgement. Listen to great and small alike. Fear no one, for judgement belongs to God. Any matter that is too difficult for you, bring to me and I will hear it." (Deut. 1:16–17)

Tzedek, "justice," is a key word in the book of Deuteronomy – most famously in the verse, "Justice, justice you shall pursue, so that you may thrive and occupy the land that the Lord your God is giving you" (Deut. 16:20).

The distribution of the word *tzedek* and its derivate *tzedaka* in the Five Books of Moses is anything but random. It is overwhelmingly concentrated in the first and last books, Genesis (where it appears sixteen times) and Deuteronomy (eighteen times). In Exodus it occurs only four times and in Leviticus five. All but one of these are clustered in two chapters: Exodus 23 (where three of the four occurrences are in two verses, 23:7–8) and Leviticus 19 (where all five incidences are in the same chapter). In Numbers, the word does not appear at all.

This distribution is one of many indications that the five Mosaic books are constructed as a chiasmus – a literary unit of the form ABCBA. The structure is this:

A: Genesis – the prehistory of Israel (the distant past)
  B: Exodus – the journey from Egypt to Mount Sinai
    C: Leviticus – the code of holiness
  B: Numbers – the journey from Sinai to the banks of the Jordan
A: Deuteronomy – the post-history of Israel (the distant future)

The leitmotif of *tzedek/tzedaka* appears at the key points of this structure – the two outer books of Genesis and Deuteronomy, and the central chapter of the work as a whole, Leviticus 19. This positioning shows that the word is a dominant theme of the Mosaic books as a whole.

Indeed, it is the only reason given by the Torah itself for God's choice of Abraham to be the father of a new nation: "For I have chosen him so that he will instruct his children and his household after him to keep the way of the Lord by doing what is right and just [*tzedaka umishpat*] so that the Lord may bring about for Abraham what He has promised him" (Gen. 18:19). Justice is at the very heart of the Judaic project. Albert Einstein famously spoke of the "almost fanatical love of justice" that was one of "the features of the Jewish tradition which make me thank my stars that I belong to it."[1]

Tzedek/tzedaka is almost impossible to translate, because of its many shadings of meaning: justice, charity, righteousness, integrity, equity, fairness, and innocence. It means more than strictly legal justice, for which the Bible uses words like *mishpat* and *din*. One example illustrates the point: "If a man is poor, you may not go to sleep holding his security. Return it to him at sundown, so that he will be able

1. Albert Einstein, *The World As I See It*, trans. Alan Harris (San Diego: The Book Tree, 2007), 90.

to sleep in his garment and bless you. To you it will be reckoned as *tzedaka* before the Lord your God" (Deut. 24:12–13). *Tzedaka* cannot mean legal justice in this verse. It speaks of a situation in which a poor person has only a single cloak or covering, which he has handed over to the lender as security against a loan. The lender has a legal right to keep the cloak until the loan has been repaid. However, acting on the basis of this right is simply not the right thing to do. It ignores the human situation of the poor person, who has nothing else with which to keep warm on a cold night.

The point becomes even clearer when we examine the parallel passage in Exodus, which states: "If you take your neighbour's cloak as a pledge, return it to him by sunset, because his cloak is the only covering he has for his body. What else will he sleep in? When he cries out to Me, I will hear, for I am compassionate" (Ex. 22:25–26). The same situation which in Deuteronomy is described as *tzedaka*, in Exodus is termed compassion or grace (*ḥanun*). The late Aryeh Kaplan translated *tzedaka* in Deuteronomy 24 as "charitable merit."[2] It is best rendered as "the right and decent thing to do" or "justice tempered by compassion."

Maimonides reflects on this in the penultimate chapter of *Guide for the Perplexed*. He writes:

> The term *tzedaka* is derived from *tzedek*, "righteousness." It denotes the act of giving everyone his due, and of showing kindness to every being according as it deserves. In Scripture, however, the expression *tzedaka* is not used in the first sense, and does not apply to the payment of what we owe to others. When we therefore give the hired labourer his wages, or pay a debt, we do not perform an act of *tzedaka*. But we do perform an act of *tzedaka* when we fulfil those duties towards our fellow-men which our moral conscience imposes upon us – e.g., when we heal the wound of the sufferer…[3]

2. Aryeh Kaplan, *The Living Torah: The Five Books of Moses and the Haftarot* (Brooklyn, NY: Moznaim, 1981), ad loc.
3. Maimonides, *Guide for the Perplexed*, III:53.

In other words, *tzedaka* means doing what is morally right, rather than simply what the law strictly requires. It means justice tempered by compassion.

Simon May, in his *Love: A History*, has wise things to say about this. He speaks about "the remarkable and radical justice that underlies the love commandment of Leviticus ['You shall love your neighbour as yourself']." This is, he says, "not a cold justice in which due deserts are mechanically handed out, but a justice that brings the other, as an individual with needs and interests, into a relationship of respect." He concludes: "Justice and love therefore become inseparable."[4]

Hence the tragic irony of Portia's speech in *The Merchant of Venice*:

> The quality of mercy is not strained;
> It droppeth as the gentle rain from heaven
> Upon the place beneath. It is twice blest;
> It blesseth him that gives and him that takes...
> And earthly power doth then show likest God's
> When mercy seasons justice. Therefore, Jew,
> Though justice be thy plea, consider this,
> That, in the course of justice, none of us
> Should see salvation: we do pray for mercy;
> And that same prayer doth teach us all to render
> The deeds of mercy.[5]

Shakespeare is here giving expression to the medieval stereotype of Christian mercy (Portia) as against Jewish justice (Shylock). He fails to realise – how could he, given the prevailing culture?[6] – that "justice" and "mercy" are not opposites in Hebrew but are bonded together in a single word, *tzedek* or *tzedaka*. To add to the irony, the very language

4. Simon May, *Love: A History* (New Haven, CT: Yale University Press, 2011), 17.
5. *The Merchant of Venice*, act IV, scene 1.
6. There were no Jews in England in Shakespeare's lifetime. They had been expelled in 1290 and were not allowed to return until 1656. *The Merchant of Venice* was written between 1596 and 1599.

and imagery of Portia's speech ("It droppeth as the gentle rain from heaven") is taken from Deuteronomy:

> Let my teaching drop as rain,
> My words descend like dew,
> Like showers on new grass,
> Like abundant rain on tender plants...
> The Rock, His work is perfect,
> For all His ways are just;
> A God of faith without iniquity
> Righteous and upright is He. (Deut. 32:2–4)

The false contrast between Jew and Christian in *The Merchant of Venice,* a contrast even the supremely humanitarian Shakespeare could not overcome, is eloquent testimony to the cruel misrepresentation of Judaism in Christian theology until recent times.

Why then is justice so central to Judaism? Because it is impartial. Law as envisaged by the Torah makes no distinction between rich and poor, powerful and powerless, home-born and stranger. Equality before the law is the translation into human terms of equality before God. Time and again the Torah insists that justice is not a human artefact: "Fear no one, for judgement belongs to God" (Deut. 1:17). Because it belongs to God, it must never be compromised – by fear, bribery, or favouritism. It is an inescapable duty, an inalienable right.

Judaism is a religion of love: you shall love the Lord your God; you shall love your neighbour as yourself; you shall love the stranger for you were once strangers. But it is also a religion of justice, for without justice, love corrupts (who would not bend the rules, if he could, to favour those he loves?). It is also a religion of compassion, for without compassion law itself can generate inequity. Justice plus compassion equals *tzedek,* the first precondition of a decent society.

Profits and Prophets

There are few more blazing passages in the whole of religious literature than the first chapter of the book of Isaiah, the great "vision," *ḥazon*, that gives its name to the Shabbat before Tisha B'Av, the saddest day of the Jewish year. It is more than great literature. It expresses one of the great prophetic truths, that a society cannot flourish without honesty and justice. A flourishing society depends on the existence of trust and trustworthiness on the part of its members. A free society is a moral achievement.

The Talmud states that when we leave this life and arrive at the World to Come, the first question we will be asked will not be a conventionally religious one: "Did you set aside times for learning Torah?" Rather, it will be: "Did you act honestly [*be'emuna*] in business?" (Shabbat 31a). I used to wonder how the rabbis felt certain about this. Death is, after all, "the undiscovered country, from whose bourn no traveller returns."[1] The answer, it seems to me, is this passage from Isaiah:

> See how the faithful city has become a harlot! She once was full of justice; righteousness used to dwell in her – but now murderers!

1. *Hamlet,* act III, scene 1.

> Your silver has become dross, your choice wine is diluted with water. Your rulers are rebels, companions of thieves; they all love bribes and chase after gifts. They do not defend the cause of the fatherless; the widow's case does not come before them. (Is. 1:21–23)

Jerusalem's fate was sealed not by conventional religious failure but by the failure of people to act honestly. They engaged in sharp business practices that were highly profitable but hard to detect – mixing silver with baser metals, diluting wine. People were concerned with maximising profits, indifferent to the fact that others would suffer. The political system, too, had become corrupt. Politicians were using their office and influence to personal advantage. People knew this or suspected it – Isaiah does not claim to be telling people something they did not already know; he did not expect to surprise his listeners. The fact that people had come to expect no better from their leaders was itself a mark of moral decline.

This, says Isaiah, is the real danger: that widespread dishonesty and corruption will sap the morale of a society, make people cynical, open up divisions between the rich and powerful and the poor and powerless, erode the fabric of society, and make people wonder why they should make sacrifices for the common good if everyone else seems to be bent on personal advantage. A nation in this condition is sick and in a state of incipient decline.

What Isaiah saw and said with primal force and devastating clarity is that sometimes (organised) religion is not the solution but itself part of the problem. It has always been tempting, even for a nation of monotheists, to slip into magical thinking: that we can atone for our sins or those of society by frequent attendance at the Temple, the offering of sacrifices, and conspicuous shows of piety. Few things, implies Isaiah, make God angrier than this:

> "The multitude of your sacrifices – what are they to Me?" says the Lord.... "When you come to appear before Me, who has asked this of you, this trampling of My courts? Stop bringing meaningless offerings! Your incense is detestable to Me...I cannot bear your evil assemblies. Your New Moon festivals and your

> appointed feasts My soul hates. They have become a burden to Me; I am weary of bearing them. When you spread out your hands in prayer, I will hide My eyes from you; even if you offer many prayers, I will not listen." (Is. 1:11–15)

The corrupt not only believe they can fool their fellow humans; they believe they can fool God as well. When moral standards begin to break down in business, finance, trade, and politics, a kind of collective madness takes hold of people. The sages said *Adam bahul al mamono* (Pesaḥim 11b), meaning, roughly, "Money makes us do wild things." People come to believe that they are leading a charmed life, that luck is with them, that they will neither fail nor be found out. They even believe they can bribe God to look the other way. In the end it all comes crashing down and those who suffer most tend to be those who deserve it least.

Isaiah is making a prophetic point, but one that has implications for economics and politics today and can be stated even in secular terms: the market economy is and must be a moral enterprise. Absent that, and eventually it will fail.

There used to be a belief among superficial readers of Adam Smith, prophet of free trade, that the market economy did not depend on morality at all: "It is not from the benevolence of the butcher, the brewer, or the baker that we expect our dinner, but from their regard to their own interest."[2] It was the brilliance of the system that it turned self-interest into the common good by what Smith called, almost mystically, an "invisible hand." Morality was not part of the system. It was unnecessary.

This was a misreading of Smith, who took morality very seriously indeed and wrote – before *The Wealth of Nations* – a book called *The Theory of Moral Sentiments*. He believed that relations between individuals must be moral if the market was to function for the common good.[3] But it was also a misreading of economics. This was made clear, two centuries later, by a paradox in Game Theory known as the Prisoner's

---

2. Adam Smith, *An Inquiry into the Nature and Causes of the Wealth of Nations* (1776), book 1, chapter 2.
3. See Russell Roberts, *How Adam Smith Can Change Your Life: An Unexpected Guide to Human Nature and Happiness* (New York: Penguin Portfolio, 2014).

Dilemma. Without going into details, this imagined two people faced with a choice (to stay silent, confess, or accuse the other). The outcome of their decision would depend on what the other person did, and this could not be known in advance. It can be shown that if both people act rationally in their own interest, they will produce an outcome that is bad for both of them. This seems to refute the basic premise of market economics, that the pursuit of self-interest serves the common good.

The negative outcome of the Prisoner's Dilemma can only be avoided if the two people repeatedly find themselves in the same situation. Eventually they realise they are harming one another and themselves. They learn to cooperate, which they can do only if they trust one another, and they will do this only if the other has earned that trust by acting honestly and with integrity.

In other words, *the market economy depends on moral virtues that are not themselves produced by the market, and may be undermined by the market itself.* For if the market is about the pursuit of profit, and if we can gain at other people's expense, then the pursuit of profit will lead first to shady practices ("Your silver has become dross, your choice wine is diluted with water"), then to the breakdown of trust, then to the collapse of the market itself.

A classic example of this was evident after the financial crash in 2008. For a decade, banks had engaged in doubtful practices, notably subprime mortgages and the securitisation of risk through financial instruments so complex that even bankers themselves later admitted they did not fully understand them. They continued to authorise them despite Warren Buffet's warning in 2002 that subprime mortgages were "instruments of mass financial destruction." The result was the crash. But that was not the source of the recession that followed. The recession took place because the banks no longer trusted one another. Credit was no longer freely available and in one country after another the economy stalled.

The key word, used by both Isaiah and the sages, is *emuna*, meaning faithfulness and trust. In the *haftara*, Isaiah twice uses the phrase *kirya ne'emana*, "faithful city." The sages, as we saw, say that in heaven we will be asked, "Did you conduct your business *be'emuna*?" – meaning, in such a way as to inspire trust. The market economy depends on trust. Even in English, the word "credit" comes from a Latin root meaning "trust, faith, belief." "Confidence," on which the market depends, is likewise from a Latin root meaning "to have full trust."

Absent trust and trustworthiness, and depend instead on contracts, lawyers, regulations, and supervisory authorities, and there will be yet more scandals, collapses, and crashes, since the ingenuity of those who seek to sidestep the rules always exceeds that of those whose job it is to apply them. The only safe regulatory authority is conscience, the voice of God within the human heart forbidding us to do what we know is wrong but think we can get away with.

Isaiah's warning is as timely now as it was twenty-seven centuries ago. When morality is missing and economics and politics are driven by self-interest alone, trust fails and society's fabric unravels. That is how all great civilisations began their decline, and there is no exception.

In the long term, the evidence shows that it is sounder to follow prophets than profits.

Va'etḥanan
ואתחנן

Parashat Va'etḥanan contains some of the most sublime theological passages in the whole of Judaism. Moses tells the people that their laws and history are unique, and will be seen as such by other nations. Their laws were given by God; their history was written by God – there is no other nation of which either can be said.

Moses then begins his second great speech. He reminds the people of the Ten Commandments and the revelation at Mount Sinai and commands them to set God at the centre of their lives in the passage that became the first paragraph of the *Shema*, the supreme expression of the love of God. This was to be more than an emotion. It was to be constantly spoken of to children, worn by men in the form of *tefillin*, and placed as *mezuzot* "on the doorposts of your house" (Deut. 6:9).

The first of the following essays looks at Moses' declaration that the Torah would be Israel's "wisdom … in the eyes of the nations" (Deut. 4:6), and how it came true. The second looks at the distinctive politics of Deuteronomy, namely, its concept of a nation formed by covenant. This too had great impact on the formative history of the free societies of the West. The third and fourth are about the word *shema*, central to our *Parashat Va'etḥanan* and to Deuteronomy as a whole. One is about its dimensions of meaning, focusing on the fact that it is the word the Torah uses instead of a verb meaning "to obey." The other is about Judaism as a culture of listening more than seeing, of the ear rather than the eye. The fifth is about the unexpected statement by Moses that the Israelites are "the fewest of all peoples."

In the Eyes of the Nations

In Moses' day the Israelites must have appeared to an outside observer as a small, undistinguished people, children of slaves who did not yet possess a home. Even many generations later, after they had conquered the land, appointed a king, and built the Temple, they were a minor power compared to the great empires around them. They never reached the scale or prestige of Mesopotamia or Egypt, Assyria or Babylon.

Yet Moses was convinced that something had happened to them of world-transforming significance. They had been touched, adopted, chosen by God for a great task, one that would affect not only them but also those who came in contact with them. The God of Israel was not like the gods of other nations. The faith of Israel was not like the religions of other people. Of this Moses was sure. He knew with a certainty that comes only from prophecy of the highest order that what had happened to Israel would reverberate far beyond Israel:

> Observe [these decrees] carefully, for this is your wisdom and understanding in the eyes of the nations, who will hear about all these decrees and say, "Surely this great nation is a wise and understanding people." What other nation is so great as to have

> their gods near them the way the Lord our God is near us whenever we pray to Him? And what other nation is so great as to have such righteous decrees and laws as this law I am setting before you today? (Deut. 4:6–8)

According to Nahmanides (Catalonia, 1194–1270), the meaning of this passage is that "the statutes and ordinances have the great benefit that they will bring honour from others to those who observe them. Even their enemies will praise them." Other nations will admire Israel's way of life. Rabbi Ovadia Sforno (Italy, c. 1475–1550) interprets it differently: through the Torah "you will be able to refute a heretic by intellectual proofs." It is not so much that others will admire Israel as that they will acknowledge the divine source of its laws. The Jewish people will be living proof that God exists and has communicated with mankind.

Rabbi Shmuel David Luzzatto (known also as Shadal; Italy, 1800–1865), writing in a later age, sees the text from a different perspective. "This is a refutation," he writes,

> of those who say that the statutes Moses gave Israel were adopted from the Egyptians and the other peoples of his time. Moses' contemporaries would have known far better than we do if this had been the case. How then could Moses have been so foolish or presumptuous to say to the Israelites that the nations, when they heard of these statutes, would say that Israel is a wise and understanding nation? Rather they would say that Israel is a foolish and inferior nation, because its laws were stolen from others.

Moses, suggests Luzzatto, knew that there was something *different* about the laws of Israel. This could not have been the case if Israel had simply adopted or adapted the practices of its time.

Whichever interpretation we take, the implication of Moses' words is clear. The Torah would have an impact far beyond the boundaries, literal or metaphorical, of Israel. At no time during the biblical era could this be said to be true, but it did come true nonetheless. The Greeks, struck by the intensity with which Jews studied Torah, called them "a nation of philosophers." Then came Christianity and Islam, two faiths tracing their ancestry to Abraham and drawing much of their inspiration from the Hebrew Bible. Already in the twelfth century, Moses Maimonides could write (in a passage long censored and only recently restored):

> The whole world is already filled with the words of [the Christian] messiah and the words of the commandments, and these words have spread to the farthest islands and among many unenlightened peoples, and they discuss these words and the commandments of the Torah.[1]

The effect of Christianity and Islam was to spread elements of the Jewish message – albeit in ways with which Jews could not fully agree – throughout the world. Today these religions represent more than half of the seven billion people on the face of the earth. The "Judaeo-Christian ethic" and the Abrahamic faiths have shaped much of the civilisation of the West. The Torah *did* become "your wisdom and understanding in the eyes of the nations."

What is particularly interesting is that this became most marked in the modern age – specifically in the seventeenth and eighteenth centuries – as Western nations searched for a way to create free societies after the wars of religion that had scarred the face of Europe following the Reformation. In England, as we will see in the next essay, figures like John Milton, Thomas Hobbes, and John Locke formulated new understandings of political authority and limited, "constitutional" monarchy, and did so because they were inspired by the Hebrew Bible in general and the book of Deuteronomy in particular.

A century later, the philosopher and inspiration of the French Revolution, Jean-Jacques Rousseau, wrote eloquently about Moses as perhaps the greatest political leader of all time. He undertook

> the astonishing enterprise of instituting as a national body a swarm of wretched fugitives who had no arts, no weapons, no talents, no virtues, no courage, and who, since they had not an inch of territory of their own, were a troop of strangers upon the face of the earth.

1. Maimonides, *Mishneh Torah, Hilkhot Melakhim* 11:4.

Despite the sheer improbability of success, writes Rousseau, Moses dared to make out of this wandering and servile troop a body politic, a free people, and while it wandered in the wilderness without so much as a stone on which to rest its head, he gave it the lasting institution, proof against time, fortune, and conquerors, which five thousand years have not been able to destroy or even to weaken, and which still subsists today in all its force, even though the body of the nation no longer does. The result is that "this singular nation, so often subjugated, so often scattered and apparently destroyed," has, despite all this, "maintained itself down to our days, scattered among other nations without ever merging with them." Its identity, "its morals, its laws, its rites subsist and will endure as long as the world itself does, in spite of the hatred and persecution by the rest of mankind."[2]

Across the Atlantic, John Adams, second president of the United States, paid similar tribute to the contribution of the Hebrew Bible to liberty:

> I will insist that the Hebrews have done more to civilize men than any other nation. If I were an atheist, and believed in blind eternal fate, I should still believe that fate had ordained the Jews to be the most essential instrument for civilizing the nations. If I were an atheist of the other sect, who believe or pretend to believe that all is ordered by chance, I should believe that chance had ordered the Jews to preserve and propagate to all mankind the doctrine of a supreme, intelligent, wise, almighty sovereign of the universe, which I believe to be the great essential principle of all morality, and consequently of all civilization.[3]

The Jewish story, as told in the books of Exodus and Deuteronomy, came to be adopted as the American story: a tale of flight from persecution (for "the Egyptians" read "the English"), across a body of water (for "the Red

2. "Considerations on the Government of Poland and on its Projected Reformation" (1772), in *Rousseau: The Social Contract and Other Later Political Writings* (Cambridge, UK: Cambridge University Press, 1997), 180.
3. President John Adams to F. A. Vanderkemp, February 16, 1809, in *The Works of John Adams,* ed. C. F. Adams (Boston: Little, Brown, 1854), 9:609–10.

Sea" read "the Atlantic"), in search of a new Promised Land. Americans were, in Abraham Lincoln's words, the "almost chosen people,"[4] and their destiny, like the Israelites of old, was to serve as a model for the rest of the world of a free and just society. Few expressed this more eloquently than Herman Melville in his 1849 novel *White Jacket*:

> We Americans are the peculiar, chosen people – the Israel of our time; we bear the ark of the liberties of the world. God has predestined, mankind expects, great things from our race; and great things we feel in our souls. The rest of the nations must soon be in our rear. We are the pioneers of the world; the advance-guard, sent on through the wilderness of untried things, to break a new path in the New World that is ours.[5]

It remains an astonishing fact that, some three thousand years after Moses first uttered those words, the Torah would be "your wisdom and understanding in the eyes of the nations." It came true, not only in the form of the two other monotheistic religions that took inspiration from Judaism, but also and specifically in the age of the Enlightenment, when in America and France revolutionary spirits sought to create new forms of society in which there was a separation of Church and State and room for religious diversity. Even then, the Torah served as a model for how to undertake the journey from slavery to freedom, from oppression to law-governed liberty.

It was not the people who inspired, but their Torah. That was what Moses was trying to teach them throughout the book of Deuteronomy. It is not your righteousness that makes you special, nor your size, he says (Deut. 9:5–6; 7:7). In the language of today: there is nothing special about Jews; there is everything special about Judaism. It is your laws, given to you by God Himself, that will lift you to greatness. It will be your story that will inspire others to undertake the long walk to freedom.

---

4. Address to the New Jersey State Senate (Trenton, New Jersey, February 21, 1861).
5. Herman Melville, *White Jacket; or The World in a Man-of-War* (London: Richard Bentley, 1850), 239.

The Politics of Responsibility

In the previous essay I looked at how Moses' prophecy – that the Torah would become "your wisdom and understanding in the eyes of the nations" (Deut. 4:6) – came true. In this essay I want to examine the specific idea that had this influence: the concept of covenant.

The book of Deuteronomy makes repeated reference to the word *brit*, the Torah's word for covenant. It appears no less than twenty-seven times. What is more, as I explained in the introduction, the entire book is structured, albeit on a monumental scale, along the lines of an ancient Near Eastern covenant. But it is the transfiguration of the idea as it enters biblical thought that is spiritually radical and intellectually revolutionary.

Covenants were a familiar feature of the ancient Near East. Essentially, they were peace treaties, sometimes between individuals, clans, and tribes, at other times between nations. So, for instance, Abraham made a covenant with Avimelekh, king of Gerar (Gen. 21:27), as did Isaac (26:28). Jacob made a covenant with Laban (31:44).

Archaeological discoveries in the twentieth century brought to light covenants between neighbouring powers in the general region of Mesopotamia dating from the third millennium BCE, that is, before the time of Abraham. These could be between nations of roughly equal strength, known as parity treaties, or they could be between a strong power and a weaker one, known as a suzerainty treaty. The covenant between God and the Israelites at Mount Sinai (Ex. 19–24; Lev. 25–26), and the renewal of that covenant in Deuteronomy (1–31), have the basic form of a suzerainty treaty, obviously so since God is infinitely powerful and the Israelites at the time were almost powerless.

So the form of covenant is borrowed. But in the Mosaic books, and in Judaism thereafter, its substance is entirely unprecedented. Instead of being a secular, political document, it becomes the fundamental theological frame through which the relationship between God and humanity is understood.

There are three divine-human covenants in the Torah. The first is between God and Noah, and through him with all humanity, after the Flood (Gen. 9). The second is between God and Abraham and his descendants (Gen. 17). The third is between God and the Israelites at Mount Sinai.

The three covenants are different in character. The covenant with Noah involves relatively few stipulations, traditionally known as the Seven Noahide Laws. The covenant at Sinai goes to the opposite extreme, involving an extensive and detailed set of commands, traditionally numbered as 613. Equally significantly, we can trace a marked transformation in the respective roles of the two parties. In the covenant with Noah, it was God who acted. Noah was not asked for his consent. In the covenant with Abraham, something *was* asked: Abraham was to circumcise himself and his family as a token of his assent. In the covenant at Mount Sinai, only when the Israelites had signalled their assent – "The people all responded together: We will do everything the Lord has said" (Ex. 19:8) – did God proceed with the revelation of the Ten Commandments. This was what the American Declaration of Independence would later call "the consent of the governed."

In the renewal of the covenant in the book of Deuteronomy, it was Moses, not God, who initiated the process. Thus we see a slow change from the first to the last book of the Torah, from divine to human initiative. This is the spiritual equivalent of the transition from childhood to adulthood. First God taught humans how to act, then, on the far side of the Jordan, humans fully and freely took that responsibility on themselves.

Covenant in the Hebrew Bible represents a unique form of politics. As I noted earlier,[1] most political structures develop either organically, through a long process of history, or as a result of conquest. In both cases, the society that emerges is essentially hierarchical. There is a ruler, or an elite, or both. They make and enforce the laws, and the freedom of the people as a whole is always subject to their will or whim. Politics, in these societies, is about power, and those who have it rule the rest. In Thucydides' famous words, "The strong do what they wish and the weak suffer what they must."[2]

Covenant is an attempt to break away from this entire universe of relationships. Covenantal politics is distinctive in the following ways:

1. It is a politics of collective responsibility. The parties to the covenant are, said Moses, "your leaders, your tribes, your elders and officials, all the men of Israel, your children, your wives, the strangers in your camp, from woodcutter to water-drawer" (Deut. 29:9–10). This is what is meant in the preamble to the American Constitution by the phrase, "We, the people."
2. It is a politics rooted in the principled equality of dignity of all citizens.[3] This is what Abraham Lincoln meant when he spoke, in the Gettysburg Address, of "a new nation, conceived in Liberty, and dedicated to the proposition that all men are created equal."
3. It is a moral politics – a politics in which we can be called to account on the grounds of justice. Hence the importance, in biblical politics, of the prophetic voice. This is what Martin Luther King Jr. was invoking when, in his great speech at the Lincoln Memorial on August 28, 1963, he quoted the prophet Amos (5:4): "We are not satisfied, and we will not be satisfied until 'justice rolls down like waters, and righteousness like a mighty stream.'"[4]

---

1. See above, "The World We Make with Words."
2. Thucydides, 5.89.
3. See Joshua Berman, *Created Equal: How the Bible Broke with Ancient Political Thought* (Oxford: Oxford University Press, 2008).
4. Martin Luther King Jr., "I Have a Dream" Speech (Lincoln Memorial, Washington, DC, August 28, 1963).

4. It is a politics rooted not in power but in a mutual pledge. As Philip Selznick puts it: "Faith based on covenant might be called a constitutional faith," founded in the "giving and receiving of promises."[5]
5. It is a politics rooted in remembrance and covenantal renewal.

Covenant politics did not appear in the West until the sixteenth century. Several things had to happen before it could do so. First was the invention of printing by Johannes Gutenberg in Mainz in 1439, followed in England in 1476 by William Caxton. Books became less expensive and more accessible. Literacy spread. Then in 1517 came the Reformation, with its emphasis on "sola Scriptura," the authority of "Scripture alone." Then came the translation of the Bible into the vernacular. We tend to forget that the Hebrew Bible is a subversive work. It does not preach submission. It speaks of prophets unafraid to challenge kings, of Saul who lost his throne because he disobeyed the word of God. So ruling authorities had good reason for preventing the Bible from being available in a language ordinary people could understand. Translating it into the vernacular was forbidden in the sixteenth century. In the 1530s the great Tyndale translation appeared. Tyndale paid for this with his life. He was arrested, found guilty of heresy, strangled, and burned at the stake in 1536.

However, it is hard to stop the spread of information that new technologies make possible. English Bibles continued to be printed and sold in massive numbers, most notably the Geneva translation of 1560 that was read by Shakespeare, Cromwell, Milton, and John Donne, as well as by the early English settlers of America.[6]

The Geneva Bible contained a commentary in the margin. Its comments were brief but sometimes explosive. This applied in particular to the story of the Hebrew midwives, Shifra and Puah, in Exodus 1 – the first recorded instance of civil disobedience, the refusal to obey

---

5. Philip Selznick, *The Moral Commonwealth* (Berkeley, CA: University of California Press, 1992), 478.
6. For the impact of the Hebrew Bible on English politics in the revolutionary era, see Christopher Hill, *The English Bible and the Seventeenth-Century Revolution* (New York: Penguin, 1993).

an immoral order. Pharaoh had instructed the midwives to kill every male Israelite child, but they did not. Commenting on this, the Geneva Bible says, "Their disobedience in this was lawful." When Pharaoh then commanded the Egyptians to drown male Israelite children, the Geneva Bible comments: "When tyrants cannot prevail by deceit, they burst into open rage." This was nothing less than a justification for rebellion against a tyrannical and unjust king.

The Tyndale and Geneva Bibles led to a group of thinkers known as the Christian Hebraists, of whom the most famous – he has been called Renaissance England's chief rabbi – was John Selden (1584–1654). Selden and his contemporaries studied not only Tanakh, but also the Babylonian Talmud (especially Tractate Sanhedrin) and Maimonides' *Mishneh Torah,* and applied Judaic principles to the politics of their day.

Their work has been described in a fine study, *The Hebrew Republic,* by Harvard political philosopher Eric Nelson.[7] Nelson argues that the Hebrew Bible influenced European and American politics in three ways. First, the Christian Hebraists tended to be republican rather than royalist. They took the view – held in Judaism by Abrabanel – that the appointment of a king in Israel in the days of Samuel was a (tolerated) sin rather than the fulfilment of a mitzva. Second, they placed at the heart of their politics the idea that one of the tasks of government is to redistribute wealth from the rich to the poor, an idea alien to Roman law. Third, they used the Hebrew Bible – especially its separation of powers between the king and the high priest – to argue for the principle of religious toleration.

It was this historic encounter between Christians and the Hebrew Bible in the seventeenth century that led to the birth of liberty in both England and America. The Calvinists and Puritans who led both the English and American Revolutions were saturated in the politics of the Hebrew Bible, especially of the book of Deuteronomy.

The first document in American political history, the Mayflower Compact of 1620, is constructed as a covenant on the biblical model: its signatories declared that they "solemnly and mutually, in the Presence of

7. Eric Nelson, *The Hebrew Republic: Jewish Sources and the Transformation of European Political Thought* (Cambridge, MA: Harvard University Press, 2010).

God and one another, covenant and combine ourselves together into a civil Body Politick, for our better Ordering and Preservation." The first great speech in American politics, John Winthrop's 1630 discourse in which he invoked the "City upon a Hill" before boarding the *Arbella* with a group of colonists,[8] was based on Moses' covenant renewal speech in Deuteronomy 30. Winthrop invited his fellow settlers to "enter into a covenant" with God and to "follow the counsel of Micah, to do justly, to love mercy and to walk humbly with our God." If they were faithful to its terms, he said, they would find "that the God of Israel is among us."[9]

In more modern times, the best expression of this faith was given by Lyndon Baines Johnson in his presidential inaugural in 1965:

> They came here – the exile and the stranger, brave but frightened – to find a place where a man could be his own man. They made a covenant with this land. Conceived in justice, written in liberty, bound in union, it was meant one day to inspire the hopes of all mankind; and it binds us still. If we keep its terms, we shall flourish…[10]

Thus the biblical idea of covenant, especially as adopted by Calvinists and Puritans, laid the foundations of freedom in the modern world, beginning with Calvin's Geneva, spreading to Holland and Scotland, and then, in the first half of the seventeenth century, to the English Revolutionaries and the Pilgrim Fathers in America.

There are, however, dangers in covenantal politics. First, it can lead to overconfidence, the belief that "God is on our side." This was the message of the false prophets whom Jeremiah denounced in his day. Second, it can lead to moral self-righteousness. People can come

8. From Winthrop's "A Model of Christian Charity" speech (Holyrood Church, Southampton, March 21, 1630).
9. This speech has been invoked by recent American presidents: John F. Kennedy, Address to the General Court of Massachusetts (The State House, Boston, January 9, 1961); Ronald Reagan, "A Vision for America" Address (UC Santa Barbara, November 3, 1980); Barack Obama, Commencement Address (University of Massachusetts, Boston, June 2, 2006).
10. Lyndon Baines Johnson, Inaugural Address (Washington, DC, January 20, 1965).

to think: We are the chosen or almost chosen people, therefore we are morally better than the rest. The prophet Malachi addresses this with biting irony: "From where the sun rises to where it sets, My name is great among the nations … but you profane it" (Mal. 1:11–12).[11] The twentieth-century American who delivered this message was Reinhold Niebuhr, in his powerful critique, *The Irony of American History*.[12] Third, it can easily slip into nationalism: the worship not of God but of the nation, the people, or the land.[13] Fourth, politicians and their supporters can forget the fundamental truth of covenantal politics, well summed up by John Schaar, writing about the political beliefs of Abraham Lincoln:

> We are a nation formed by a covenant, by dedication to a set of principles and by an exchange of promises to uphold and advance certain commitments among ourselves and throughout the world. Those principles and commitments are the core of American identity, the soul of the body politic. They make the American nation unique, and uniquely valuable, among and to the other nations. But the other side of the conception contains a warning very like the warnings spoken by the prophets to Israel: if we fail in our promises to each other, and lose the principles of the covenant, then we lose everything, for they are we.[14]

Jewish tradition instituted one of the most powerful reminders of this truth ever uttered: the first chapter of the book of Isaiah, read as the *haftara* on the Shabbat before Tisha B'Av, with its solemn warning that

11. See the classic commentators for a range of interpretations, but the general message is clear. The prophet is telling the people that they have no grounds for self-righteousness.
12. Reinhold Niebuhr, *The Irony of American History* (New York: Scribners, 1952). A generation later, the sociologist Robert Bellah wrote a book along similar lines, *The Broken Covenant* (New York: Seabury Press, 1975).
13. The strongest Jewish critic of nationalism in modern times was the late Yeshayahu Leibowitz. Essential here is the distinction made by George Orwell between patriotism, of which he approved, and nationalism, which he feared (see, for example, *Notes on Nationalism* [London: Penguin, 2018]). Note that veneration of the State rather than of God was the fateful contribution of Rousseau to modern politics (see *The Social Contract*, trans. H. J. Tozer [Ware, UK: Wordsworth, 1998], 37–43).
14. Quoted in Selznick, *Moral Commonwealth*, 481.

corruption and injustice destroy a nation. If that happens, no amount of prayers or sacrifices will save it.

Covenantal politics, first set out in the book of Deuteronomy, thus became, as Moses knew it would, "your wisdom and understanding in the eyes of the nations," though it took the better part of three thousand years for it to happen. Covenant is the most powerful path to lasting freedom yet discovered. But its challenge remains: if we fail in our promises to each other, and lose the principles of the covenant, then we lose everything, for they are we.

The Meanings of Shema

"Listen, Israel, the Lord is our God, the Lord is one" (Deut. 6:4). These words are the supreme testimony of Jewish faith. Each word in this sentence needs careful study, but in this and the next essay I want to focus on only one, the first: the verb *Shema*. In the next essay I ask why we are commanded to listen, rather than to see. In this I want to understand the range of meanings of the verb itself. This will prove fundamental to our understanding of Judaism.

The Mosaic books are, among other things, a set of commandments, 613 of them. That is the primary meaning of the word Torah – *law*. The Torah is not fundamentally about the salvation of the soul. It is about the redemption of society. It is about how to construct a social order that will honour the dignity of the individual, the sanctity of life, and the twin imperatives of justice and compassion. It is about our life together, not about the inner life of the soul, for which we have the book of Psalms.

Hence the Torah's emphasis on law: not secular law, such as every society has, but *Torah min hashamayim,* law as prescribed by Heaven itself. As Psalm 147 puts it: "He has revealed His word to Jacob, His laws and decrees to Israel. He has done this for no other nation"

(Ps. 147:19–20). Law is the basis of liberty. Without it, there is chaos, violence, injustice, and the will to power. Judaism is a religion of law, not because it is solely concerned with justice rather than love. To the contrary, Torah is the source of the three great love commands in Western civilisation: you shall love the Lord your God with all your heart, might, and soul; you shall love your neighbour as yourself; you shall love the stranger for you were once strangers. But love alone cannot structure grace in society.

It would seem to follow logically that a book of commands must have a verb that means "to obey." That is the whole purpose of an imperative. Obedience stands in relation to command as truth does to making a statement. *Yet there is no verb in biblical Hebrew that means to obey*. This is an astonishing fact.

So glaring is the lacuna that when Hebrew was revived in modern times a verb had to be found that meant "to obey." It was obviously necessary, for example, in the case of Israel's defence forces. An army depends on obedience to the command of a superior officer. The word chosen was *letzayet*. But this is an Aramaic word that does not appear in this sense anywhere in the Hebrew Bible. The Torah itself uses a quite different word, namely, *shema*, meaning, "to hear, to listen," and several other things besides.

The root SH-M-A is absolutely fundamental to the book of Deuteronomy, where it appears in one or other forms some ninety-two times (by way of comparison, it appears only six times in the whole of Leviticus). It conveys a wide range of meanings, clustered around five primary senses:

1. to listen, to pay focused attention, as in "Be silent, Israel, and listen [*ushema*]" (Deut. 27:9);
2. to hear, as in "I heard [*shamati*] Your voice in the garden and I was afraid" (Gen. 3:10);
3. to understand, as in "Come, let us go down and confuse their language so they will not understand [*yishme'u*] each other" (Gen. 11:7);
4. to internalise, register, take to heart, as in "And as for Ishmael I have heard you [*shmatikha*]" (Gen. 17:20), meaning, "I have

taken into account what you have said; I will bear it in mind; it is a consideration that weighs with Me";

5. to respond in action, as in "Whatever Sarah says to you, do as she tells you [*shema bekolah*]" (Gen. 21:12).

It is this last sense in which *shema* comes closest to meaning "to obey."

It has yet other meanings in rabbinic Hebrew, such as "to infer," "to accept," "to take into account as evidence," and "to receive as part of the Oral Tradition." No English word has this range of meanings. Perhaps the closest are "to hearken" and "to heed" – neither of them terms in common use today. Psychotherapists nowadays sometimes speak of "active listening," and this is part of what is meant by *shema*.

The best way to discover what is unique about a civilisation is to search for words in its lexicon that are untranslatable into other languages. It is said that the Bedouin have many words for sand and the Inuit many terms for snow. The Greek word *megalopsuchos* – literally, the "great-souled" person, one blessed with wealth, status, and effortless superiority – has no equivalent in either Judaism or Christianity, two cultures that valued, as Greece did not, humility. *Shema* is untranslatable – understandably so since it belongs to biblical Hebrew, the world's supreme example of a culture of the ear (on this, see the next essay).

This is a fact of great consequence and should affect our entire understanding of Judaism. The existence of the verb *lishmo'a* and the absence of the verb *letzayet* tells us that biblical Israel, despite its intense focus on divine commandments, is not a faith that values blind, unthinking, unquestioning obedience. Though there were those who disagreed, for the most part Jews understood the commands as more, and other, than the arbitrary will of God. To the contrary, they were given by God for our benefit, not His.

There is a reason for the commands. In some cases they are rooted in the fact that God created the universe and the laws that govern it; therefore we must respect the integrity of nature. In other cases they are grounded in history. Our ancestors were slaves in Egypt. They knew from indelible personal experience what it is to live in an unjust, tyrannical regime. Therefore a society based on Torah must be just, compassionate, generous. Slaves must rest one day in seven. One year in seven, debts must be cancelled. The landless poor should not go without food at harvest time – and so on.

The God of revelation is also the God of creation and redemption. Therefore when God commands us to do certain things and refrain from others, it is not because His will is arbitrary but because He cares for the integrity of the world as His work (creation), and for the dignity of the human person as His image (redemption). There is a profound congruence between the commandments and the laws that govern nature and history. An arbitrary ruler demands blind obedience. God is not an arbitrary ruler (Avoda Zara 3a); therefore He does not demand blind obedience. Instead, He wishes us as far as possible to understand *why* He has commanded *what* He has commanded.

Hence the emphasis, in Exodus and Deuteronomy, on children asking questions. In an authoritarian culture, questions are discouraged: "Theirs not to reason why/Theirs but to do and die," as Tennyson put it.[1] Had this been the case in Judaism, the Torah would have had a verb that meant the same as *letzayet*, not one with the meanings of *shema*.

On Passover the *least* mature child, not the most, is "one who does not know how to ask." Indeed we are commanded to teach him or her to ask. Even the verb three lines after "Hear O Israel" – usually translated as "You shall *teach these things diligently* to your children" – means, according to Rashi, "You shall *sharpen* your children" – meaning, teach them the full depth of their meaning, rather than superficially (Rashi to Deut. 6:7).

To be sure – this should go without saying – obedience to the commandments should never be *conditional* on understanding them. It is a contradiction in terms to say that one who does not understand or agree with a law is free to break it. Anyone who thinks this has not understood what a law is. But ours is certainly a searching, questioning, rational, intellectual faith, one that calls for the full exercise of the mind.

Shema Yisrael does not mean "Hear, O Israel." It means something like: "Listen. Concentrate. Give the word of God your most focused attention. Strive to understand. Engage all your faculties, intellectual

1. Alfred, Lord Tennyson, "The Charge of the Light Brigade," found in *The Charge of the Light Brigade and Other Poems* (Mineola, NY: Dover, 1992), 52.

and emotional. Make His will your own. For what He commands you to do is not irrational or arbitrary but for your welfare, the welfare of your people, and ultimately for the benefit of all humanity."

In Judaism faith is a form of listening – to the song creation sings to its Creator, and to the message history delivers to those who strive to understand it. That is what Moses says time and again in Deuteronomy: Stop looking; listen. Stop speaking; listen. Create a silence in the soul. Still the clamour of instinct, desire, fear, anger. Strive to listen to the still, small voice beneath the noise. Then you will know that the universe is the work of the One beyond the furthest star yet closer to you than you are to yourself – and then you will love the Lord your God with all your heart, all your soul, and all your might. In God's unity you will find unity, within yourself and between yourself and the world, and you will no longer fear the unknown.

Listening Is an Art

Rabbi Jacob Leiner (1814–1878), leader of the hasidic community in Radzyn, Poland, was the son of the Ishbitzer Rebbe, Rabbi Mordechai Joseph Leiner, whose Torah commentary *Mei Hashilo'aḥ* has become popular in recent years. Rabbi Jacob wrote a commentary of his own, called *Beit Yaakov,* and in the course of a sermon on the month of Av made a profound point about the differences between the senses:

> From a human perspective it often seems as if seeing is a more precise form of knowledge than hearing. In fact, however, hearing has a greater power than seeing. Sight discloses the external aspect of things, but hearing reveals their inwardness. The aspect of God which prevails is "Be silent, Israel, and listen" (Deut. 27:9). The idea of being silent is that the person practises a self-imposed limitation on his senses, no longer looking at the events in this world, and he is then able clearly to understand that "you have now become the people of the Lord your God" – something one can hear during this month.[1]

1. Rabbi Jacob Leiner, *Beit Yaakov,* Rosh Ḥodesh Menahem Av.

Though God cannot be seen, argues the *Beit Yaakov,* He can still be heard, and hearing represents a depth encounter more intimate and transformational than seeing.

Perhaps without intending to, the *Beit Yaakov* has provided us with a point of entry into one of the most important and least understood differences between the two great civilisations of the West. Matthew Arnold, in his *Culture and Anarchy,* called them Hellenism and Hebraism. The political philosopher Leo Strauss spoke of Athens and Jerusalem. We know them best as ancient Greece and ancient Israel.

Greece of the fifth to third centuries BCE was in many respects the greatest culture of antiquity. It excelled in art, architecture, sculpture, and theatre – in short, the visual arts. In these it achieved a greatness never surpassed. The most glittering subsequent artistic flowering of Europe, in Renaissance Italy, was essentially a rediscovery of the world and skills of ancient Greece.

Jews excelled at none of these things, yet their contribution to the West was no less great. The reason is that their interest lay altogether elsewhere, not in sight but in sound, not in seeing but hearing. Judaism is the supreme example of a culture not of the eye but of the ear.

This is how Hans Kohn put it in his *The Idea of Nationalism.* In his opinion, the ancient Greeks were

> the people of sight, of the spatial and plastic sense…as if they thought to transpose the flowing, fleeting, ever related elements of life into rest, space, limitation…. The Jew did not see so much as he heard…. His organ was the ear…. When Elijah perceived God, he heard only a still, small voice. For that reason the Jew never made an image of his God.[2]

That is why the key word of Judaism is *shema.* God is not something we see, but a voice we hear. This is how Moses put it elsewhere in *Parashat Va'etḥanan,* describing the supreme revelation at Mount Sinai: "Then the Lord spoke to you out of the fire. You *heard the sound* of words but

2. Hans Kohn, *The Idea of Nationalism: A Study in Its Origins and Background* (New York: Macmillan, 1945), 30–32.

saw no form; there was only a voice" (Deut. 4:12). This has deep implications for the whole of Judaism. Its way of understanding the world and relating to it is fundamentally different from that of the Greeks and of the philosophical tradition (Socrates, Plato, Aristotle, and others) of which they were the founders. A listening culture is not the same as a seeing culture.

To this day, the West, when it speaks of understanding, uses metaphors of sight.[3] We talk of *insight, foresight,* and *hindsight*; of making an *observation*, of people of *vision*. When we express an opinion, we say, "It *appears* to me that…" When we want someone to concentrate, we say, "*Look*." When we understand something we say, "I *see*." The very word "idea" comes from the same Latin root as the word "video." These come to the West from ancient Greece.

In the Hebrew Bible, by contrast, instead of saying that someone thinks, the verse will say that he "said in his or her heart." Thought is not a form of sight but of speech. This becomes all the more emphatic in the Babylonian Talmud, as the Nazir, Rabbi David Cohen, pointed out in his book *Kol HaNevua*.[4] When the Talmud brings a prooftext, it says *ta shema*, "come and hear." When it draws an inference, it says *shema mina*, "hear from this." When it wants to signal agreement, it says *shome'a ani*, "I hear," and when someone disagrees with a proof, it says *lo mashma lei*, meaning, roughly, "he did not hear it." Tradition is called *mipi hashemua*, "that which has been heard and transmitted orally." All of these are verbs of listening, attending with the ear. For the Greeks, truth is what we see. For Jews, it is what we hear.

Pagan cultures *saw* God, or rather, the gods. They were there in visible phenomena: the sun, the storm, the earth, the sea, the great forces that surround us and reduce us to a sense of insignificance. The polytheistic imagination views reality as the clash of powerful forces, each of which is indifferent to the fate of humankind. A tidal wave does

3. See George Lakoff and Mark Johnson, *Metaphors We Live By* (Chicago: University of Chicago Press, 1980).
4. David Cohen, *Kol HaNevua: HaHigayon HaIvri HaShimi* (Jerusalem: Mossad HaRav Kook, 1970).

not stop to think whom it will drown. The free market makes no moral distinctions. Climate change affects the innocent and guilty alike.

A world confined to the visible is an impersonal world, deaf to our prayers, blind to our hopes, a world without overarching meaning, in which we are temporary interlopers who must protect ourselves as best we can against the random cruelties of fate. Today's secular culture – dominated by television, smartphones, tablets, and computer screens – is also massively visual, a world of images and icons. It, too, like the paganisms of old, finds it hard to discern any meaning in history.

Judaism, by contrast, is the supreme example of a person-centred civilisation – and persons communicate by words. They speak and listen. Conversation joins soul to soul. We communicate, therefore we commune.

The patriarchs and prophets of ancient Israel were the first to understand that God is not part of the visible world but beyond. Hence the prohibition against graven images, visual representations, and icons. Hence, too, the great encounter between God and the prophet Elijah at Mount Horeb:

> The Lord said, "Go out and stand on the mountain in the presence of the Lord, for the Lord is about to pass by." Then a great and powerful wind tore the mountains apart and shattered the rocks before the Lord, but the Lord was not in the wind. After the wind there was an earthquake, but the Lord was not in the earthquake. After the earthquake came a fire, but the Lord was not in the fire. And after the fire came a still, small voice. When Elijah heard it, he pulled his cloak over his face and went out and stood at the mouth of the cave. (I Kings 19:11–13)

You can watch a storm, a fire, an earthquake, but you cannot see a still, small voice. Indeed the Hebrew is more pointed still: the words *kol demama daka* actually mean "the sound of a thin silence," which I define as *a voice you can hear only if you are listening.*

In fact, even when the Hebrew Bible seems to be talking about sight, often this is not the case. So, for example, the book of Isaiah opens with the words, "The *vision* of Isaiah," but it continues: "*Hear* me, you heavens! *Listen*, earth!" (Is. 1:2). The *parasha* known as *Re'eh* begins with the words, "*See*, I am setting before you today a blessing and a curse" (Deut. 11:26), but then immediately continues: "The blessing if you *listen* to the commands of the Lord your God...the curse if you do not *listen* to the commands of the Lord your God" (11:27–28). Even seeing, in Tanakh, is a form of listening.

This had huge consequences for Judaism, the greatest of which is that at the heart of reality is not so much a *power* as a *personal reality*, the God who speaks to us in revelation, and to whom we speak in prayer. This was at the heart of the experience Blaise Pascal had on the night of November 23, 1654, which changed his life, turning him from the most brilliant mathematician of his age into the person who dedicated the rest of his life to spirituality and faith. The famous words he wrote in his diary were: "God of Abraham, God of Isaac, God of Jacob, not of philosophers and scholars."[5]

Faith in Judaism is not about ontology (what exists?) or epistemology (what can we know?) but about relationships – about the people with whom we converse. The famous Turing Test, devised by Alan Turing in 1950 and still the best criterion for artificial intelligence, is whether we can have a conversation with X (who delivers text messages in response to ours) and not know whether X is a computer or a human being. Our humanity lies in the ability to communicate through words.

Sigmund Freud, who had a troubled relationship with Judaism, nonetheless devised the most Jewish cure ever invented. Despite the fact that he called psychoanalysis the "talking cure," it is in fact the *listening cure*: it is the ability of the analyst to listen that helps the patient to bring to articulation sentiments that would otherwise be shrouded in silence. Indeed the sentence "I hear you" has recently come into English usage – mainly in urban America – to mean "I understand." Almost certainly this can be traced to the impact of psychoanalysis on American culture (what Philip Rieff called "the triumph of the therapeutic"[6]).

5. Blaise Pascal, *Pensées*, trans. A. J. Krailsheimer (Harmondsworth: Penguin, 1966), 309.
6. See Philip Rieff, *The Triumph of the Therapeutic* (London: Chatto and Windus, 1966).

The emphasis on listening lies at the heart of the unique intimacy Jews feel with God. In terms of power, there is no possible relationship between an infinite Creator and His finite creations. But in terms of speech, there is. God asks us, as He asked Adam and Eve in the Garden, *Ayeka*, "Where are you?" At times we cry out to Him, "Where are You?" Because there is speech, there is relationship. Between two beings who can communicate with one another there is connection, even if the One is infinitely great and the other infinitely small. Words bridge the metaphysical abyss between soul and soul.

Once we understand this, the significance of many biblical passages becomes clear. God's greatness is that He hears the unheard. As Ishmael lay dying of thirst, "God *heard* the boy crying, and the angel of God called to Hagar from heaven and said to her, 'What is the matter, Hagar? Do not be afraid; God has *heard* the boy crying, there where he lies'" (Gen. 21:17). The very name Ishmael means "God *hears*." One of the tasks of a leader, according to Moses, is to "hear between your brothers" (Deut. 1:16; to this day, a court case is called "a hearing"). The great social legislation in Exodus states that "if you take your neighbour's cloak as a pledge, return it to him by sunset, because his cloak is the only covering he has for his body. What else will he sleep in? *When he cries out to Me, I will hear*, for I am compassionate" (Ex. 22:25–26). Hearing is the basis of both justice and compassion.

When the Torah wants to convey the degradation suffered by the Israelites in Egypt, it says, "They did not *listen* to Moses because of their broken spirit and cruel bondage" (Ex. 6:9). They could no longer hear the good news of their impending liberation. When Solomon asked God for the greatest gift He could bestow on him, he said, "Grant Your servant *a listening heart* to govern Your people and to distinguish between right and wrong" (I Kings 3:9).

We can now also understand one of the strangest sayings of the rabbis: "If a person is taking a walk while reciting Mishnaic teachings, and interrupts his studies to say, How beautiful is that tree, or How fine is that field, it is as if he had committed a mortal sin" (Mishna Avot 3:7). It is not that Judaism does not wish us to enjoy the beauties of nature. In fact, in the siddur there is a special blessing to be said on seeing trees in blossom. The sin is that such a person *abandons the world of sound* (Mishna, i.e., "Oral Torah") *in favour of the world of sight.*

Listening is an art, a skill, a religious discipline, the deepest reflex of the human spirit. One who truly listens can sometimes hear, beneath the noise of the world, the deep speech of the universe, the song creation sings to its Creator:

> The heavens declare the glory of God,
> The skies proclaim the work of His hands.
> Day pours forth speech to day,
> Night communicates knowledge to night.
> There is no speech or language
> Where their voice is not heard. (Ps. 19:2–4)

In the silence of the desert (*midbar*) the Israelites were able to hear the word (*davar*). One trained in the art of listening can hear not only the voice of God but also the silent cry of the lonely, the afflicted, the poor, the needy, the neglected, the unheard. For speech is the most personal of all gestures, and listening the most human – and at the same time, the most divine – of all gifts. God listens, and asks us to listen.

That is why the greatest of all commands – the one we read in *Parashat Va'etḥanan,* the first Jewish words we learned as children, the last words spoken by Jewish martyrs as they went to their deaths, words engraved on the Jewish soul – is *Shema Yisrael,* "Listen, Israel." And now we understand why, as we say those words, we cover our eyes – to shut out, if only for a moment, the world of sight, so that we can more fully enter the world of sound, the world not of Creation but of Revelation, not of God's work but of His word – the world we cannot see but which, if we create an open, attentive silence in the soul, we can hear.

Why Is the Jewish People So Small?

Near the end of *Va'etḥanan,* so inconspicuously that we can sometimes miss it, is a statement with such far-reaching implications that it challenges the impression that has prevailed thus far in the Torah, giving an entirely new complexion to the biblical image of the people Israel: "The Lord did not set His affection on you and choose you because you were more numerous than other peoples, for you are the fewest of all peoples" (Deut. 7:7).

This is not what we have heard thus far. In Genesis God promised the patriarchs that their descendants would be like the stars of the heaven, the sand on the seashore, the dust of the earth, uncountable. Abraham will be the father, not just of one nation but of many. At the beginning of Exodus we read of how the covenantal family, numbering a mere seventy when they went down to Egypt, were "fertile and prolific, and their population increased. They became so numerous that the land was filled with them" (Ex. 1:7). Three times in the book of Deuteronomy, Moses describes the Israelites as being "as many as the stars of the sky" (1:10; 10:22; 28:62). King Solomon speaks of himself as being part of "the people You have chosen, a great people, too numerous to count or number" (I Kings 3:8). The prophet Hosea says that "the Israelites will be like the sand on the seashore, which cannot be measured or counted" (Hos. 2:1).

In all these texts and others it is the size, the numerical greatness, of the people that is emphasised. What then are we to make of Moses' words that speak of its smallness? *Targum Yonatan* interprets it not to be about numbers at all but about self-image. He translates it not as "the fewest of all peoples" but as "the most lowly and humble of peoples." Rashi gives a similar reading, citing Abraham's words, "I am but dust and ashes" (Gen. 18:27), and Moses and Aaron's, "Who are we?" (Ex. 16:7).

Rashbam and Hizkuni (Rabbi Hezekiah ben Manoah; France, mid-thirteenth century) give the more straightforward explanation that Moses is contrasting the Israelites with the seven nations they would be fighting in the land of Canaan/Israel. God would lead the Israelites to victory despite the fact that they were outnumbered by the local inhabitants. Rabbenu Baḥya (Spain, 1255–1340) quotes Maimonides, who says that we would have expected God, King of the universe, to have chosen the most numerous nation in the world as His people, since "the glory of the king is in the multitude of people" (Prov. 14:28). God did not do so. Thus Israel should count itself extraordinarily blessed that God chose it, despite its smallness, to be His *am segula*, His special treasure.

Rabbenu Baḥya finds himself forced to give a more complex reading to resolve the contradiction of Moses, in Deuteronomy, saying *both* that Israel is the smallest of peoples *and* "as many as the stars of the sky" (Gen. 22:17). He turns it into a hypothetical subjunctive, meaning: God *would still have chosen you, even if* you had been the smallest of the peoples.

Sforno gives a simple and straightforward reading: God did not choose a nation for the sake of His honour. Had He done so He would undoubtedly have chosen a mighty and numerous people. His choice had nothing to do with honour and everything to do with love. He loved the patriarchs for their willingness to heed His voice; therefore He loves their children.

Yet there is something in this verse that resonates throughout much of Jewish history. Historically Jews were and are a small people – today, less than 0.2 per cent of the population of the world. There were two reasons for this. First is the heavy toll taken through the ages by exile and persecution, directly by Jews killed in massacres and pogroms, indirectly by those who converted – in fourteenth- and fifteenth-century Spain and nineteenth-century Europe – in order to avoid persecution (tragically, even conversion did not work; racial anti-Semitism persisted in both cases). The Jewish population is a mere fraction of what it might have been had there been no Hadrian, no Crusades, and no anti-Semitism.

The second reason is that Jews did not seek to convert others. Had they done so they would have been closer in numbers to Christianity (2.4 billion) or Islam (1.6 billion). In fact, Malbim reads something like this into our verse. The previous verses have said that the Israelites were about to enter a land with seven nations, Hittites, Girgashites, Amorites, Canaanites, Perizzites, Hivites, and Jebusites. Moses warns them against intermarriage with the other nations, not for racial but for religious reasons: "They will turn your children away from following Me to serve other gods" (Deut. 7:4). Malbim interprets our verse as Moses saying to the Israelites: Do not justify out-marriage on the grounds that it will increase the number of Jews. God is not interested in numbers.

There was a moment when Jews might have sought to convert others.[1] The period in question was the Roman Empire in the first century. Jews numbered some 10 per cent of the empire, and there were many Romans who admired aspects of their faith and way of life. The pagan deities of the Hellenistic world were losing their appeal and plausibility, and throughout the centres of the Mediterranean, individuals were adopting Jewish practices. Two aspects of Judaism stood in their way: the commandments and circumcision. In the end, Jews chose not to compromise their way of life for the sake of making converts. The Hellenistic people who sympathised with Judaism mostly adopted Pauline Christianity instead. Consistently throughout history, Jews have chosen to be true to themselves and to stay small rather than make concessions for the sake of increasing numbers.

1. To be sure, there was one instance when they did. The Hasmonean priest-king John Hyrcanus I forcibly converted the Edomites, known as the Idumeneans. Herod was one of their number.

Notwithstanding all these interpretations and explanations, Tanakh itself offers one extraordinary episode that sheds a different light on the whole issue. It occurs in the seventh chapter of the book of Judges. God has told Gideon to assemble an army and do battle with the Midianites. He gathers a force of 32,000 men. God tells him, "You have too many men. I cannot deliver Midian into their hands, or Israel would boast against Me, 'My own strength has saved me'" (Judges 7:2).

God tells Gideon to say to the men: Whoever is afraid and wishes to go home may do so. Twenty-two thousand men leave. Ten thousand remain. God tells Gideon, "There are still too many men." He proposes a new test. Gideon is to take the men to a river and see how they drink the water. Ninety-seven hundred kneel down to drink, and are dismissed. Gideon is left with a mere three hundred men. "With the three hundred men that lapped [the water] I will save you and give the Midianites into your hands," God tells him (Judges 7:1–8). By a brilliant and unexpected strategy, the three hundred put the entire Midianite army to flight.

The Jewish people are small but have achieved great things to testify in themselves to a force beyond themselves. It has achieved things no other nation its size could have achieved. Its history has been living testimony to the force of divine providence and the impact of high ideals. That is what Moses meant when he said:

> Ask now about the former days, long before your time, from the day God created human beings on the earth; ask from one end of the heavens to the other. Has anything so great as this ever happened, or has anything like it ever been heard of? Has any other people heard the voice of God speaking out of fire, as you have, and lived? Has any god ever tried to take for himself one nation out of another nation, by testings, by signs and wonders, by war, by a mighty hand and an outstretched arm, or by great and awesome deeds, like all the things the Lord your God did for you in Egypt before your very eyes? (Deut. 4:32–34)

Israel defies the laws of history because it serves the Author of history. Attached to greatness, it becomes great.

Through the Jewish people, God is telling humankind that you do not need to be numerous to be great. Nations are judged not by their size but by their contribution to human heritage. Of this the most compelling proof is that a nation as small as the Jews could produce an ever-renewed flow of prophets, priests, poets, philosophers, sages, saints, halakhists, aggadists, codifiers, commentators, rebbes, and *rashei yeshivot.* It has also yielded some of the world's greatest writers, artists, musicians, filmmakers, academics, intellectuals, doctors, lawyers, businesspeople, and technological innovators. Out of all proportion to their numbers, Jews could and can be found working as lawyers fighting injustice, economists fighting poverty, doctors fighting disease, teachers fighting ignorance, and therapists fighting depression and despair.

You do not need numbers to enlarge the spiritual and moral horizons of humankind. You need other things altogether: a sense of the worth and dignity of the individual, of the power of human possibility to transform the world, of the importance of giving everyone the best education they can have, of making each feel part of a collective responsibility to ameliorate the human condition. Judaism asks of us the willingness to take high ideals and enact them in the real world, unswayed by disappointments and defeats.

This is still evident today, especially among the people of Israel in the State of Israel. Traduced in the media and pilloried by much of the world, Israel continues to produce human miracles in medicine, agriculture, technology, and the arts, as if the word "impossible" did not exist in the Hebrew language. Israel remains a small nation, surrounded, as in biblical times, by "nations larger and stronger than you" (Deut. 7:1). Yet the truth remains, as Moses said: "The Lord did not set His affection on you and choose you because you were more numerous than other peoples, for you are the fewest of all peoples."

This small people has outlived all the world's great empires to deliver to humanity a message of hope: you need not be large to be great. What you need is to be open to a power greater than yourself. It is said that King Louis XIV of France once asked Blaise Pascal, the brilliant mathematician and theologian, to give him proof of the existence of God. Pascal is said to have replied, "Your Majesty, the Jews!"

Ekev
עקב

In *Ekev*, Moses continues his second address, setting out in broad terms the principles of the covenant the Israelites made with God, and what it demands of them as a chosen nation in a Promised Land. If they are faithful to the covenant, they will be blessed materially as well as spiritually. But they should not attribute their success to themselves or their righteousness. Moses reminds them of the people's sins during the wilderness years, the Golden Calf, the Korah rebellion, and other such episodes. He reminds them, too, of God's forgiveness. Remembering their history, they are to love and revere God and teach their children to do likewise. This entire complex of beliefs is summarised in the passage that became the second paragraph of the *Shema* (Deut. 11:13–21). Israel's fate depends on Israel's faith.

The first of the following essays is about why Moses, in Deuteronomy, speaks so persistently about the importance of collective memory and the danger of forgetfulness. What has this to do with politics and society? The second is about another of Deuteronomy's key words: love. Why is this so central to Judaism, and why does Moses speak about it here more than in the Torah's previous books? The third is about the emphasis, here and in the previous *parasha*, on the duty of parents to educate their children; Israel was to become a nation of educators. The fourth concerns an unusual description of Israel's geography and climate. Why was *this* land chosen to become the holy land? Is there a connection between landscape and spirituality? The last essay reflects on a passage in the *parasha* that became the basis for the rabbinic teaching that "where you find greatness, there you find humility."

The Politics of Memory

In *Ekev* Moses sets out a political doctrine of such wisdom that it can never become redundant or obsolete. He does it by way of a pointed contrast between the ideal to which Israel is called, and the danger with which it is faced. This is the ideal:

> Observe the commands of the Lord your God, walking in His ways and revering Him. For the Lord your God is bringing you into a good land – a land with streams and pools of water, with springs flowing in the valleys and hills; a land with wheat and barley, vines and fig trees, pomegranates, olive oil and honey; a land where bread will not be scarce and you will lack nothing; a land where the rocks are iron and you can dig copper out of the hills. *When you have eaten and are satisfied,* bless the Lord your God for the good land He has given you. (Deut. 8:6–10)

And this is the danger:

> Be careful that you *do not forget* the Lord your God, failing to observe His commands, His laws, and His decrees that I am

> giving you this day. Otherwise, *when you eat and are satisfied,* when you build fine houses and settle down, and when your herds and flocks grow large and your silver and gold increase and all you have is multiplied, then your heart will become proud and *you will forget* the Lord your God, who brought you out of Egypt, out of the land of slavery.... You may say to yourself, "My power and the strength of my hands have produced this wealth for me." But *remember* the Lord your God, for it is He who gives you the ability to produce wealth, and so confirms His covenant, which He swore to your forefathers, as it is today. (Deut. 8:11–17)

The two passages follow directly on from one another. They are linked by the phrase "when you have eaten and are satisfied," and the contrast between them is a fugue between the verbs "to remember" and "to forget."

Good things, says Moses to the next generation, will happen to you. Everything, however, will depend on how you respond. *Either* you will eat and be satisfied and bless God, *remembering* that all things come from Him – *or* you will eat and be satisfied and *forget* to whom you owe all this. You will think it comes entirely from your own efforts: "My power and the strength of my hands have produced this wealth for me." Although this may seem a small difference, it will, says Moses, make *all* the difference. On this alone will turn your future as a nation in its own land.

Moses' argument is brilliant and counter-intuitive. You may think, he says, that the hard times are behind you. You have wandered for forty years without a home. There were times when you had no water, no food. You were exposed to the elements. You were attacked by your enemies. You may think this was the test of your strength. It was not. *The real challenge is not poverty but affluence, not slavery but freedom, not homelessness but home.*

Many nations have been lifted to great heights when they faced difficulty and danger. They fought battles and won. They came through crises – droughts, plagues, recessions, defeats – and were toughened by them. When times are hard, people grow. They bury their differences. There is a sense of community and solidarity, of neighbours and strangers pulling together. Many people who have lived through a war remember it as the most vivid time of their life.

The real test of a nation is not if it can survive a crisis but if it can survive the *lack* of a crisis. Can it stay strong during times of ease and plenty, power and prestige? That is the challenge that has defeated every civilisation known to history. Let it not, says Moses, defeat you.

Moses' foresight was little less than stunning. The pages of history are littered with the relics of nations that seemed impregnable in their day, but which eventually declined and fell and lapsed into oblivion – and always for the reason Moses prophetically foresaw. *They forgot.*[1] Memories fade. People lose sight of the values they once fought for – justice, equality, independence, freedom. The nation, its early battles over, becomes strong. Some of its members grow rich. They become lax, self-indulgent, over-sophisticated, decadent. They lose their sense of social solidarity. They no longer feel it their duty to care for the poor, the weak, the marginal, the losers. They begin to feel that such wealth and position as they have is theirs by right. The bonds of fraternity and collective responsibility begin to fray. The less well-off feel an acute sense of injustice. The scene is set for either revolution or conquest. Societies succumb to external pressures when they have long been weakened by internal decay. That was the danger Moses foresaw and about which he warned.

His analysis has proved true time and again, and it has been restated by several great analysts of the human condition. In the fourteenth century, the Islamic scholar Ibn Khaldun (1332–1406) argued that when a civilisation becomes great, its elites get used to luxury and comfort, and the people as a whole lose what he called their *asabiyyah*, their social solidarity. The people then become prey to a conquering enemy, less civilised than they are but more cohesive and driven.

The Italian political philosopher Giambattista Vico (1668–1744) described a similar cycle: People, he said, "first sense what is necessary, then consider what is useful, next attend to comfort, later delight in

1. For a recent study of this idea applied to contemporary politics, see David Andress, *Cultural Dementia: How the West Has Lost Its History and Risks Losing Everything Else* (London: Head of Zeus, 2018).

pleasures, soon grow dissolute in luxury, and finally go mad squandering their estates."[2] Affluence begets decadence.

In the twentieth century few said it better than Bertrand Russell in his *History of Western Philosophy*. He believed that the two great peaks of civilisation were reached in ancient Greece and Renaissance Italy, but he was honest enough to see that the very features that made them great contained the seeds of their own demise:

> What had happened in the great age of Greece happened again in Renaissance Italy: traditional moral restraints disappeared, because they were seen to be associated with superstition; the liberation from fetters made individuals energetic and creative, producing a rare fluorescence of genius; but the anarchy and treachery which inevitably resulted from the decay of morals made Italians collectively impotent, and they fell, like the Greeks, under the domination of nations less civilized than themselves but not so destitute of social cohesion.[3]

Moses, however, did more than prophesy and warn. He also taught how the danger could be avoided, and here too his insight is as relevant now as it was then. He spoke of the vital significance of *memory* for the moral health of a society.

Throughout history there have been many attempts to ground ethics in universal attributes of humanity. Some, like Immanuel Kant, based it on reason. Others based it on duty. Bentham rooted it in consequences ("the greatest happiness for the greatest number"[4]). David Hume attributed it to certain basic emotions: sympathy, empathy, compassion. Adam Smith predicated it on the capacity to stand back from situations and judge them with detachment ("the impartial spectator"). Each of these has its virtues, but none has proved fail-safe.

---

2. Giambattista Vico, *New Science: Principles of the New Science Concerning the Common Nature of Nations* (London: Penguin, 1999), 489.
3. Bertrand Russell, *History of Western Philosophy* (London: Routledge, 2004), 6.
4. *The Collected Works of Jeremy Bentham: A Comment on the Commentaries and A Fragment on Government*, ed. James Henderson Burns and Herbert Lionel Adolphus Hart (London: Athlone Press, 1977), 393.

Judaism took and takes a different view. *The guardian of conscience is memory*. Time and again the verb *zakhor*, "remember," resonates through Moses' speeches in Deuteronomy:

> *Remember* that you were slaves in Egypt ... therefore the Lord your God has commanded you to observe the Shabbat day. (Deut. 5:15)
>
> *Remember* how the Lord your God led you all the way in the desert these forty years ... (Deut. 8:2)
>
> *Remember* this and never forget how you provoked the Lord your God to anger in the desert ... (Deut. 9:7)
>
> *Remember* what the Lord your God did to Miriam along the way after you came out of Egypt. (Deut. 24:9)
>
> *Remember* what the Amalekites did to you along the way when you came out of Egypt. (Deut. 25:17)
>
> *Remember* the days of old, consider the years of ages past. (Deut. 32:7)

As Yosef Hayim Yerushalmi notes in his great treatise, *Zakhor: Jewish History and Jewish Memory*, "Only in Israel and nowhere else is the injunction to remember felt as a religious imperative to an entire people."[5] *Civilisations begin to die when they forget. Israel was commanded never to forget.*

In an eloquent passage, the American scholar Jacob Neusner once wrote:

> Civilization hangs suspended, from generation to generation, by the gossamer strand of memory. If only one cohort of mothers and fathers fails to convey to its children what it has learned

5. Yosef Hayim Yerushalmi, *Zakhor: Jewish History and Jewish Memory* (Seattle: University of Washington Press, 1982), 11.

> from its parents, then the great chain of learning and wisdom snaps. If the guardians of human knowledge stumble only one time, in their fall collapses the whole edifice of knowledge and understanding.[6]

The politics of free societies depends on the handing on of memory. That was Moses' insight, and it speaks to us with undiminished power today.

6. Jacob Neusner, *Conservative, American, and Jewish* (Lafayette, LA: Huntington House, 1993), 35.

The Morality of Love

Something implicit in the Torah from the very beginning becomes explicit in the book of Deuteronomy. God is the God of love. More than we love Him, He loves us. Here, for instance, is the beginning of *Parashat Ekev*:

> If you pay attention to these laws and are careful to follow them, then the Lord your God will keep his *covenant of love* [*et habrit ve'et haḥesed*] with you, as He swore to your ancestors. He will *love* you and bless you and increase your numbers. (Deut. 7:12–13)

Again in the *parasha* we read:

> To the Lord your God belong the heavens, even the highest heavens, the earth, and everything in it. Yet the Lord *set His affection* on your ancestors and *loved* them, and He chose you, their descendants, above all the nations – as it is today. (Deut. 10:14–15)

And here is a verse from *Parashat Va'etḥanan*: "Because He *loved* your ancestors and chose their descendants after them, He brought you out of Egypt by His Presence and His great strength" (Deut. 4:37).

The book of Deuteronomy is saturated with the language of love. The root A-H-V appears in Exodus twice, in Leviticus twice (both in Lev. 19), in Numbers not at all – and in Deuteronomy twenty-three times. Deuteronomy is a book about societal beatitude and the transformative power of love.

Nothing could be more misleading and invidious than the contrast between Christianity as a religion of love and forgiveness and Judaism as a religion of law and retribution. As I have noted elsewhere,[1] and as David Konstan has argued in *Before Forgiveness*, the idea of forgiveness as opposed to mere appeasement was born in Judaism.[2] Interpersonal forgiveness began when Joseph forgave his brothers for selling him into slavery. Divine forgiveness entered the Jewish calendar with the institution of Yom Kippur as the supreme day of divine pardon following the sin of the Golden Calf.

Similarly with love: when the New Testament speaks of love it does so by direct quotation from Leviticus: "You shall love your neighbour as yourself" (19:18) and Deuteronomy: "You shall love the Lord your God with all your heart, all your soul, and all your might" (6:5). As philosopher Simon May puts it in his splendid book, *Love: A History*:

> The widespread belief that the Hebrew Bible is all about vengeance and "an eye for an eye," while the Gospels supposedly invent love as an unconditional and universal value, must therefore count as one of the most extraordinary misunderstandings in all of Western history. For the Hebrew Bible is the source not

1. See, for example, "What It Takes to Forgive" (http://rabbisacks.org/takes-forgive-vayechi-5778/) and "The Day Forgiveness Was Born (http://rabbisacks.org/covenant-conversation-5772-vayigash-the-day-forgiveness-was-born/).
2. David Konstan, *Before Forgiveness: The Origins of a Moral Idea* (Cambridge, UK: Cambridge University Press, 2010).

> just of the two love commandments but of a larger moral vision inspired by wonder for love's power.[3]

His judgement is unequivocal: "If love in the Western world has a founding text, that text is Hebrew."[4]

More than this: in *Ethical Life: The Past and Present of Ethical Cultures,* philosopher Harry Redner distinguishes four basic visions of the ethical life in the history of civilisations.[5] One he calls *civic ethics,* the ethics of ancient Greece and Rome. Second is the *ethic of duty,* which he identifies with Confucianism, Krishnaism, and late Stoicism. Third is the *ethic of honour,* a distinctive combination of courtly and military decorum to be found among Persians, Arabs, and Turks as well as in medieval Christianity (the "chivalrous knight") and Islam.

The fourth vision of the ethical life, which he calls simply *morality,* he traces to Leviticus and Deuteronomy. He defines it simply as "the ethic of love," and represents what made the West morally unique:

> The biblical "love of one's neighbor" is a very special form of love, a unique development of the Judaic religion and unlike any to be encountered outside it. It is a supremely altruistic love, for to love one's neighbor as oneself means always to put oneself in his place and to act on his behalf as one would naturally and selfishly act on one's own.[6]

To be sure, Buddhism also makes space for the idea of love, though it is differently inflected, more impersonal, and unrelated to a relationship with God.

What is radical about this idea is that, first, the Torah insists, against virtually the whole of the ancient world, that the elements that constitute reality are neither hostile nor indifferent to humankind. We

3. Simon May, *Love: A History* (New Haven, CT: Yale University Press, 2011), 19–20.
4. Ibid., 14.
5. Harry Redner, *Ethical Life: The Past and Present of Ethical Cultures* (New York: Rowman and Littlefield, 2001).
6. Ibid., 50.

are here because Someone wanted us to be, One who cares about us, watches over us, and seeks our well-being.

Second, the love with which God created the universe is not just divine. It is to serve as the model for us in our humanity. We are bidden to love the neighbour and the stranger, to engage in acts of kindness and compassion, and to build a society based on love. Here is how *Parashat Ekev* puts it:

> For the Lord your God is God of gods and Lord of lords, the great, mighty, and awesome God who shows no partiality and accepts no bribes. He defends the cause of the fatherless and the widow, and loves the stranger, giving him food and clothing. So you must love the stranger, for you yourselves were strangers in the land of Egypt. (Deut. 10:18–19)

In short: *God created the world in love and forgiveness and asks us to love and forgive others.* I believe that to be the most profound moral idea in human history.

There is, however, an obvious question. Why is it that love, which plays so great a part in the book of Deuteronomy, is so much less in evidence in the earlier books of Exodus, Leviticus (with the exception of Lev. 19), and Numbers?

The best way of answering that question is to ask another: Why is it that forgiveness plays no part – at least on the surface of the narrative – in the book of Genesis?[7] God does not forgive Adam and Eve or Cain (though He mitigates their punishment). Forgiveness does not figure in the stories of the Flood, the Tower of Babel, or the destruction of Sodom and the cities of the plain (Abraham's plea is that the cities be spared if they contain fifty or ten righteous people; this is not a plea for forgiveness). Divine forgiveness makes its first appearance in the book of Exodus after Moses' successful plea in the wake of the Golden Calf, and is then institutionalised in the form of Yom Kippur (Lev. 16), but not before. Why so?

---

7. I exclude, here, midrashic readings of these texts, some of which do make reference to forgiveness.

The simple, radical answer is: *God does not forgive human beings until human beings learn to forgive one another*. Genesis ends with Joseph forgiving his brothers. Only thereafter does God forgive human beings.

Turning to love: Genesis contains many references to it. Abraham loves Isaac. Isaac loves Esau. Rebecca loves Jacob. Jacob loves Rachel. He also loves Joseph. There is interpersonal love in plentiful supply. *But almost all the loves of Genesis turn out to be divisive*. They lead to tension between Jacob and Esau, between Rachel and Leah, and between Joseph and his brothers. Implicit in Genesis is a profound observation missed by most moralists and theologians. Love in and of itself – real love, personal and passionate, the kind of love that suffuses much of the prophetic literature as well as the Song of Songs, the greatest love song in Tanakh, as opposed to the detached, generalised love called *agape* which we associate with ancient Greece – is not sufficient as a basis for society. It can divide as well as unite.

Hence it does not figure as a major motif until we reach the integrated social-moral-political vision of Deuteronomy which combines love and justice. *Tzedek*, justice, turns out to be another key word of Deuteronomy, appearing eighteen times. It appears only four times in Exodus, not at all in Numbers, and in Leviticus only in chapter 19, the only chapter that also contains the word "love." In other words, *in Judaism love and justice go hand in hand*. Again this is noted by Simon May:

> [W]hat we must note here, for it is fundamental to the history of Western love, is the remarkable and radical justice that underlies the love commandment of Leviticus. Not a cold justice in which due deserts are mechanically handed out, but the justice that brings the other, as an individual with needs and interests, into a relationship of respect. All our neighbours are to be recognised as equal to ourselves before the law of love. Justice and love therefore become inseparable.[8]

8. May, *Love: A History*, 17.

Love without justice leads to rivalry, and eventually to hate. Justice without love is devoid of the humanising forces of compassion and mercy. We need both. This unique ethical vision – the love of God for humans and of humans for God, translated into an ethic of love towards both neighbour and stranger – is the foundation of Western civilisation and its abiding glory.

It is born here in the book of Deuteronomy, the book of law-as-love and love-as-law.

A Nation of Educators

In a justly famous passage the American writer Mark Twain made this observation about the Jew:

> He has made a marvelous fight in this world, in all the ages; and has done it with his hands tied behind him.... The Egyptian, the Babylonian, and the Persian rose, filled the planet with sound and splendor, then faded to dream-stuff and passed away; the Greek and the Roman followed, and made a vast noise, and they are gone; other peoples have sprung up and held their torch high for a time, but it burned out, and they sit in twilight now, or have vanished. The Jew saw them all, beat them all, and is now what he always was, exhibiting no decadence, no infirmities of age, no weakening of his parts, no slowing of his energies, no dulling of his alert and aggressive mind. All things are mortal but the Jew; all other forces pass, but he remains. What is the secret of his immortality?[1]

1. Mark Twain, "Concerning the Jews," *Harper's Magazine*, September 1899.

Twain's question is a good one. What is the secret of Jewish survival throughout the ages under conditions that were often those of exile, dispersion, homelessness, powerlessness, and persecution? Normally nations survive because they have a land; they have the power of self-determination; they inhabit a culture that is of their own making; they have the requisites of continuity. For the better part of two thousand years, Jews did not. No other nation has kept its identity under such circumstances.

The answer is set out in Deuteronomy in the two passages that form the first two paragraphs of the *Shema,* the first in *Parashat Va'etḥanan,* the second in *Parashat Ekev*. Here is the second of those texts:

> Teach [these things] to your children, speaking of them when you sit at home and when you travel on the way, when you lie down and when you rise. Write them on the doorframes of your houses and on your gates, so that your days and the days of your children may be many in the land that the Lord swore to give your forefathers, as many as the days that the heavens are above the earth. (Deut. 11:19–21)

Jews survived because they set as their highest priority handing on their heritage to the next generation. They placed education at the very heart of faith. Their heroes were teachers, their citadels were houses of study, and their passion learning and the life of the mind. And it began, as the passage makes clear, in the context of the home. To be a parent, in Judaism, is to be a teacher. Education is the conversation between the generations.

There is a profound reason for this. The Torah envisaged a society that would be more than just a reflection of the kind of values that drive most human groups: the search for wealth and power. Instead, as a holy people in a holy land, Jews were to care about the poor and powerless. They were to become a nation driven by high ideals. They would seek to be an inspiration to others. They were charged with becoming a society that would bear testimony to something greater than themselves, namely, to God Himself.

But if one thing is clear from the Torah's narrative thus far, it is that the transformation of a people takes a long time. The generation born in slavery who left Egypt proved to be unequal to the task of conquering a land. The journey to the Promised Land that should have taken days or weeks turned out to last for forty years. Larger transformations take longer still. There is little doubt that the underlying message of the Torah is hostile to the idea of slavery. A religion whose founding experience was the liberation of slavery cannot be one that seeks to turn other people into slaves. Yet slavery was not abolished in the United States until 1865, and even then not without a civil war.

If any change in the human condition takes longer than a generation, education becomes fundamental. We need to hand on our memories, values, ideals, laws, and customs to our children, and they to theirs, if each generation is to continue the journey to a destination not yet reached. The handing on of tradition is usually thought of as something valued by conservative thinkers, such as Edmund Burke. But it can also be a radical gesture, when we hand on to our children our own not-yet-fully-realised ideals.

This emphasis on education has given Judaism, from the very beginning, a future orientation that is unusual among the great religions of the world. Jews have always cared about children and placed them as their highest joy. Rather than look back to a vanished past, they have looked forward to a distant but promised future. A people that places children at the apex of its agenda does not grow old. It learns to see the world through the eyes of a child – with hope and wonder and aspiration unsullied by cynicism and despair.

It was not until 1870 that Britain – then the most advanced and prosperous in the world – introduced universal compulsory education. Jews had done so eighteen centuries before. This is how the Talmud describes the educational programme of the person it credits with the achievement, R. Yehoshua b. Gamla:

> May the name of that man, Yehoshua b. Gamla, be blessed, because, were it not for him, the Torah would have been forgotten from Israel. For at first, if a child had a father, his father taught him, and if he had no father, he did not learn at all.... They then made an ordinance that teachers of children should be appointed in Jerusalem.... Even so, however, if a child had a father, the father

> would take him up to Jerusalem and have him taught there, and if not, he would not go up to learn there. They therefore ordained that teachers should be appointed in each prefecture, and that boys should enter school at the age of sixteen or seventeen. However, if the teacher punished them they used to rebel and leave the school. Eventually Yehoshua b. Gamla came and ordained that teachers of young children should be appointed in each district and each town, and that children should enter the school at the age of six or seven. (Bava Batra 21a)

At roughly the same time – the first century – the historian Josephus testifies:

> Should any one of our nation be asked about our laws, he will repeat them as readily as his own name. The result of our education in our laws from the very dawn of intelligence is that they are, as it were, engraved on our souls. Hence to break them is rare, and no one can evade punishment by the excuse of ignorance.[2]

So it was at virtually every period of Jewish history and almost every place where there was a Jewish community. One testimony is particularly poignant. By the fifteenth century, Spanish Jewry had long passed its Golden Age. The Spanish equivalent of Kristallnacht – synagogues set on fire, Jewish businesses looted, and Jews killed – took place in 1391. From then until their expulsion in 1492, Jews lived under the shadow of persecution. Their civil rights were curtailed. They were constantly urged to convert to Christianity. Some did so, while practising Judaism in secret. Jews called them *conversos* or *anusim* (forced converts). The Spanish contemptuously called them Marranos, meaning "pigs," or "swine." Many of them became victims of the Inquisition and were burned at the stake.

At the height of this crisis, a gathering of Jews was convened at Valladolid, Spain, in 1432. It ordained a series of taxes on meat, wine, weddings, and circumcisions, to raise funds for public education:

2. Josephus, *Contra Apionem*, ii, 177–78.

> We also ordain that every community of fifteen householders [or more] shall be obliged to maintain a qualified elementary teacher to instruct their children in Scripture. They shall provide him with sufficient income for a living in accordance with the number of his dependants. The parents shall be obliged to send their children to that teacher, and each shall pay him in accordance with his means. If this revenue from the parents should prove inadequate, the community shall be obliged to supplement it with an amount necessary for his livelihood in accordance with the time and the place.[3]

Until modern times, there was no parallel to this Jewish insistence on education as the fundamental right and duty of every person, every child.

Nor did this begin in the days of Moses. It started even earlier, at the dawn of Jewish time, when God said of Abraham, "For I have chosen him, *so that he will instruct his children* and his household after him to keep the way of the Lord by doing what is right and just" (Gen. 18:19). Abraham was chosen to be a father and a teacher.

Where did it come from, this passion for learning and teaching, education and literacy? My own view is that it happened when and where it did because Judaism was born at the time and place of the invention of the alphabet. Until then, writing systems like Mesopotamian cuneiform and Egyptian hieroglyphics had so many symbols that only a small minority of the population had the time and resources to learn to read and write. They became the cognitive elite. The masses remained illiterate. The invention of the alphabet made it possible to change that. The first known alphabet was the Proto-Semitic script. The word *alphabet* itself comes from the names of the first two letters in Semitic languages (and subsequently in Greek): *aleph, bet*. This reduced the symbol set to a mere twenty-two characters, and thus made universal literacy possible for the first time.

This also gave shape and substance to the Jewish belief, revolutionary in its time, in the equal dignity of every person under the

3. Salo Wittmayer Baron, *The Jewish Community* (Westport, CT: Greenwood Press, 1972), 2:172.

sovereignty of God. Many attempts have been made to create an egalitarian society. Some have focused on equality of income, others on equality of power. Judaism concentrated on something else altogether: equal access to education. Knowledge is fundamental to human dignity, and a society that cares for the latter must make the former available to all.

Above all, though, education is a key expression of the fundamental idea of Deuteronomy, that Judaism is a covenant across the generations. Even when, after Moses' death, the Israelites crossed the Jordan and entered the Promised Land, they were still on a journey, spiritual if not physical, to the good society that would be a home for the Divine Presence. We are still on that journey to a world at peace under the sovereignty of God. That is why Moses was so insistent that we hand on our ideals and aspirations to our children. What we have not yet achieved, our children or grandchildren may. Teaching our children, we entrust our future to them as those who came before us placed their trust in us.

The Mesopotamians built ziggurats, the Egyptians built pyramids, the Greeks built the Parthenon, and the Romans the Coliseum. Jews built schools. That is why we are still here. That, in answer to Mark Twain's question, is the secret of our immortality.

Geography and Destiny

The Torah is a work of wondrous depth and subtlety, so much so that we can easily miss some of its most profound intimations. There is a fine example in *Parashat Ekev*. It concerns the character of the land of Israel. Ultimately, however, it is a haunting glimpse into the nature of Jewish destiny itself, then and now.

The picture we have had of the Promised Land, from the beginning of the Exodus until now, is that it is a land "flowing with milk and honey." Interestingly, the mid-twentieth-century scholar Reuven Margaliot once pointed out that when the land of Israel is praised in the Torah, it is always in terms of its vegetation, never in terms of its animal products. Why, then, is there an apparent exception in the case of the most famous phrase of all, the land "flowing with milk and honey"? The honey referred to, he notes, is not from bees but from the date palm. On that, many commentators concur. Margaliot's radical suggestion relates to "milk." We know from many texts that Israel was famed for its grapes and wine. But the biblical *yayin*, "wine," standardly refers to red wine. *Ḥalav* – the word we translate as "milk" – says Margoliot, means white wine, and is called *ḥalav* because of its milky appearance.[1]

Even the spies, despite their gloomy report, cannot deny its fruitfulness: "We went into the land to which you sent us, and it does flow with milk and honey! Here is its fruit" (Num. 13:27). Early in the *parasha* Moses delivers a magnificent poem to this effect:

> For the Lord your God is bringing you into a good land – a land with streams and pools of water, with springs flowing in the valleys and hills, a land of wheat and barley, vines and fig trees, pomegranates, olive oil and honey, a land where bread will not be scarce, and you will lack nothing. (Deut. 8:7–8)

Thus far the Promised Land conjured up in our imagination is indeed a land of promise, another Eden, an earthly paradise. However, as the lawyers say: always read the small print. It comes several chapters later and is fateful in its implications. For the first time in forty years, Moses uses a quite different tone when speaking about the land of Israel:

> The land you are entering to take over is not like the land of Egypt, from which you have come, where you planted your seed and irrigated it by foot as in a vegetable garden. But the land you are crossing the Jordan to take possession of is a land of mountains and valleys that drinks rain from heaven. It is a land the Lord your God cares for; the eyes of the Lord your God are continually on it from the beginning of the year to its end. (Deut. 11:10–12)

The point is made briefly, almost in passing, yet it makes all the difference. It is indeed a fine land – but it is not like other fine lands. Civilisation began when human beings first turned from hunting and gathering to agriculture and the domestication of animals. This led to the first concentrations of population, the birth of cities, city states, and then nations and empires.

---

1. Reuven Margaliot, *HaMikra VeHaMesora* (Jerusalem: Mossad HaRav Kook, 5749), 62–64.

The Torah sketches this process in broad outlines. It began in Mesopotamia, in the fertile plain between the Tigris and Euphrates, and then in Egypt, in the Nile delta. These were ideal places for the development of agriculture because water was supplied by rivers, and irrigation was a simple matter of making ditches and channels. Water, on which crops depended, was reliable (the one danger in the low-lying lands of Mesopotamia was of floods – hence the presence of flood narratives, not only in the Torah but in all literatures of that place and time).

The land of Israel, says Moses, is not like that. It is not a fertile plain. It is a land of hills and valleys. It depends on rain – and rain in the Middle East, then and now, is unpredictable. Suddenly, with this discordant note, we recall a whole series of earlier episodes in the book of Genesis in which we read the words, "And there was a famine in the land." This led first Abraham, then Isaac, then Jacob and his children into a series of journeys and exiles (the book of Ruth begins with another famine, which forces Elimelekh and his family to the land of Moab).

Life in Israel will never be as stable, permanent, and secure as it is elsewhere. Those who live there are vulnerable, if to nothing else, then to periodic drought. They will exist in a permanent state of insecurity, never knowing in advance whether the seeds they plant will grow or not. Israel is the land of promise, but it will always depend on He-who-promises.

Is geography destiny? Judah Halevi thought so. He writes the following in *The Kuzari* about the land of Israel:

> Its fertility or barrenness, its happiness or misfortune, depend upon the divine influence which your conduct will merit, whilst the rest of the world will continue its natural course. For if the Divine Presence is among you, you will perceive by the fertility of your country, by the regularity with which your rainfalls appear in their due seasons, by your victories over your enemies in spite of your inferior numbers, that your affairs are not managed by simple laws of nature, but by the divine will. You will also see that drought, death, and wild beasts pursue you as a result of disobedience, although the whole world lives in peace. This

> shows you that your concerns are arranged by a higher power than mere nature.[2]

Unpacking this in non-mystical terms, we can say that the character of a country – its topography and climate – affects the kind of society people build, and hence the culture and ethos that emerge. In Mesopotamia and Egypt, the most powerful reality was the regularity of nature, the succession of the seasons, which seemed to mirror the slow revolution of the stars. The cultures to which both places gave rise were cosmological and their sense of time cyclical. The universe seemed to be ruled by the heavenly bodies whose hierarchy and order were replicated in the hierarchy and order of life on earth. This is the mindset of the world of myth.

Israel, by contrast, was a land without regularities. There was no guarantee that next year would be like this, or this year like last, no certainty that the rain would fall and the earth yield its crops or the trees their fruit. Thus in Israel a new sense of time was born – the time we call historical. Those who lived, or live, in Israel exist in a state of radical contingency. They can never take the future for granted. They depend on something other than nature. David Ben-Gurion knew this. He once said: "In Israel, in order to be a realist, you must believe in miracles."[3] To put it at its simplest: In Egypt, where the source of life was the Nile, you looked down. In Israel, where the source of life is rain, you had no choice but to look up.

This is a theme we have met before. In the course of the first war the Israelites had to fight for themselves, against Amalek, we read: "As long as Moses held up his hands, the Israelites prevailed, but whenever he lowered his hands, the Amalekites prevailed" (Ex. 17:11). On this, the Mishna comments: "Did the hands of Moses make or break war? Rather, the text implies that whenever the Israelites looked up and dedicated their hearts to their Father in heaven, they prevailed, but otherwise they fell" (Mishna Rosh HaShana 3:8).

Israel – the land "that drinks rain from heaven" – is a place whose inhabitants would be ever mindful of their dependence on the fact that

---

2. *Kuzari*, I:109.
3. Interview on CBS, October 5, 1956.

"the eyes of the Lord your God are continually on it from the beginning of the year to its end." It is the place where you have to look up to survive.

And so it was. Israel's existence as a nation in its land was never secure. Its greatest moment, under King Solomon, did not last. Immediately after his death, the people split into two kingdoms, neither of which could, or did, sustain their independence for long.

Israel is by its very nature a vulnerable place, a strategic location at the meeting point of three continents, always at the mercy of surrounding empires but never the basis of an empire itself. Thus were the terms of the covenant – and the prophetic interpretation of history – fixed from the outset. Israel would have to depend on exceptional strength on the part of its inhabitants. It was never big enough to sustain a large population. The prophets knew that the very existence of Israel as a sovereign nation was predicated on a people lifted to greatness by a sense of mission and high ideals.

Every individual would count. Therefore every individual had to feel part of the whole, respected and given the means of a dignified life. Injustice, gross inequality, or a failure of concern for the weak and marginal would endanger society at its very roots. There was no margin for error or discontent. Without indomitable courage based on the knowledge that God was with them, the people would fall prey to larger powers.

When the prophet Zechariah said, "Not by strength nor by might but by My spirit, says the Lord" (Zech. 4:6), he was formulating an axiom of Jewish history. There neither was nor would be a time when Israel could rely on numbers, or vast tracts of territory, or easily defensible borders. So it was then. So it is now.

We do not live in an age of prophets, yet Israel exists today in the same circumstances as those which gave birth to the prophets. As I write these words, the state is seventy years old. But it is also more than three thousand years old. The terms of its existence have not changed. Israel always longed for security but rarely found it. Neither its climate nor its geography made for an easy life.

That is the nature of Jewish faith – not security but the courage to live with insecurity, knowing that life is a battle, but that if we do justice and practise compassion, if we honour great and small, the powerful and the powerless alike, if our eyes do not look down to the earth and its seductions but to heaven and its challenges, this small, vulnerable people is capable of great, even astonishing, achievements.

When Moses told the Israelites the full story about the land, he was telling them – whether or not they understood it at the time – that it was a place where not just wheat and barley but the human spirit also grew. It was the land where people were lifted beyond themselves because, time and again, they would have to believe in something and someone beyond themselves. Not accidentally but essentially, by its climate, topography, and location, Israel is the holy land, the place where, merely to survive, the human eye must turn to heaven and the human ear to heaven's call.

Greatness and Humility

A sequence of verses in *Parashat Ekev* gave rise to a beautiful Talmudic passage, one that has found a place in the siddur. It is among the readings we say after the evening service on Saturday night as Shabbat comes to an end. Here is the text on which it is based:

> For the Lord your God is God of gods and Lord of lords, the great, mighty, and awe-inspiring God, who shows no favouritism and accepts no bribe. He upholds the cause of the orphan and widow, and loves the stranger, giving him food and clothing. (Deut. 10:17–18)

The juxtaposition of the two verses – the first about God's supremacy, the second about His care for the low and lonely – could not be more striking. The Power of powers cares for the powerless. The Infinitely Great shows concern for the small. The Being at the heart of being listens to those at the margins: the orphan, the widow, the stranger, the poor, the outcast, the neglected. On this idea, the third-century teacher R. Yoḥanan built the following homily:

> R. Yoḥanan said, Wherever you find the greatness of the Holy One, Blessed Be He, there you find His humility. This is written in the Torah, repeated in the Prophets, and stated a third time in the Writings.
>
> It is written in the Torah: "For the Lord your God is God of gods and Lord of lords, the great, mighty, and awe-inspiring God, who shows no favouritism and accepts no bribe" (Deut. 10:17). Immediately afterwards it is written: "He upholds the cause of the orphan and widow, and loves the stranger, giving him food and clothing" (10:18).
>
> It is repeated in the Prophets, as it says: "So says the High and Exalted One, who lives forever and whose name is Holy: I live in a high and holy place, but also with the contrite and lowly in spirit, to revive the spirit of the lowly, and to revive the heart of the contrite" (Is. 57:15).
>
> It is stated a third time in the Writings: "Sing to God, make music for His name, extol Him who rides the clouds – God is His name – and exult before Him" (Ps. 68:5). Immediately afterwards it is written: "Father of the fatherless and judge of widows, is God in His holy habitation" (68:6). (Megilla 31a)

It is this passage that found its way into the (Ashkenazi) service at the end of Shabbat. Its presence there is to remind us that, as the day of rest ends and we return to our weekday concerns, we should not be so caught up in our own interests that we forget others less favourably situated. To care only for ourselves and those immediately dependent on us is not "the way of God."

Greatness is humility. Three episodes taught me this in ways I will never forget. The first was this: During the twenty-two years in which I served as chief rabbi, Elaine and I used to give dinner parties for people from within – and also from outside of – the Jewish community. Usually, at the end, the guests would thank the hosts. Only once, though, did a guest not only thank us but also ask to be allowed to go into the kitchen to thank those who had made and served the meal. It was a fine act of sensitivity. What was most interesting was who it was who did so. It was John Major, at that time the British prime minister. Greatness is humility.

The second episode took place in the oldest synagogue in Britain: Bevis Marks, in the heart of the City of London. Built in 1701, it was the first purpose-built synagogue in London, created by the Spanish and Portuguese Jews who were the first to return to England (or practise their Judaism in public; some had been Marranos) after Oliver Cromwell gave permission in 1656 for Jews to return. They had been expelled by Edward I in 1290. Modelled on the Great Synagogue in Amsterdam, it has stayed almost unchanged ever since. Only the addition of electric lights has marked the passing of time – and even so, on special occasions, services are candlelit as they were in those early days.

For the tercentenary service in 2001, Prince Charles came to the synagogue. There he met members of the community as well as leaders of Anglo-Jewry. What was impressive was that he spent as much time talking to the young men and women who were doing security duty as he did to the great and good of British Jewry. For security reasons, people volunteer to stand guard at communal events – part of the work of one of our finest organisations, the Community Security Trust. Often, people walk past them, hardly noticing their presence. But Prince Charles did notice them, and made them feel as important as anyone else on that glittering occasion. Greatness is humility.

The late Vivienne Wohl died tragically young. She and her husband Maurice had been blessed by God with material success. They were wealthy, but they did not spend their money on themselves. They gave *tzedaka* on a massive scale – within and beyond the Jewish community, in Britain, Israel, and elsewhere. In Israel, for example, they donated the nineteen-acre rose garden next to the Knesset and the striking Daniel Libeskind-designed cultural centre at Bar-Ilan University. They endowed medical facilities in Tel Aviv and Jerusalem, as well as at King's College and University College, London. They supported Jewish schools in Britain and yeshivot in Israel – and all this hardly touches the surface of their philanthropy. They were among the greatest philanthropists of our time.

What was really moving, though, was how they became a couple in the first place, because Vivienne was thirty years younger than Maurice. When they met, Maurice was in his late forties, a dedicated businessman seemingly destined for a life of bachelorhood. Vivienne, not yet twenty, was the daughter of friends of Maurice who had asked whether she could work for him during a vacation.

One day, Maurice offered to take her for lunch. On their way to the restaurant, they passed a beggar in the street. Maurice gave him a coin, and walked on. Vivienne stopped and asked Maurice if he would be kind enough to give her in advance a substantial sum – she named the figure – from that week's wages. Maurice handed over the money. She then walked back and gave it all to the beggar. "Why did you do that?" asked Maurice. "Because what you gave him was not enough to make a change to his life. He needed something more."

When the week came to an end, Maurice said to Vivienne, "I am not going to give you your full wages this week, because you gave away part of the money as a mitzva and I do not want to rob you of it." But it was then that he decided that he must marry her, because, as he told me shortly before he died, "Her heart was bigger than mine."

Among those who felt most bereaved by her death were the waiters and waitresses of a well-known hotel in Israel where they often stayed. It transpired that she had come to know all of them – where they came from, what their family situation was, the difficulties they were going through, the problems they faced. She remembered not only their names but also the names of their spouses and children. Whenever any of them needed help, she made sure it came, quietly, unobtrusively. It was a habit she had wherever she went.

I have had the privilege of knowing other philanthropists, but none who knew the names of the children of the waiters at the hotel where they stayed, none who cared more for those whom others hardly noticed or who gave help more quietly, more effectively, more humanly. Greatness is humility.

This idea – counter-intuitive, unexpected, life-changing – is one of the great contributions of the Torah to Western civilisation and it is set out in the words of *Parashat Ekev*, when Moses told the people about the "God of gods and Lord of lords, the great, mighty, and awe-inspiring God" whose greatness lay not just in the fact that He was creator of the universe and shaper of history, but that "He upholds the cause of the orphan and widow, and loves the stranger, giving him food and clothing."

Physically, the taller you are the more you look down on others. Morally, the reverse is the case. The more we look up to others, the higher we stand. For us, as for God, greatness is humility.

Re'eh
ראה

In *Parashat Re'eh*, Moses turns from the general principles of the covenant to the specific details, prefacing them with a warning of the choice that lies before them: blessings if they are faithful to God's laws, curses if they are not. They are to proclaim these to the nation, on Mount Gerizim and Mount Ebal, when they enter the land. They must destroy all traces of idolatry, and establish a central site that God will choose where they will worship, offer sacrifices, and eat consecrated food. Moses then issues further warnings about idolatry, false prophets, clean and unclean animals, tithes, and the Sabbatical year, when debts are to be cancelled and Hebrew slaves set free. The *parasha* concludes with the laws of the three pilgrimage festivals when the nation is to celebrate and the men "appear before the Lord" at the central place of worship.

The first of the following essays is about the choice itself, between the blessing and the curse. Not only individually but also collectively the nation must exercise its free will to choose the good and stay faithful to God. A free society must be a responsible society. The second is about a recurring theme of the *parasha*: joy. It is not enough to be free; we must celebrate our freedom, seeing what we have as God's gift, not to be taken for granted. The third and fourth essays are about *tzedaka*, charity-as-justice, the great command alluded to in the course of the command to release debts in the seventh year. One is about what makes this idea untranslatable into Western languages. The other is about the deep psychological dimension of *tzedaka* legislation. Not only must we relieve physical poverty; we must also alleviate the humiliation it brings. The fifth essay is about the festival added to the Jewish calendar in the Middle Ages – Simḥat Torah – and the moving story it tells us about the spirituality of joy even in the midst of uncertainty and exile.

The Politics of Freedom

Having set out the broad principles of the covenant, Moses now turns to the details, which extend over many chapters and several *parashot*. The long review of the laws that will govern Israel in its land begins and ends with Moses posing a momentous choice. Here is how he frames it in *Parashat Re'eh*:

> See, I am setting before you today a blessing and a curse – the blessing if you listen to the commands of the Lord your God that I am giving you today, the curse if you do not listen to the commands of the Lord your God and turn from the way that I command you today by following other gods, which you have not known. (Deut. 11:26–28)

And here is how he puts it at the end:

> See, I have set before you today life and good, death and evil.... I call heaven and earth to witness against you today, that I have set before you life and death, blessing and curse. Therefore choose life, that you and your children may live. (Deut. 30:15, 19)

Maimonides takes these two passages as proof of our belief in free will,[1] which indeed they are. But they are more than that. They are also a political statement. The connection between individual freedom (which Maimonides is talking about) and collective choice (which Moses is talking about) is this: if humans are free then they need a free society within which to exercise that freedom. The book of Deuteronomy represents the first attempt in history to create a free society.

Moses' vision is deeply political – but in a unique way. It is not politics as the pursuit of power or the defence of interests or the preservation of class and caste. It is not politics as an expression of national glory and renown. There is no desire in Moses' words for fame, honour, expansion, empire. There is not a word of nationalism in the conventional sense. Moses does not tell the people that they are great. He tells them that they have been rebellious, that they have sinned, and that their failure of faith during the episode of the spies cost them forty extra years of delay before entering the land. Moses would not have won an election. He was not that kind of leader.

Instead Moses summons the people to humility and responsibility. We are the nation, he says, in effect, that has been chosen by God for a great experiment. Can we create a society that is not Egypt, not empire, not divided into rulers and ruled? Can we stay faithful to the more-than-human hand that has guided our destinies since I first stood before Pharaoh and asked for our freedom? For if we truly believe in God – not God as a philosophical abstraction but God in whose handwriting our history has been written, God to whom we pledged allegiance at Mount Sinai, God who is our only sovereign – then we can do great things.

These things are great not in conventional terms, but in moral terms. For if all power, all wealth, all might belong to God, then none of these things can rightfully set us apart one from another. We are all equally precious in His sight. We have been charged by Him to feed the poor and bring the orphan and widow, the landless Levite and non-Israelite stranger, into our midst, sharing our celebrations and days of rest. We have been commanded to create a just society that honours human dignity and freedom.

1. Maimonides, *Mishneh Torah, Hilkhot Teshuva* 5:3.

Moses insists on three things. First, we are free. The choice is ours. Blessing or curse? Good or evil? Faithfulness or faithlessness? You decide, says Moses. Never has freedom been so starkly defined, not just for an individual but for a nation as a whole. We do not find it hard to understand that as individuals we are confronted by moral choices. Adam and Eve were. So was Cain. Choice is written into the human condition.

But to be told this as a nation – this is something new. There is no defence, says Moses, in protestations of powerlessness, in saying we could not help it, we were outnumbered, we were defeated, it was the fault of our leaders or our enemies. No, says Moses, your fate is in your hands. The sovereignty of God does not take away human responsibility. To the contrary, it places it centre stage. If you are faithful to God, says Moses, you will prevail over empires. If you are not, nothing else – neither military strength nor political alliances – will help you.

If you betray your unique destiny, if you worship the gods of the surrounding nations, then you will become like them. You will suffer the fate of all small nations in an age of superpowers. Do not blame others or chance or ill-fortune for your defeat. The choice is yours; the responsibility is yours alone.

Second, we are collectively responsible. The phrase "All Israelites are responsible for one another" (Shevuot 39a) is rabbinic but the idea is already present in the Torah. This too is radical. There is no "great man" theory of history in Judaism, nothing of what Carlyle called "heroes and hero-worship."[2] The fate of Israel depends on the response of Israel, all Israel, from "the heads of your tribes, your elders and officers" to your "hewers of wood and drawers of water" (Josh. 9:23). This is the origin of the American phrase (which has no counterpart in the vocabulary of British politics) "We, the people."

Unlike all other nations in the ancient world and most today, the people of the covenant did not believe that their destiny was determined by kings, emperors, a royal court, or a governing elite. It was and is determined by each of us as moral agents, conjointly responsible

2. Thomas Carlyle, *On Heroes, Hero-Worship, and The Heroic in History* (London: Cassell, 1908).

for the common good. This is what Michael Walzer means when in his recent book *In God's Shadow* he calls biblical Israel an "almost democracy."[3]

Third, it is a God-centred politics. There was no word for this in the ancient world so Josephus had to coin one. He called it "theocracy." However, this word has been much abused and taken to mean what it does not, namely, rule by clerics, priests. That is not what Israel was. Again, an American phrase comes to mind. Israel was "one nation under God." If any single word does justice to the vision of Deuteronomy it is not theocracy but *nomocracy*, "the rule of laws, not men."

Biblical Israel is the first example in history of an attempt to create a free society. Not free in the modern sense of liberty of conscience; that concept was born in the seventeenth century in a Europe that had been scarred for a century by religious wars between Catholics and Protestants. Liberty of conscience is the attempt to solve the problem of how people with markedly different religious beliefs (all of them Christians, as it happened) can live peaceably with one another. That is not the problem to which biblical Israel was an answer.

Instead it was an answer to the question: How can freedom and responsibility be shared equally by all? How can limits be placed on the power of rulers to turn the mass of people into slaves – not necessarily literally slaves but as a labour force to be used to build monumental buildings or engage in empire-building wars? It was the great nineteenth-century historian Lord Acton who rightly saw that freedom in this sense was born in biblical Israel:

> The government of the Israelites was a Federation, held together by no political authority, but by the unity of race and faith, and founded, not on physical force, but on a voluntary covenant.... The throne was erected on a compact, and the king was deprived of the right of legislation among the people that recognised no lawgiver but God.... The inspired men who rose in unfailing succession to prophesy against the usurper and the tyrant, constantly

3. Michael Walzer, *In God's Shadow: Politics in the Hebrew Bible* (New Haven, CT: Yale University Press, 2012), 201.

> proclaimed that the laws, which were divine, were paramount over sinful rulers.... Thus the example of the Hebrew nation laid down the parallel lines on which all freedom has been won.[4]

It is a beautiful, powerful, challenging idea. If God is our only sovereign, then all human power is delegated, limited, subject to moral constraints. Jews were the first to believe that an entire nation could govern itself in freedom and equal dignity. This has nothing to do with political structures (monarchy, oligarchy, democracy – Jews have tried them all), and everything to do with collective moral responsibility.

Jews never quite achieved the vision, but never ceased to be inspired by it. Moses' words still challenge us today. God has given us freedom; it is for us to use it to create a just, generous, gracious society. God does not do it for us but He teaches us how it is done. As Moses said: The choice is ours.

4. Lord Acton, *Essays in the History of Liberty* (Indianapolis: Liberty Classics, 1985), 7–8.

Collective Joy

If we were to ask what key word epitomises the society Jews were to make in the Promised Land, several concepts would come to mind: justice, compassion, reverence, respect, holiness, responsibility, dignity, loyalty. Surprisingly, though, another word figures centrally in Moses' speeches in Deuteronomy. It is a word that appears only once in each of the other books of the Torah: Genesis, Exodus, Leviticus, and Numbers.[1] Yet it appears twelve times in Deuteronomy, seven of them in *Parashat Re'eh*. The word is *simḥa*, joy.

It is an unexpected word. The story of the Israelites thus far has not been a joyous one. It has been marked by suffering on the one hand, rebellion and dissension on the other. Yet Moses makes it eminently clear that joy is what the life of faith in the land of promise is about. Here are the seven instances in this *parasha*, and their contexts:

1. *The central Sanctuary, initially Shilo*: "There in the presence of the Lord your God you and your families shall eat *and rejoice* in

1. Gen. 31:27; Ex. 4:14; Lev. 23:40; Num. 10:10.

everything you have put your hand to, because the Lord your God has blessed you" (Deut. 12:7).

2. *Jerusalem and the Temple*: "And there *you shall rejoice* before the Lord your God, you, your sons and daughters, your menservants and maidservants, and the Levites from your towns, who have no allotment or inheritance of their own" (Deut. 12:12).
3. *Sacred food that may be eaten only in Jerusalem*: "Instead, you are to eat them in the presence of the Lord your God at the place the Lord your God will choose – you, your sons and daughters, your menservants and maidservants, and the Levites from your towns – and *you are to rejoice* before the Lord your God in everything you put your hand to" (Deut. 12:18).
4. *The second tithe*: "Use the silver to buy whatever you like: cattle, sheep, wine, or other fermented drink, or anything you wish. Then you and your household shall eat there in the presence of the Lord your God *and rejoice*" (Deut. 14:26).
5. *The festival of Shavuot*: "*And rejoice* before the Lord your God at the place He will choose as a dwelling for His name – you, your sons and daughters, your menservants and maidservants, the Levites in your towns, and the strangers, the fatherless, and the widows living among you" (Deut. 16:11).
6. *The festival of Sukkot*: "*Be joyful* at your feast – you, your sons and daughters, your menservants and maidservants, and the Levites, the strangers, the fatherless, and the widows who live in your towns" (Deut. 16:14).
7. *Sukkot, again*. "For seven days, celebrate the feast to the Lord your God at the place the Lord your God will bless you in all your harvest and in all the work of your hands, and *your joy* will be complete [*vehayita akh same'aḥ*]" (Deut. 16:15).

Why does Moses emphasise joy specifically in the book of Deuteronomy? It is there, in the speeches Moses delivered in the last month of his life, that he scaled the heights of prophetic vision never reached by anyone else before or since. It is as if, standing on a mountaintop, he sees the whole course of Jewish history unfold below him, and from that dizzying altitude he brings back a message to the people gathered around him: the next generation, the children of those he led out of Egypt, the people who will cross the Jordan he will not cross and enter the land he is only able to see from afar.

What he tells them is unexpected, counter-intuitive. In effect he says this: "You know what your parents suffered. You have heard about their slavery in Egypt. You yourselves have known what it is to wander in the wilderness without a home or shelter or security. You may think those were the greatest trials, but you are wrong. You are about to face a harder trial. The real test is security and contentment."

Absurd though this sounds, it has proved true throughout Jewish history. In the many centuries of dispersion and persecution, from the destruction of the Second Temple to the nineteenth century, no one raised doubts about Jewish continuity. They did not ask, "Will we have Jewish grandchildren?" Only since Jews achieved freedom and equality in the Diaspora and independence and sovereignty in the State of Israel has that question come to be asked. When Jews had little to thank God for, they thanked Him, prayed to Him, and came to the synagogue and the house of study to hear and heed His word. When they had everything to thank Him for, many turned their backs on the synagogue and the house of study.

Moses was giving prophetic expression to the great paradox of faith: *It is easy to speak to God in tears. It is hard to serve God in joy*. It is the warning he delivered as the people came within sight of their destination: the Promised Land. Once there, they were in danger of forgetting that the land was theirs only because of God's promise to them, and only for as long as they remembered their promise to God.

Simḥa is usually translated as joy, rejoicing, gladness, happiness, pleasure, or delight. In fact, *simḥa* has a nuance untranslatable into English. Joy, happiness, pleasure, and the like are all states of mind, emotions. They belong to the individual. We can feel them alone. *Simḥa*, by contrast, is not a private emotion. It means *happiness shared*. It is a social state, a predicate of "we," not "I." There is no such thing as feeling *simḥa* alone.

Moses repeatedly labours the point. When you rejoice, he says time and again, it must be "you, your sons and daughters, your menservants and maidservants, and the Levites, the strangers, the fatherless, and the widows in your towns." A key theme of *Parashat Re'eh* is the idea of a central Sanctuary "in the place the Lord your God will choose." As we know from later Jewish history, during the reign of King David this was Jerusalem, where David's son Solomon eventually built the Temple.

What Moses is articulating for the first time is the idea of *simḥa* as communal, social, and national rejoicing. The nation was to be brought together not just by crisis, catastrophe, or impending war, but by collective celebration in the presence of God. The celebration itself was to be deeply moral. Not only was this a religious act of thanksgiving; it was also to be a form of social inclusion. No one was to be left out: not the stranger, or the servant, or the lonely (the orphan and widow). In a remarkable passage in the *Mishneh Torah*, Maimonides makes this point in the strongest possible terms:

> And while one eats and drinks himself, it is his duty to feed the stranger, the orphan, the widow, and other poor and unfortunate people, for he who locks the doors to his courtyard and eats and drinks with his wife and family, without giving anything to eat and drink to the poor and the bitter in soul – his meal is not a rejoicing in a divine commandment, but a rejoicing in his own stomach. It is of such persons that Scripture says, "Their sacrifices shall be to them as the bread of mourners, all that eat thereof shall be polluted; for their bread is a disgrace to their own appetite" (Hos. 9:4). Rejoicing of this kind is a disgrace to those who indulge in it, as Scripture says, "And I will spread dung upon your faces, even the dung of your sacrifices" (Mal. 2:3).[2]

Moses' insight remains valid today. The West is more affluent than any previous society has ever been. Our life expectancy is longer, our standards of living higher, and our choices wider than at any time since Homo sapiens first walked on earth. Yet Western societies are not measurably happier. The most telling indices of unhappiness – drug and alcohol abuse, depressive illness, stress-related syndromes, eating disorders, and the rest – have risen by between 300 and 1,000 per cent in the space of two generations. Why so?

2. Maimonides, *Mishneh Torah, Hilkhot Yom Tov* 6:18.

In 1968 I met the Lubavitcher Rebbe, Rabbi Menachem Mendel Schneersohn, of blessed memory, for the first time. While I was there, the Hasidim told me the following story. A man had written to the Rebbe in roughly these terms: "I am depressed. I am lonely. I feel that life is meaningless. I try to pray, but the words do not come. I keep mitzvot but find no peace of mind. I need the Rebbe's help." The Rebbe sent a brilliant reply without using a single word. He simply circled the first word of every sentence and sent the letter back. The word in each case was "I."

Our contemporary consumer is constructed in the first-person singular: I want, I need, I must have. There are many things we can achieve in the first-person singular but one we cannot, namely, *simḥa* – because *simḥa* is the joy we share, the joy we have only *because* we share. That, said Moses before the Israelites entered their land, would be their greatest challenge. Suffering, persecution, a common enemy, unite a people and turn it into a nation. But freedom, affluence, and security turn a nation into a collection of individuals, each pursuing his or her own happiness, often indifferent to the fate of those who have less, the lonely, the marginal, and the excluded. When that happens, societies start to disintegrate. At the height of their good fortune, the long slow process of decline begins.

The only way to avoid it, said Moses, is to share your happiness with others, and, in the midst of that collective, national celebration, serve God.[3] Blessings are not measured by how much we own or earn or spend or possess but by how much we share. *Simḥa* is the mark of a sacred society. It is a place of collective joy.

3. The great French sociologist Émile Durkheim (whose father, grandfather, and great-grandfather were all rabbis) argued, in *The Elementary Forms of the Religious Life* (trans. Karen E. Fields [New York: Free Press, 1995]), that religion is born in the experience of "collective effervescence," which is closely related to *simḥa* in the biblical sense.

The Untranslatable Virtue

In *Parashat Re'eh* we encounter a passage that is the source of one of Judaism's most majestic institutions, the principle of *tzedaka*:

> If there is a poor man among your brothers in any of the towns of the land that the Lord your God is giving you, do not be hard-hearted or tight-fisted towards your poor brother. Rather, be open-handed and freely lend him sufficient for his need in that which he lacks.... Give generously to him and do so without a grudging heart; then because of this the Lord your God will bless you in all your work and in everything you put your hand to. There will always be poor people in the land. Therefore I command you to be open-handed towards your brothers and towards the poor and needy in your land." (Deut. 15:7–11)

Note that the passage does not use the word *tzedaka*, despite the fact that the root TZ-D-K is one of Deuteronomy's key words, appearing eighteen times. Nor is it explicitly about *tzedaka* as such. Instead it is about *Shemitta*, the seventh year in which debts were cancelled. We will explain below why this is so.

The broad principle of *tzedaka* lies at the heart Judaism's understanding of *mitzvot bein adam leḥavero,* the duties we have to other people. It appears in a key passage in Genesis, the only place in which the Torah explains why God singled out Abraham to be the founder of a new faith:

> Then the Lord said, "Shall I hide from Abraham what I am about to do? Abraham will surely become a great and powerful nation, and all the nations of the earth will be blessed through him. For I have chosen him so that he will instruct his children and his household after him to keep the way of the Lord by doing what is right [*tzedaka*] and just [*mishpat*], so that the Lord will bring about for Abraham what He has promised him." (Gen. 18:17–19)

The "way of the Lord" is defined here by two words, *tzedaka* and *mishpat.* They are both forms of justice, but are quite different in their logic. *Mishpat* means *retributive justice.* It refers to the rule of law, through which disputes are settled by right rather than might. Law distinguishes between innocent and guilty. It establishes a set of rules, binding on all, by means of which the members of a society act in such a way as to pursue their own interests without infringing on the rights and freedoms of others. Few civilisations have robed law with greater dignity than Judaism. It is the most basic institution of a free society. It is no coincidence that in Judaism, God reveals Himself primarily in the form of laws, for Judaism is concerned not just with salvation (the soul in its relationship with God) but also with redemption (society as a vehicle for the Divine Presence). A law-governed society is a place of *mishpat.*

But *mishpat* alone cannot create a good society. To it must be added *tzedaka, distributive justice.* One can imagine a society which fastidiously observes the rule of law, and yet contains so much inequality that wealth is concentrated in the hands of the few, and many are left without the most basic requirements of a dignified existence. There may be high unemployment and widespread poverty. Some may live in palaces while others go homeless. That is not the kind of order that the Torah contemplates. There must be justice not only in how the law is applied, but also in how the means of existence – wealth as God's blessing – are distributed. That is *tzedaka.*

Why then is it set out so briefly in the Torah itself? The answer is that the Torah is a set of timeless ideals that are to be realised in the course of time, and not all times are the same. The immediate focus of the Torah from the Exodus onwards is the creation of a society in the land of Israel – the society that actually emerged from the days of Joshua to the close of the biblical era. Its economy was primarily agricultural, as were all ancient economies. Therefore, the Torah sets out its programme of distributive justice in great detail in terms of an agrarian order.

There was the seventh year, when debts were cancelled. In the seventh year of service, Jewish slaves went free. There was the Jubilee in which ancestral lands returned to their original owners. There were the "corner of the field," the "forgotten sheaf," the "gleanings" of grain and wine harvest, and the tithes in the third and sixth years that were given to the poor. In these ways and others, the Torah established the first form of what in the twentieth century came to be known as a welfare state – with one significant difference. It did not depend on a *state*. It was part of *society*, implemented not by power but by moral responsibility, not by governments but by individuals in local communities. We see what this was like in practice in the book of Ruth, in which Boaz comes to the aid of two women in need. That is what a covenantal society should be. It was an exceptionally beautiful structure.

But the genius of the Torah is that it does not predicate its social vision on a single era or a particular economic order. Alongside the specifics is a broad statement of timeless ideals. That is the role of the verses quoted above, which served as the basis for rabbinic legislation on *tzedaka*. *Tzedaka* refers to more than gifts of produce. It includes gifts of money, the medium of exchange in all advanced societies whatever their economic base. That is why in post-biblical times, when Israel was no longer a nation in its own land, and most of its people no longer lived and worked on farms, *tzedaka* took on new forms, as gifts of money or food or other resources. The implementation changed but the principle remained the same.

Maimonides, in his halakhic code the *Mishneh Torah*, makes a fascinating observation: "We have never seen or heard of a Jewish community without a *tzedaka* fund." He adds:

> We are obligated to be more scrupulous in fulfilling the commandment of *tzedaka* than any other positive commandment because *tzedaka* is the sign of the righteous, the seed of Abraham our father, as it is said, "For I have chosen him so that he will instruct his children ... to do *tzedaka*" (Gen. 18:19). The throne of Israel and the religion of truth is upheld only through *tzedaka*, as it is said, "In *tzedaka* shall you be established" (Is. 54:14). Israel is redeemed only through *tzedaka*, as it is said, "Zion shall be redeemed with judgement and those that return by *tzedaka*" (Is. 1:27) .... All Jews and those attached to them are like brothers, as it is said, "You are sons of the Lord your God" (Deut. 14:1), and if a brother will not show mercy to his brother, who then will have mercy on him?[1]

Tzedaka was thus, both in ideal and reality, constitutive of Jewish community life, the moral bond between Jew and Jew (though it should be noted that Jewish law also obligates Jews to give *tzedaka* to non-Jews under the rubric of *darkhei shalom*, the "ways of peace"[2]). It is foundational to the concept of covenantal society: society as an ethical enterprise is constructed on the basis of mutual responsibility.

Thus far, deliberately, I have left the word *tzedaka* untranslated. It cannot be translated, and this is not accidental. Civilisations differ from one another in their structure of ideals, even their most fundamental understandings of reality. They are not different ways of saying or doing the same things, mere garments, as it were, covering the same basic modes of existence. If we seek to understand what makes a civilisation distinctive, the best place to look is at the words that are untranslatable.

Tzedaka cannot be translated because it joins together two concepts that in other languages are opposites, namely, charity and justice. Suppose, for example, that I give someone £100. Either he is entitled to it or he is not. If he is, then my act is a form of justice. If he is not, it is an act of charity. In English (as with the Latin terms *caritas* and *iustitia*) a gesture of charity cannot be an act of justice, nor can an act of justice

1. Maimonides, *Mishneh Torah, Hilkhot Matenot Aniyim* 10:1.
2. Tosefta, Gittin 3:13.

be described as charity. *Tzedaka* is therefore an unusual term, because it means both.

The idea of *tzedaka* arises from the theology of Judaism, which insists on the difference between possession and ownership. Ultimately, all things are owned by God, Creator of the world. What we possess, we do not own – we merely hold it in trust for God. The clearest example is the provision in Leviticus: "The land must not be sold permanently because the land is Mine; you are merely strangers and temporary residents in relation to Me" (Lev. 25:23).

If there were absolute ownership, there would be a difference between justice (what we are bound to give others) and charity (what we give others out of generosity). The former would be a legally enforceable duty, the latter, at best, the prompting of benevolence or sympathy. In Judaism, however, because we are not owners of our property but merely guardians on God's behalf, we are bound by the conditions of trusteeship, one of which is that we share part of what we have with others in need. Hence the following unique law: "Someone who does not wish to give *tzedaka* or an appropriate amount of *tzedaka* may be compelled to do so by a Jewish court of law."[3] Charity is always voluntary. *Tzedaka* is compulsory. Therefore *tzedaka* does not mean charity. What would be seen as charity in other legal systems is, in Judaism, a strict requirement of the law, enforceable by the courts.

The nearest English equivalent to *tzedaka* is the phrase that came into existence alongside the idea of a welfare state, namely, social justice (significantly, Friedrich Hayek regarded the concept of social justice as incoherent and self-contradictory[4]). Behind both is the idea that no one should be without the basic requirements of existence, and that those who have more than they need must share some of that surplus with those who have less. This is fundamental to the kind of society the Israelites were charged with creating, namely, one in which everyone has a basic right to a dignified life and equal worth as a citizen in the covenantal community under the sovereignty of God.

---

3. Maimonides, *Mishneh Torah, Hilkhot Matenot Aniyim* 7:10.
4. Friedrich Hayek, *Law, Legislation, and Liberty: The Mirage of Social Justice* (Chicago: University of Chicago Press, 1973).

With its combination of charity and justice, *tzedaka* is a unique institution. It is deeply humanitarian, but it could not exist without the essentially religious concepts of divine ownership and social covenant. The prophet Jeremiah says of King Josiah, "He judged the cause of the poor and needy; then it was well. Is this not to know Me? says the Lord" (Jer. 22:16). To know God is to act with justice and compassion, to recognise His image in other people, and to hear the silent cry of those in need.

The Psychology of Dignity

Listen to these stories. Behind them lies an extraordinary insight into the nature of Jewish ethics.

When R. Yona saw a man of good family who had lost his money and was ashamed to accept charity, he would go and say to him, "I have heard that an inheritance has come your way in a city across the sea. So here is an article of some value. Sell it and use the proceeds. When you are more affluent, you will repay me." As soon as the man took it, R. Yona would say, "It's yours as a gift."[1]

Mar Ukba had a poor man in his neighbourhood into whose door socket he used to throw four coins every day. Once the poor man thought, "I will go and see who does me this kindness." That day Mar Ukba stayed late at the house of study and his wife was coming home with him. As soon as the poor man saw them moving the door (to leave the coins) he ran out after them, but they fled from him and hid. Why did they do this? Because it was taught: One should throw himself into a fiery furnace rather than publicly put his neighbour to shame (Ketubbot 67b).

1. Leviticus Rabba 34:1.

When R. Yannai saw a certain man giving a coin to a poor person in front of everyone, he said: It would have been better not to have given it to him than to have given it and put him to shame (Ḥagiga 5b).

These stories all have to do with the mitzva of *tzedaka,* whose source, as we saw in the previous essay, is in *Parashat Re'eh*. What they tell us is something radical and of the highest importance. Judaism conceives poverty not only in material terms, that the poor lack the means of sustenance. It also sees it in psychological terms. Poverty humiliates. It robs people of dignity. It makes them dependent on others. It deprives them of self-respect.

So *tzedaka* is addressed not only to people's physical needs but also to their psychological ones. The rabbis based their approach on a finely nuanced understanding of the key verse in the *parasha,* "Be open-handed and freely lend him *sufficient for his need in that which he lacks*" (Deut. 15:8):

> *Sufficient for his need*: This means that you are commanded to maintain him, but you are not commanded to make him rich. *That which he lacks*: This means even a horse to ride on and a slave to run before him. It is told of Hillel the Elder that he bought for a certain poor man of good family a horse to ride on and a slave to run before him. On one occasion he could not find a slave to run before him, so he himself ran before him for three miles. (Ketubbot 67b)

The first provision ("sufficient for his need") refers to an absolute subsistence level. In Jewish law this was taken to include food, housing, basic furniture, and, if necessary, funds to pay for a wedding. The second ("that which he lacks") means relative poverty – relative, however, not to others but to the individual's own previous standard of living. Someone who was once rich and is now poor has received a devastating psychological blow. Hence the story of Hillel, whose power lies in the fact that he himself was notoriously poor, yet he gave of his money and time to help a rich man who had lost all his wealth regain his self-respect.

This duality is evident throughout the laws of *tzedaka*. They are directed to the brute fact of poverty, but they also address with great sensitivity the psychology of poverty. It demeans, shames, and humiliates, and a good society will not allow humiliation.[2]

Protecting dignity and avoiding humiliation was a systematic element of rabbinical law. So, for example, the rabbis ruled that even the richest should be buried plainly so as not to shame the poor (Moed Katan 27b). On certain festive days, girls, especially those from wealthy families, had to wear borrowed clothes, "so as not to shame those who do not have" (Mishna Taanit 4:8). The rabbis intervened to lower the prices of religious necessities so that no one would be excluded from communal celebrations (Pesaḥim 30a). Work conditions had to be humane. Freedom presupposes self-respect, and a free society will therefore be one that robs no one of that basic human entitlement.

Many of the world's religions have praised poverty, even embraced it as a virtue. They tell stories of saints who give away all they have and spend their lives with next to nothing. Judaism rejects this absolutely. The sages refused to romanticise poverty or anaesthetise its pain. They had no inclination to turn religion into what Marx called the opium of the people. Poverty is not, in Judaism, a blessed condition. It is, the rabbis said, "a kind of death"[3] and "worse than fifty plagues" (Bava Batra 116a). They said, "Nothing is harder to bear than poverty, because he who is crushed by poverty is like one to whom all the troubles of the world cling and upon whom all the curses of Deuteronomy have descended. If all other troubles were placed on one side and poverty on the other, poverty would outweigh them all."[4]

This psychological insight is eloquently expressed in the third paragraph of the Grace after Meals: "Please, O Lord our God, do not make us dependent on the gifts or loans of other people, but only on Your full, open, holy, and generous hand so that we may suffer neither shame nor humiliation for ever and all time."

As a result, Jewish law focuses not only on how much we must give but also on the manner in which we do so. Hence the stories at the

2. See Avishai Margalit, *The Decent Society* (Cambridge, MA: Harvard University Press, 1998).
3. Nedarim 7b; Y. Bava Batra 116a; Exodus Rabba 31:14.
4. Exodus Rabba 31:14.

beginning of this essay, and others like them. From them Maimonides inferred a series of general principles. Ideally the donor should not know to whom he or she is giving, nor the recipient know from whom he or she is receiving. If a poor person does not want to accept *tzedaka*, we should practise a form of benign deception and give it to him under the guise of a loan.[5]

Maimonides sums up the general principle thus:

> Whoever gives charity to the poor with bad grace and averted eyes has lost all the merit of his action even though he gives him a thousand gold pieces. He should give with good grace and with joy and should sympathise with him in his plight, as it is said, "Have I not wept for those in trouble? Has not my soul grieved for the poor?" (Job 30:25).[6]

This is the logic behind two laws that are otherwise inexplicable. The first is "even a poor person who is dependent on *tzedaka* is obliged to give *tzedaka*."[7] The law seems absurd. Why should we give money to the poor so that they may give to the poor? It makes sense only on this assumption, that giving is essential to human dignity and *tzedaka* is the obligation to ensure that everyone has that dignity.

The second is the famous ruling of Maimonides that

> the highest degree of charity, exceeded by none, is when a person assists a poor Jew by providing him with a gift or a loan or by accepting him into a business partnership or by helping him find employment – in a word, by putting him in a situation where he can dispense with other people's aid.[8]

5. Maimonides, *Mishneh Torah, Hilkhot Matenot Aniyim* 7:9.
6. Ibid. 10:4.
7. Ibid. 7:5.
8. Ibid. 10:7.

Giving someone a job or making him your partner would not normally be considered charity at all. It costs you nothing. But this further serves to show that *tzedaka* does not mean charity. It means giving people the means to live a dignified life, and any form of employment is more dignified, within the Jewish value system, than dependence.

This ruling of Maimonides in the twelfth century precisely articulates a practice rediscovered in our time: microloans enabling poor people to start small businesses. For this, Muhammad Yunus was awarded the 2006 Nobel Peace Prize. Explaining their decision, the Nobel Committee said that "lasting peace cannot be achieved unless large population groups find ways in which to break out of poverty" and that Yunus had shown that "even the poorest of the poor can work to bring about their own development."[9]

Maimonides went to the heart of the matter when he said, "The well-being of the soul can only be obtained after that of the body has been secured."[10] Poverty is not a noble state. You cannot reach spiritual heights if you have no food to eat or roof for your head, if you lack access to medical attention or are beset by financial worries.

Jewry has had many distinguished economists, from David Ricardo (whom Keynes called the greatest mind that ever addressed itself to economics), to John von Neumann (a physicist who invented Game Theory), to Paul Samuelson, Milton Friedman, and Alan Greenspan. They have won an astonishing 38 per cent of Nobel Prizes in the field. Why so? Because Jews have long known that economics is one of the fundamental determinants of a society; that economic systems are not written into the structure of the universe, but are constructed by human beings and can be changed by human beings; and that poverty is not a fact of nature but can be alleviated, minimised, reduced.

Economics is not a religious discipline. Yet underlying the Jewish passion for economics is a religious imperative: "There will always be poor people in the land. Therefore I command you to be open-handed towards your brothers and towards the poor and needy in your land" (Deut. 15:11).

---

9. See "The Nobel Peace Prize for 2006," *The Nobel Prize*, October 13, 2006, https://www.nobelprize.org/prizes/peace/2006/press-release/.
10. Maimonides, *Guide for the Perplexed*, III:27.

Insecurity and Joy

On October 14, 1663, the famous diarist Samuel Pepys paid a visit to the Spanish and Portuguese Synagogue in Creechurch Lane in the city of London. Jews had been exiled from England in 1290 but in 1656, following an intercession by Rabbi Menasseh ben Israel of Amsterdam, Oliver Cromwell concluded that there was in fact no legal barrier to Jews living there. So for the first time since the thirteenth century Jews were able to worship openly.

The first synagogue, the one Pepys visited, was simply a private house belonging to a successful Portuguese Jewish merchant, Antonio Fernandez Carvajal, that had been extended to house the congregation. Pepys had been in the synagogue once before, at the memorial service for Carvajal, who died in 1659. That occasion had been sombre and decorous. What he saw on his second visit was something else altogether, a scene of celebration that left him scandalised. This is what he wrote in his diary:

> After dinner my wife and I, by Mr. Rawlinson's conduct, to the Jewish Synagogue: where the men and boys in their vayles [i.e., *tallitot*], and the women behind a lattice out of sight; and some things stand up, which I believe is their Law, in a press [i.e., the

> ark] to which all coming in do bow; and at the putting on their vayles do say something, to which others that hear him do cry Amen, and the party do kiss his vayle. Their service all in a singing way, and in Hebrew. And anon their Laws that they take out of the press are carried by several men, four or five several burthens in all, and they do relieve one another; and whether it is that every one desires to have the carrying of it, I cannot tell, thus they carried it round about the room while such a service is singing.... But, Lord! to see the disorder, laughing, sporting, and no attention, but confusion in all their service, more like brutes than people knowing the true God, would make a man forswear ever seeing them more and indeed I never did see so much, or could have imagined there had been any religion in the whole world so absurdly performed as this.[1]

Poor Pepys. No one told him that the day he chose to come to the synagogue was Simḥat Torah, nor had he ever seen in a house of worship anything like the exuberant joy of the day when we dance with the Torah scroll as if the world were a wedding and the book a bride. Nor had he any reason to suppose that Jews had any reason to rejoice. I want in this essay to tell the story behind the story of Pepys' incomprehension and surprise, because it is a moving, unexpected one.

There is a line in *Ne'ila,* the concluding service of Yom Kippur, that epitomises the situation of Jewry during the tragic centuries of exile and persecution. It was written by Rabbenu Gershom (c. 960–1040) in Metz, in what is today northwest France. The age of the Crusades had not yet begun. Europe had not yet descended into the mad frenzy of anti-Semitism that was to mark Jewish history for almost a thousand years until the Holocaust. Yet we already sense in the poem he wrote an anticipation of what was to come. The line reads simply: "There is nothing left but this Torah."

Jews had lost almost everything. They had no land, no home, no power, no rights, and no security. They never knew when the local

1. Found in Robert Latham, ed., *The Shorter Pepys* (Berkeley, CA: University of California Press, 1985).

population would turn against them, massacring or expelling them. All they had was a book, the Torah. It was the record of their past and their promise of a future. God may have abandoned them but He would not do so forever: "When they are in the land of their enemies, I will not reject them or abhor them so as to destroy them completely, breaking My covenant with them. I am the Lord their God" (Lev. 26:44). Jews had "nothing left but this Torah." It was their faint, flickering flame of hope.

And it was "this Torah" that inspired Jews in exile to create the one festival added to the calendar between the second century BCE, when Ḥanukka was introduced, and May 14, 1948, when Yom HaAtzma'ut, Israel's Independence Day, was observed for the first time. That festival was Simḥat Torah, the Day of "Rejoicing in the Torah," added around the time that Rabbenu Gershom was writing his poem. It celebrates the end of the annual reading of the Torah and the beginning of a new cycle.

Simḥat Torah is quintessentially a festival of the Diaspora, for two reasons. It is the second day of Shemini Atzeret, the festival immediately following the seventh day of Sukkot – and in Israel, there is no second day. The other reason is that, at that time, only in the Diaspora was the Torah read in an annual cycle. In Israel it was read in a three- or three-and-a-half-year cycle, so there was no annual celebration of ending and beginning anew. But note the name of the festival: not "concluding" or "beginning" the Torah, but rather "rejoicing" in it. That is what the Jews of the dark centuries chose to leave as their legacy to the calendar: not a day of tears, but one of joy.

That is what Samuel Pepys saw that October night that left him bewildered: the joy of Simḥat Torah. For how could anyone in those days associate Jews and Judaism with joy? They were, for Christians, the "wandering Jew," condemned like Cain to be endless exiles on earth, pariahs among peoples. There was hardly a city in Europe from which they had not at some time been expelled. As Rabbenu Gershom had said, they had nothing left but a book, yet they danced with it and sang to it as though it were alive, their one true love.

Aristotle wrote, in the *Nicomachean Ethics,* that happiness is the ultimate purpose of human existence. People seek many things: pleasure, wealth, honour, fame. But if we ask why they seek them, the answer will always in the end turn out to be because they yield happiness. We seek everything else as a means to an end. Only happiness is an end in itself, something we desire for its own sake alone.[2]

Judaism sees things differently. To be sure, happiness – *osher*, or as it generally appears in Tanakh, *ashrei* – is a value in Judaism. It is the first word of the book of Psalms, and appears thirty-two times in that book. However, it appears only twice in the Torah: when Leah says, "Happy am I [*be'ashri*], for the daughters will call me blessed" (Gen. 30:13), and when Moses, in his final blessing, says, "Happy are you [*ashrekha*] Israel" (Deut. 33:29). The Torah's key word for positive emotion is not happiness but *simḥa*, joy. As we saw in an earlier essay, "Collective Joy," it is this of which Moses speaks no less than seven times in *Parashat Re'eh*, twelve times in Deuteronomy as a whole.

There are fundamental differences between happiness and joy. Happiness is a calm feeling, joy an exuberant one. One can feel happiness alone, but joy in the Torah is always something shared with others. Happiness – in Aristotle's sense – is a judgement on life as a whole, while joy lives in the moment. Happiness depends on things going well, but one can experience joy even in the midst of adversity. King David, in Psalms, speaks of danger, fear, dejection, sometimes even despair, but his songs usually end in the major key:

> Weeping may stay for the night,
> but rejoicing comes in the morning…
> You turned my wailing into dancing;
> You removed my sackcloth and clothed me with joy,
> that my heart may sing Your praises and not be silent.
> Lord my God, I will praise You forever. (Ps. 30:6–13)

There remains, though, a fundamental question about the joy of Simḥat Torah. As we saw in that earlier essay, Moses speaks of joy as the key emotion of the people of the covenant in the Promised Land. *Simḥa* is what you feel when you have finally arrived at the land that is yours. How

2. Aristotle, *Nicomachean Ethics*, 1097a30–34.

then could the Jews of the Diaspora discover, celebrate, and sanctify joy when they were exiled from home? The answer, it seems to me, is implicit in what *Re'eh* tells us about Sukkot, the festival to which Simḥat Torah is joined. The verb "to rejoice" appears three times in the *parasha* in connection with a festival: not at all in connection with Passover, once in relation to Shavuot, but twice in connection with Sukkot: "Be joyful at your festival ... and your joy will be complete" (Deut. 16:14–15). It is for this reason that Sukkot (and Shemini Atzeret) are called *zeman simḥatenu*, "the time of our joy."

This is starkly counter-intuitive. We could understand why Passover should be a festival of joy: it recalls our ancestors' liberation from slavery. Similarly with Shavuot: it celebrates the giving of the Torah, God's great gift to us as a people. But why Sukkot? It represents not a positive event, but forty years of wandering in the wilderness without a permanent home. A sukka is, by halakhic definition, a temporary dwelling. Sukkot, when we live for seven days in a hut with only leaves for a roof, exposed to the wind, cold, and rain, is the festival of insecurity. Why then is it, supremely, the "time of our joy"?

That is what makes *simḥa* the supreme religious emotion. You do not have to be religious to be happy. But there is something profoundly spiritual about our capacity to live in a state of total insecurity and yet feel the joy of simply being, under the shelter of the Divine Presence. Yes, there is danger, risk, uncertainty, vulnerability. But we are here, with a world to live in, family and friends to love and be loved by, and we are not alone, for with us is the Torah, God's unbreakable word, and though we walk through the valley of the shadow, we walk towards the redemptive light.

In the Diaspora, even the greatest mansion is, for Jews, only a sukka, a temporary dwelling. Yet we can still rejoice, remembering what our ancestors knew, that the wilderness is simply a series of way stations on the road to home. Kierkegaard once wrote: "It takes moral courage to grieve. It takes religious courage to rejoice."[3] Life is full of problems and pains, but beyond them is the sense of wonder that we

3. Søren Kierkegaard, *Journals and Papers*, ed. and trans. Howard V. Hong and Edna Hong (Bloomington, IN: Indiana University Press, 1970), 2:2179.

are alive in a universe filled with beauty, and so long as we have the Torah, we still have hope. Pepys may not have understood what he was seeing in the synagogue, but Robert Louis Stevenson would have done, for it was he who said what Jews have always known: "Find out where joy resides and give it a voice far beyond singing. For to miss the joy is to miss all."[4]

4. Robert Louis Stevenson, "The Lantern Bearers," in *Across the Plains* (Carlisle, MA: Applewood Books, 1892), 247.

Shofetim
שפטים

Having dealt with many of the aspects of worship in the Promised Land, Moses now turns to the institutions of governance. He begins with the overarching imperative of justice: there must be courts, judges, and officers in every city. Justice must be accessible and impartial. Procedures must be followed for the prosecution of idolatry, and there is to be a supreme court to deal with hard cases. There are to be three main types of leader: a king, priests and Levites, and prophets. Warnings are issued against sorcery and witchcraft, and against false prophets. Cities of refuge are to be provided as sanctuaries for those who kill accidentally or unintentionally. Conspiring witnesses who testify falsely are to be punished. Moses then turns to the laws of warfare. The *parasha* concludes with the atonement procedure to be followed in the case of an unsolved murder.

The first of the following essays looks at the Torah's revolutionary approach to the separation of powers. The second is about how to identify a false prophet. The third is about the Torah's subtle, complex approach to the institution of monarchy. The fourth looks at the dramatic effects of this teaching on the West, once rabbinic teachings were made accessible through the work of the Christian Hebraists in the sixteenth and seventeenth centuries. The fifth is about Judaism's approach to environmental ethics, based on a text relating to the conduct of war.

The Three Crowns

In *Shofetim*, we reach an answer to the problem that has preoccupied the Torah since the beginning: how to achieve, in human affairs, a combination of freedom and order.

In the beginning, God created order. Then He created humanity, endowing it with His greatest gift: freedom. But humans used freedom to damage, even destroy, the order God had created in the world. First, Adam and Eve eat the forbidden fruit. Then Cain, the first human child, commits the first murder. With breathtaking speed, humanity, by the eve of the Flood, had turned the world into a place full of violence. For a moment, God "regretted that He had made man on earth" (Gen. 6:6). That is freedom without order – in a word, chaos.

God commands Abraham to leave Mesopotamia and live a different kind of life in a different kind of land. Yet throughout Genesis, Abraham's descendants are only an extended family, not yet a nation capable of building a society. And as Genesis makes clear, even the most faithful family cannot avoid the impact of violence and chaos. Lot discovers this in Sodom. Abraham and Isaac encounter societies in which they fear for their lives because of the attractiveness of their wives. Jacob's daughter Dina is raped and abducted. By the end of Genesis, we understand why God has promised the patriarchs a land and so many descendants that they will form a nation. *Only in a just society can justice flourish. Only in a free society can individual liberty be sustained.* That is why the Torah is a formula for the construction of a society, not (primarily) a roadmap for the salvation of the soul.

Exodus shows us the other side of the coin. The Israelites have become a nation. But they are in exile, in Egypt, the longest-lived and most technologically advanced empire of the ancient world. There they discover order without freedom – in a word, slavery. That was their formative experience. Liberated by God, their task was to create a new kind of social order that would be a place of freedom. But how do you honour freedom without creating anarchy and chaos? That is the question to which the Torah, especially the book of Deuteronomy – and in particular the *parasha* of *Shofetim* – is the answer.

We know part of the answer already. At Mount Sinai the Israelites had consented to become a nation under the sovereignty of God. They had agreed to a covenant with God, meaning that they had accepted responsibility for honouring God's laws and becoming a "holy" – that is, distinctive – nation unlike others. This in itself was revolutionary. Until then, kings made covenants with other kings. God (or "the gods") did not make covenants with human beings, let alone with an entire nation.

Now, though, the question was: What kind of government was the nation to have? What kind of structure would best secure freedom and order? How, if human beings were to be invested with power, could you protect against the corruptions of power? The answer *Parashat Re'eh* gives is simple and revolutionary. There was not to be one leader, but three, each of a very different kind: the king, the priest, and the prophet. First the king:

> When you enter the land the Lord your God is giving you and have taken possession of it and settled in it, and you say, "Let us set a king over us like all the nations around us," be sure to appoint over you the king the Lord your God chooses. (Deut. 17:14–15)

The king recruited an army, levied taxes, and was responsible for civic order. It was his task to defend the nation from enemies outside and lawlessness within. He was immersed in the demands of statecraft. He was a civil rather than religious leader. Nonetheless it was the king to whom tradition attached the command of reading the Law – sections of the book of Deuteronomy – at the national gathering every seven years (Deut. 31:12), thus ensuring that the people did not forget its covenant with God.

The most obvious emphasis in the Torah's account of monarchy is its insistence on limits. The king must not engage in any of the personal indulgences associated with power throughout the ages. He must not multiply wives, horses, or wealth. He must study the Torah constantly and never transgress it. This marks the birth of the idea of constitutional monarchy: *the king is not above the law*. There is also a heavy hint that monarchy is an alien import into Judaism. It is the only command in which the words "like all the nations around us" appear.

The second institution was the priesthood and the wider circle of Levites:

> The priests, who are Levites – indeed the whole tribe of Levi – are to have no allotment or inheritance with Israel.... For the Lord your God has chosen them and their descendants out of all your tribes to stand and minister in the Lord's name always. (Deut. 18:1–2)

The priest mediated between the people and God. He served in the Temple, offered sacrifices on behalf of the people, and ensured that the holy was at the heart of national life. He was also a teacher and adjudicator of the law. He was the guardian of the holy, preserver of the boundaries between sacred and secular.

Yet the priest was not the only kind of spiritual leader in biblical Israel. There was also the prophet:

> The Lord your God will raise up for you a prophet like me from among your own brothers. You must listen to him.... The Lord said to me..."I will raise up for them a prophet like you from among their brothers; I will put My words in his mouth, and he will tell them everything I command him. If anyone does not listen to

> My words that the prophet speaks in My name, I Myself will call him to account." (Deut. 18:15–19)

The prophet heard the word of God and conveyed it to the people. Priest and prophet had different sensibilities, different modes of consciousness, and used somewhat different terminologies. The priest spoke of separation and order, purity and impurity, the holy and the profane. The prophet spoke of relationships: justice and righteousness, compassion and mercy. When they spoke of sin and repentance, the priest used words like atonement and purification, while the prophet spoke of return, healing, and compassion. They had a different relationship to history. The priest lived outside of history, the prophet within it and responsive to it. The priest spoke the word of God for *all* time; the prophet spoke the word of God for *this* time.

The king used yet a third language, that of *ḥokhma*, (worldly) wisdom. Not accidentally, two of the great wisdom works of the Hebrew Bible, Proverbs and Ecclesiastes, are attributed to Solomon, the king who asked God for wisdom and eventually acquired it in greater measure "than the wisdom of all the men of the East and greater than all the wisdom of Egypt" (I Kings 5:10).

Why three leaders, not one?[1]

In the eighteenth century, the French thinker Montesquieu formulated the principle of "the separation of powers" that played a major part in the development of the modern nation-state. In *De l'esprit des lois*, he spoke of three branches of government: the legislature, the executive, and the judiciary.

More than 2,500 years earlier, the prophet Isaiah had already articulated a similar division. Speaking of God, he said, "For the Lord is our judge [=judiciary]; the Lord is our lawgiver [=legislature]; the Lord is our king; He will save us [=executive]" (Is. 33:22). For Montesquieu, the separation of powers was essential to a free society:

1. See Stuart Cohen, *The Three Crowns* (Cambridge, UK: Cambridge University Press, 1990).

> Liberty does not flourish because men have natural rights or because they revolt if their rulers push them too far; it flourishes because power is so distributed and so organized that whoever is tempted to abuse it finds legal restraints in his way.[2]

Something like this, though clearly not the same, was implicit in the threefold structure of king, priest, and prophet. The Mishna speaks of the roles as "crowns": "There are three crowns: the crown of Torah [=prophecy], the crown of priesthood, and the crown of kingship" (Mishna Avot 4:13).

Thus what we have in the Torah is the first intimation in history of the doctrine that would emerge in the West in the eighteenth century, namely the separation of powers. It was not the same as Montesquieu's – he was, after all, speaking about a secular nation-state, not a sacred society. But it shares the same concern: to avoid the concentration of power in a single individual or institution.

The Torah does not spell out explicitly why this separation was important, but we can guess. Power tends to corrupt; absolute power corrupts absolutely. Therefore, in the good society, no one should have absolute power. What is more, throughout history, leaders have been seen as sacred: demigods or children of the gods or chief intermediaries with the gods. That, in Judaism, is idolatry. No human is divine.

Hence the radical break, signalled in *Parashat Shofetim*, from the almost universal practice in the ancient world to identify the head of state with the head of the national religion. In Judaism, a king is not a high priest, and a high priest is not a king. This rule was later breached by some of the Hasmonean kings, who also had themselves appointed high priests. The sages objected. Their attitude was best expressed in their critique of the Hasmonean king and high priest, Alexander Yannai: "O King Yannai, let the royal crown be sufficient for you; leave the priestly crown to the descendants of Aaron" (Kiddushin 66a).

When a religion becomes political, or politics is turned into a religion, the result is usually disastrous for both politics and religion.

2. John Plamenatz, *Man and Society* (London: Longman, 1963), 1:194.

The other key distinction was between king and priest, on the one hand, and prophet, on the other. Monarchy and priesthood were hereditary offices in biblical Israel, the former going to descendants of David, the latter to the offspring of Aaron. Prophecy was not hereditary. It was not an "office" with rules of succession, official robes, and installation ceremonies. It was a charismatic endowment. Prophets could be either men or women. Their role was to serve as the conscience of the nation, giving voice to the word of Heaven when the people or their rulers drifted from their mission, became corrupt, adopted the practices of their pagan neighbours, and grew overconfident in the good times or despairing in bad ones.

The result was a remarkable structure which limited the powers of king and priest alike, and which gave prominence to the prophet, who had no power but lasting influence. True power, in the Judaic view of things, belongs to God alone. All earthly power is merely delegated – Heaven's conditional gift to human beings. This means that any attempt by king, priest, or prophet to subvert or contravene the revealed will of God is automatically ultra vires, lacking in authority.

Politics, in the Jewish view of things, is not the highest human good. It is necessary: "Pray for the welfare of the government," said R. Ḥanina, "for without it, men would eat one another alive."[3] But it is also, as the prophetic literature testifies, fraught with dangers of corruption and compromise. The best defence of liberty is to ensure that not all powers are concentrated in a single institution. An independent priesthood was necessary to ensure that the service of God was never enlisted for purely political ends. Prophets were necessary to "speak truth to power" and expose injustice and oppression.

The Torah's deepest and most radical political truth is as relevant today as ever before in history. Power is necessary but not sacred. People do not exist to serve the state. The state exists to serve the people, whose true service is not to man but to God.

3. Mishna Avot 3:2. This rabbinic view is strikingly similar to that set out by Hobbes in *The Leviathan* and to that of Thomas Paine in *Common Sense*.

True and False Prophets

Enumerating the various leadership roles within the nation that would take shape after his death, Moses mentions not only the priest/judge and king but also the prophet: "The Lord your God will raise up for you a prophet like me from among your own brothers. You must listen to him" (Deut. 18:15).

Moses would not be the last of the prophets. He would have successors. Historically this was so. From the days of Samuel to the Second Temple period, each generation gave rise to men – and sometimes women – who spoke God's word with immense courage, unafraid to censure kings, criticise priests, or rebuke an entire generation for its lack of faith and moral integrity.

There was, however, an obvious question: How does one tell a true prophet from a false one? Unlike kings or priests, prophets did not derive authority from formal office. Their authority lay in their personality, their ability to give voice to the word of God, their self-evident inspiration. But precisely because a prophet hears words others cannot hear and sees visions others cannot see, the real possibility of false prophets existed – like those of Baal in the days of King Ahab, or those who, in the days of Jeremiah, told the people they had nothing to fear, "saying, 'Peace, peace,' when there is no peace" (Jer. 6:14).

Charismatic authority is inherently destabilising. What was there to prevent a fraudulent, or even a sincere but mistaken, figure, able to perform signs and wonders and move the people by the power of his words, from taking the nation in a wrong direction, misleading others and perhaps even himself?

There are several dimensions to this question. One in particular is touched on in *Parashat Shofetim*, namely, the prophet's ability to foretell the future. This is how Moses puts it:

> You may say to yourselves, "How can we know when a message has not been spoken by the Lord?" If what a prophet proclaims in the name of the Lord does not take place or come true, that is a message the Lord has not spoken. That prophet has spoken presumptuously. Do not be afraid of him. (Deut. 18:21–22)

The test seems simple: if what the prophet predicts comes to pass, he is a true prophet; if not, not. In actuality, it turned out to be not that simple.

The classic case is the book of Jonah. Jonah is commanded by God to warn the people of Nineveh that their wickedness is about to bring disaster on them. Jonah attempts to flee, but fails – the famous story of the sea, the storm, and the "great fish." Eventually he goes to Nineveh and utters the words God has commanded him to say: "Forty more days and Nineveh will be destroyed" (Jonah 3:4). The people listen and repent and the city is spared. Jonah, however, is deeply dissatisfied:

> But Jonah was greatly displeased and became angry. He prayed to the Lord, "O Lord, is this not what I said when I was still at home? That is why I was so quick to flee to Tarshish. I knew that You are a gracious and compassionate God, slow to anger and abounding in love, a God who relents from sending calamity. Now, O Lord, take away my life, for it is better for me to die than to live." (Jonah 4:1–3)

Jonah's complaint can be understood in two ways. First, he was distressed that God had forgiven the people. They were, after all, wicked. They deserved to be punished. Why then did a mere change of heart release them from the punishment that was their due?

Second, he had been made to look a fool. He had told them that in forty days the city would be destroyed. It was not. God's mercy made nonsense of his prediction. Jonah was wrong to be displeased; that much is clear. God says, in the rhetorical question with which the book concludes: "Should I not be concerned about that great city?" (Jonah 4:11). Should I not be merciful? Should I not forgive?

What then becomes of the criterion Moses lays down for distinguishing between a true and false prophet: "If what a prophet proclaims in the name of the Lord does not take place or come true, that is a message the Lord has not spoken"? Jonah had proclaimed that the city would be destroyed in forty days. It was not, yet the proclamation was true. He really did speak the word of God. How can this be so?

The answer is given in the book of Jeremiah. Jeremiah had been prophesying national disaster. The people had drifted from their religious vocation, and the result would be defeat and exile. It was a difficult and demoralising message for people to hear. A false prophet, Hananiah son of Azzur, arose, preaching the opposite. Babylon, Israel's enemy, would soon be defeated. Within two years the crisis would be over. Jeremiah knew that it would not be so. Hananiah was telling the people what they wanted to hear, not what they needed to hear. He addressed the assembled people:

> He said, "Amen! May the Lord do so! May the Lord fulfil the words you have prophesied by bringing the articles of the Lord's house and all the exiles back to this place from Babylon. Nevertheless, listen to what I have to say in your hearing and in the hearing of all the people: From early times the prophets who preceded you and me have prophesied war, disaster, and plague against many countries and great kingdoms. But the prophet who prophesies peace will be recognised as one truly sent by the Lord only if his prediction comes true." (Jer. 28:6–9)

Jeremiah makes a fundamental distinction between good news and bad. It is easy to prophesy disaster. If the prophecy comes true, then you have spoken the truth. If it does not, then you can say: God relented and forgave. A negative prophecy cannot be refuted, but a positive one can. If the good foreseen comes to pass, then the prophecy is true. If it does not, then you cannot say, "God changed His mind," because God does not retract from a promise He has made of good, or peace, or return.

It is therefore only when the prophet offers a positive vision that he can be tested. That is why Jonah was wrong to believe he had failed when his negative prophecy – the destruction of Nineveh – failed to come true. This is how Maimonides puts it:

> As to calamities predicted by a prophet, if, for example, he foretells the death of a certain individual or declares that in a particular year there will be famine or war and so forth, the non-fulfilment of his forecast does not disprove his prophetic character. We are not to say, "See, he spoke and his prediction has not come to pass." For God is long-suffering and abounding in kindness and repents of evil. It may also be that those who were threatened repented and were therefore forgiven, as happened to the men of Nineveh. Possibly, too, the execution of the sentence is only deferred, as in the case of Hezekiah. But if the prophet, in the name of God, assures good fortune, declaring that a particular event would come to pass, and the benefit promised has not been realised, he is unquestionably a false prophet, for no blessing decreed by the Almighty, even if promised conditionally, is ever revoked.... Hence we learn that only when he predicts good fortune can the prophet be tested.[1]

Fundamental conclusions follow from this. A prophet is not an oracle; a prophecy is not a prediction. Precisely because Judaism believes in free will, the human future can never be unfailingly predicted. People are capable of change. God forgives. As we say in our prayers on the High Holy Days: "Prayer, penitence, and charity avert the evil decree."

1. Maimonides, *Mishneh Torah, Hilkhot Yesodei HaTorah* 10:4.

There is no decree that cannot be revoked. A prophet does not foretell. He warns. A prophet does not speak to predict future catastrophe but rather to avert it. *If a prediction comes true it has succeeded. If a prophecy comes true it has failed.*

The second consequence is no less far-reaching. The real test of prophecy is not bad news but good. Calamity, catastrophe, disaster prove nothing. Anyone can foretell these things without risking his reputation or authority. It is only by the realisation of a positive vision that prophecy is put to the test. So it was with Israel's prophets. They were realists, not optimists. They warned of the dangers that lay ahead. But they could also see beyond the catastrophe to the consolation.

A true prophet is an agent of hope.

Monarchy: An Ambivalent Institution

Parashat Shofetim contains the command to appoint a king. But it is a very strange command indeed. This is how it opens:

> When you enter the land the Lord your God is giving you and have taken possession of it and settled in it, and you say, "Let us set a king over us like all the nations around us," be sure to appoint over you the king the Lord your God chooses. (Deut. 17:14–15)

The oddity here is self-evident. The Israelites were not commanded to be "like all the nations around us." They were commanded to be different. That is the root meaning of the word "holy," *kadosh*. It means: distinctive, singular, set apart. Four times in the book of Deuteronomy Moses calls the Israelites an *am kadosh,* a holy people. The last thing a holy people does is copy its institutions from "the nations around us."

Second, the command is curiously conditional. It is only triggered when the people say, "Let us set a king over us." Why so? There is no such condition attached to the other two leadership roles in this *parasha*: the priest and the prophet. The existence of priests in Israel did not depend on the people asking for them. As for the prophet, according to the Torah, the institution did follow a request from the Israelites. Having heard the voice of God at Mount Sinai, the Israelites asked Moses to listen on their behalf and convey the divine word to them, because the direct experience of God's voice was simply too intense for them to bear (Ex. 20:16). Moses now tells the people that there will be prophets in the future also. But it will be God who will raise them up and put His words in their mouths (Deut. 18:18). The initiative will not come from the people. So why is the appointment of a king dependent on the people's request?

Third, there is no description of the powers of the king – his role, his task, his mission. Instead there is a series of restrictions. He must not accumulate horses, wives, or wealth (Deut. 17:17). He is to have his personal Torah scroll that he is to read "all the days of his life" (17:18–19) and not deviate from its teachings "to the right or to the left" (17:20). He must be humble and "not consider himself better than his fellow Israelites" (17:20). These are all negatives, not statements of positive purpose.

The problem deepens as we trace the history of monarchy as described in Tanakh. The Israelites did not immediately appoint a king after conquering the land. Instead, in times of crisis, they relied on charismatic leaders known as "judges," who led the people in battle but thereafter held no formal office. A classic example is the case of Gideon, who led the people to victory over the Midianites. The people sought to make him king, but he refused. "The Israelites said to Gideon, 'Rule over us – you, your son, and your grandson – because you have saved us from the hand of Midian.' But Gideon told them, 'I will not rule over you, nor will my son rule over you. The Lord will rule over you'" (Judges 8:22–23).

Even more perplexing is the account of the moment when the Israelites did request a king, in the days of Samuel. Samuel was distressed. He thought that the people were rejecting him. God, however, told him, "It is not you they have rejected, but they have rejected *Me* as their king" (I Sam. 8:7). God then told the prophet to spell out the consequences of appointing a king. He would take their children, their property, and their produce for his own purposes. Nonetheless, if the people persisted in wanting a king, Samuel should accede to their request.

The problem is obvious. If God wanted the people to appoint a king, why would He say that it meant that they were rejecting Him? If, to the contrary, God did not want them to appoint a king, why did He tell Samuel to accede to their request?

Eventually, Samuel did appoint a king and the monarchy was established. But the story is haunted by failure. Saul failed to carry out God's command. David unified the tribes and established Jerusalem as the kingdom's capital but committed a terrible sin. His son Solomon was wise. He consolidated the kingdom and built the Temple. But his failure was momentous. He disobeyed all the prohibitions set out in this *parasha*: not to accumulate many horses, wives, or wealth. The sages spoke of this in a piercing Talmudic passage:

> Why were the reasons of the Torah's laws not revealed? Because in two cases reasons were revealed, and they caused the greatest man in the world (Solomon) to stumble. It is written, "He shall not take many wives lest his heart be led astray" (Deut. 17:17). Solomon said, I will take many wives but my heart will not be led astray. Yet we read, "When Solomon was old, his wives turned his heart astray" (I Kings 11:4). Again it is written, He must not acquire great numbers of horses for himself lest he make the people return to Egypt. Solomon said, I will acquire many horses but I will not make the people return to Egypt. Yet we read (I Kings 10:29), "They imported a chariot from Egypt for six hundred shekels." (Sanhedrin 21b)

Solomon, the wisest of men, thought himself wiser than the Torah. Hubris led to nemesis. After his death, the kingdom split in two and was never subsequently reunited.

These are extraordinary ambivalences, and they led to a marked divergence of opinion among the commentators as to what *kind* of command was the mitzva of appointing a king. According to Maimonides, the appointment of a king is a positive command. Monarchy is the Torah's ideal form of government. God was angry with the people in the days of Samuel, not because they asked for a king but because they asked in the wrong way.

Ibn Ezra, however, sees the appointment of a king not as an obligation but as a permission: not "you should" but "you may." Abrabanel, who among the medieval rabbis was closest to kings and queens – he was a diplomat in the service of King Afonso V of Portugal, Queen Isabella of Castille, King Ferdinand of Naples, and the republic of Venice – held that the entire institution is only a concession to wayward human instincts.

This divergence reflects a profound tension that played itself out in the course of the biblical era. On the one hand, there is opposition in Judaism to the very idea of one human being exercising power over another. "To Me the children of Israel are servants," says the Torah (Lev. 25:55), on which the rabbis commented, "But not the servants of other servants [i.e., other humans]" (Bava Metzia 10a). R. Akiva said it most simply in the prayer *Avinu Malkeinu*: "Our Father, our King, we have no other king but You" (Taanit 25b).

On this view, there should be no need for a human ruler in the form of a king. Yet in practice this proved to be not a viable option. The book of Judges ends with the sentence: "In those days there was no king in Israel; everyone did what was right in his own eyes" (Judges 21:25). Without monarchy, anarchy.

Hence the view of Ibn Ezra and Abrabanel, that God gave the Israelites permission to decide how they would be governed, and, if they so chose, they were permitted to appoint a king. Abrabanel's view is strikingly similar to that of the eighteenth-century radical Thomas Paine – a key figure in both the American and French Revolutions – who wrote, "Government, like dress, is the badge of lost innocence; the palaces of kings are built on the ruins of bowers of paradise."[1]

In the twentieth century, Rav Kook, first Ashkenazic chief rabbi of pre-state Israel, wrote that in the absence of a king, sovereignty returns to the people, who are empowered to choose the form of governance they prefer – including, if they wish, a democratically elected parliament. For him the Knesset was the functional equivalent of a king: testimony that democracy is compatible with Judaism.[2]

1. Thomas Paine, *Common Sense* (Mineola, NY: Dover Publications, 1997), 3.
2. Responsa *Mishpat Kohen* (Jerusalem: Mossad HaRav Kook, 1966), responsa 144.

There is undeniably another strand in Jewish thought, represented by Maimonides, that sees monarchy as an ideal, epitomised in the figure of King David, a brilliant military tactician, adroit politician, and visionary statesman and one of the greatest religious poets of all time. With him, God made an eternal covenant, and though the Davidic monarchy came to an end, its re-establishment is at the heart of the Jewish idea of the Messiah, an anointed king of direct descent from David, who will restore Jewish sovereignty, rebuild the Temple, and inaugurate an era of peace.

Yet in pre-messianic time, we are left with a significant distinction between the eternally valid and God-given laws of morality and halakha, and the time-bound nature of politics and government. How high should the percentage of national income taken by the government in taxation be? To what extent should the rich be taxed proportionately more than the poor? How much morality should be enforced by civil law and how much left to individual conscience? How should governments be elected and how long should they last?

There is no timeless answer to these questions. Politics will always be an arena of conflict, compromise, and context, and it is a measure of the wisdom of the Torah that it does not attempt to specify a single model valid for all time. There are, however, moral limits to the use of power, and it was the role of prophets to remind kings of those limits, "speaking truth to power."

The debate about monarchy from biblical times to the present is a fine example of Judaism's refusal to simplify the complex. There was, and until the Messianic Age always will be, a conflict between the religious ideal of "We have no other King but You," and the practical requirements of politics and governance in a world still marked by violence and injustice. A good society is one in which people understand the difference between the time-bound demands of politics and the timeless truths of faith. In pre-messianic time, politics and religion are two different things, and work best unmixed.

Uneasy Lies the Head That Wears a Crown

There is a little-known and fascinating story behind one of the key passages in *Parashat Shofetim*. For it was precisely the command *to appoint* a king that led, in seventeenth-century England and eighteenth-century America, to the republican movement and the revolution *against* kings: against Charles I in the days of Cromwell, and then the break with George III that led to American independence. The story tells of how an acquaintance with the Hebrew Bible led people to call into question the whole institution of monarchy.

In the previous essay we noted the sheer strangeness of the command: "When you enter the land the Lord your God is giving you and have taken possession of it and settled in it, and you say, 'Let us set a king over us like all the nations around us,' be sure to appoint over you the king the Lord your God chooses" (Deut. 17:14–15). It is unusual to make a command conditional on the people's request, more unusual still to acquiesce to the people's desire to be "like all the nations around us." It was Israel's destiny to be different, *not* to be like everyone else. And, as we detailed there, there were other difficulties besides, most notoriously God's statement to the prophet Samuel, several centuries later, that in asking for a king the people were rejecting Him (I Sam. 8:7).

The commentators, as we saw, differed in their resolution of the problems. Maimonides held that appointing a king is a positive biblical command; Samuel and God were angry, not because the people asked for a king, but because they asked in the wrong way. Ibn Ezra held that the appointment of a king is not an obligation but a permission. Abrabanel held that the Torah's acceptance of monarchy was only a concession to wayward human instincts.

However, there was a fourth line of interpretation, significantly different from the others. It is to be found in a midrashic source, Deuteronomy Rabba. According to this, the text about monarchy in *Parashat Shofetim* is not a command or even a permission but a prediction: this is what is going to happen – as, in the days of Samuel, it did.[1]

In this fourth reading, the Torah *disapproves* of the appointment of a human king. God's permission to Samuel to give the people a king was not a form of consent but, rather, a kind of punishment. God was letting the people do what they wanted, knowing that they would suffer the consequences. Here is the midrash:

> *When you enter the land*: The rabbis said, God said to Israel: "I planned that you should be free from kings." How do we know this? As it is said, "A wild ass used to the wilderness" (Jer. 2:24) – just as the wild ass grows up in the wilderness and has no fear of man, so too I planned that you should have no fear of kings, but you did not desire so…
>
> This bears out what Scripture says: "Put not your trust in princes" (Ps. 146:3). R. Shimon said in the name of R. Yehoshua b. Levi, "Whoever put his trust in the Holy One, Blessed Be He, is privileged to become like Him. But whoever puts his trust in flesh and blood passes away and his dignity also passes away…
>
> God said, "Although they know that man is nothing, yet they forsake My glory and say, 'Let us set a king over us.' Why

1. Underlying this interpretation is the principle, "Where a person wants to go, there he is led" (Makkot 10b), meaning that God does not interfere with human free will, even if He disapproves of the people's intentions.

> did they ask for a king? By your life, in the end you will learn to your cost what you will have to suffer from your king..."[2]

Kings, concludes the midrash, brought catastrophe on Israel: David brought about a plague, Ahab's misconduct caused a drought, and Zedekiah was the cause of the destruction of the Temple. It was this *negative* approach to monarchy that entered the writings of the Christian Hebraists of the late sixteenth and early seventeenth centuries.[3] In 1625, Wilhelm Schikhard, a German Lutheran who was professor of Hebrew at the University of Tubingen, published *Mishpat HaMelekh, Jus Regium Hebraeorum,* based on rabbinic halakhic and midrashic sources. Schikhard cites Baḥya ibn Pakuda (Spain, eleventh century) to the effect that

> God the Master of the universe was enough for them, nor did He grant them kings except as a punishment.... It was not the will of the most excellent and most great God that there should be any king in Israel apart from Himself.... For what would an elect nation whose king is the Lord of the universe do with a king who is mere flesh and blood?[4]

Among Schikhard's readers was John Milton, who used this approach to explain why God says, in the book of Samuel, that by asking for a king, the Israelites had rejected Him: "The meaning is that it is a form of idolatry to ask for a king, who demands that he be worshipped and granted honours like those of God.... It was not for any man, but for God alone, to rule over men."[5]

In his view – specifically on the basis of biblical texts and rabbinic interpretation – monarchy comes close to a worship of human beings

2. Deuteronomy Rabba 5:8.
3. I owe this analysis to Eric Nelson, *The Hebrew Republic* (Cambridge, MA: Harvard University Press, 2010), 23–56.
4. See Rabbenu Baḥya to Deut. 17:15.
5. Cited in Nelson, *Hebrew Republic,* 43. For an alternative translation, see Milton, *Political Writings,* ed. Martin Dzelzainis (Cambridge, UK: Cambridge University Press, 1991), 101.

instead of worship of God alone. In 1660, on the eve of the Restoration, Milton wrote caustically that

> a king must be adored like a demigod, with a dissolute and haughty court about him, of vast expense and luxury...and all this to do nothing but...pageant himself up and down in progress among the perpetual bowings and cringings of an abject people, on either side deifying and adoring him.[6]

All this represents to him "a civil kind of idolatry."

More than a century later, the English radical Thomas Paine inspired an American public to rise in revolt against the king of England, again citing the Hebrew Bible as his text and justification. "The will of the Almighty, as declared by Gideon and the prophet Samuel, expressly disapproves of government by kings," he writes.[7] Paine quotes text after biblical text to show that God is *opposed* to the appointment of kings.

The pamphlet in which this argument is set out, *Common Sense,* published in January 1776, became the most influential in all American history. It sold some 100,000 copies in the first year, and it led to Paine being described as "the father of the American Revolution." John Adams said, "Without the pen of the author of *Common Sense,* the sword of Washington would have been raised in vain."[8]

Hence the irony of ironies: that the very passage in *Parashat Shofetim* in which we read of the command to appoint a king set in motion the first two revolutions in the modern world, the English in the 1640s and the American in the 1770s, leading to the execution of one king, and the abandonment, by Americans, of another.

What was it about the biblical conception of monarchy that was so revolutionary that it had this effect on English thinkers like Milton and Paine?

---

6. Nelson, *Hebrew Republic,* 45.
7. Thomas Paine, *Political Writings,* ed. Bruce Kuklick (Cambridge, UK: Cambridge University Press, 1989), 9.
8. Quoted in Jill Lapore, *The Story of America: Essays on Origins* (Princeton, NJ: Princeton University Press, 2012), 62.

First, the fact that the Torah links the appointment of a king to a popular request tells us that *sovereignty rests with the people.* Within the limits set by the Torah, it is they who have the right to choose how they will be governed. Political authority, for the Torah, comes from the bottom up; it is not imposed, top down (as in the doctrine of the "divine right of kings"). This was the source of the principle, set out by John Locke and adopted in the American Declaration of Independence, that governments derive their authority "from the consent of the governed." Hence also the key opening words of the American Constitution: "We, the people." This phrase belongs to the language of covenant, in which it is the people as a whole who are responsible to one another and to God for the conduct of the nation.

Second, as Michael Walzer points out, uniquely in ancient Israel the king had *no cosmological significance.* Monarchy was not written into the fabric of the universe. It was not part of the "great chain of being," in which the sun ruled the heavens, the lion ruled the beasts, and the king ruled the people. Walzer quotes Henri Frankfurt who wrote, "The relation between the Hebrew monarch and his people was as nearly secular as is possible in a society wherein religion is a living force."[9]

Third, and again unique to ancient Israel, the king had *no special legislative powers.* He did not make the law; he, like everyone else, was subject to it. The result of all these factors was that biblical Israel was what Walzer calls an "almost democracy."[10]

Underlying all this is the idea set out by Milton in *Paradise Lost*:

> [God] gave us only over beast, fish, fowl,
> Dominion absolute; that right we hold
> By his donation; but man over men
> He made not lord; such title to himself
> Reserving, human left from human free.[11]

---

9. Michael Walzer, *In God's Shadow: Politics in the Hebrew Bible* (New Haven, CT: Yale University Press, 2012), 58.
10. Ibid., 200.
11. *Paradise Lost*, 12.67–71.

Only God has the right to rule over human beings. This idea entered Europe only in the sixteenth and seventeenth centuries, after the Reformation. The invention of printing and translation of the Bible into the vernacular allowed ordinary people for the first time to encounter directly the Hebrew Bible, which had hitherto been the preserve of the Church and its clergy. Hence the remarkable phenomenon that the free societies of Britain and the United States owe their origin to ideas set out in the Hebrew Bible as interpreted by the rabbis.

This is not the only way to arrive at a free society – the Athens of Solon and Pericles in the sixth and fifth centuries BCE belonged to a quite different culture and understanding of freedom. Nonetheless, it was ancient Israel, not ancient Greece, that inspired the birth of Western liberty in the seventeenth century. It was their unshakeable belief in the power of Heaven that led Jews, and those who were influenced by their texts, to be critical in their relationship to all earthly powers.

For over all earthly powers is the sovereignty of God.

The Ecological Imperative

In the course of setting out the laws of war, the Torah adds a seemingly minor detail that became the basis of a much wider field of human responsibility, and is of major consequence today. The passage concerns a military campaign that involves laying siege to a city:

> When you lay siege to a city for a long time, fighting against it to capture it, do not destroy its trees by putting an axe to them, because you can eat their fruit. Do not cut them down. Are the trees people, that you should besiege them? However, you may cut down trees that you know are not fruit trees and use them to build siege works until the city at war with you falls. (Deut. 20:19–20)

War is, the Torah implies, inevitably destructive. That is why Judaism's highest value is peace. Nonetheless, there is a difference between necessary and needless destruction. Trees are a source of wood for siege works. But some trees, those that bear fruit, are also a source of food. Therefore, do not destroy them. Do not needlessly deprive yourself and others of a productive resource. Do not engage in a "scorched earth" tactic in the course of war.

The sages, though, saw in this command something more than a detail in the laws of war. They saw it as a *binyan av,* a specific example of a more general principle. They called this the rule of *bal tashḥit,* the prohibition against needless destruction of any kind. This is how Maimonides summarises it: "Not only does this apply to trees, but also whoever breaks vessels or tears garments, destroys a building, blocks a wellspring of water, or destructively wastes food transgresses the command of *bal tashḥit.*"[1] This is the halakhic basis of an ethic of ecological responsibility.

What determines whether a biblical command is to be taken restrictively or expansively? There were some commands that the sages so hedged around with qualifications that they were rarely if ever applied. There were others of which they said, "The laws are many but the scriptural basis is slender" (Mishna Ḥagiga 1:8). A seemingly minor law became the basis of a wide halakhic field. What led the sages in the direction they took?

The simplest answer lies in the word "Torah" itself. It means law. But it also means, more generally: teaching, instruction, direction, guidance. The Torah is a lawbook like no other, because it includes not only laws but also narratives, genealogies, history, and song. Law as the Torah conceives it is embedded in a larger universe of meanings. Those meanings help us understand the context and purpose of any given law.

So it is here. First and foremost is the fact that the earth is not ours. It belongs to its Creator, to God Himself. That is the point of the first chapter of the Torah: "In the beginning, God created…" He made it; therefore He is entitled to lay down the conditions within which we live in it as His guests.

The logic of this is immediately played out in the story of the first humans. In Genesis 1 God commands humanity: "Fill the earth and *subdue* it. *Rule* over the fish in the sea and the birds in the sky and over every living creature that moves on the ground" (1:28). "Subdue" and "rule" are verbs of dominance. In Genesis 2, however, the text uses two quite different verbs. God placed the first man in the Garden "to serve it [*le'ovdah*] and guard it [*leshomrah*]" (2:15). These belong to the language

1. Maimonides, *Mishneh Torah, Hilkhot Melakhim* 6:10.

of responsibility. The first term, *le'ovdah,* tells us that humanity is not just the master but also the servant of nature. The second, *leshomrah,* is the term used in later biblical legislation to specify the responsibilities of one who undertakes to guard something that is not his.

How are we to understand this tension between the two opening chapters? Quite simply: Genesis 1 tells us about creation and nature, the reality mapped by the natural sciences. It speaks about humanity as the biological species, Homo sapiens. What is distinctive about humans as a species is precisely our godlike powers of dominating nature and exercising control of the forces that shape the physical world. This is a matter of fact, not value, and it has increased exponentially throughout the relatively short period of human civilisation. As John F. Kennedy put it in his inaugural presidential address: "Man holds in his mortal hands the power to abolish all forms of human poverty and all forms of human life."[2] Power is morally neutral. It can be used to heal or wound, build or destroy.

Genesis 2, by contrast, is about morality and responsibility. It tells us about the moral limits of power. Not everything we *can* do *may* we do. We have the power but not the permission; we have the ability but not the right. The earth is not ours. It belongs to God who made it. Therefore we are not the owners of nature but its custodians. We are here to serve it and care for it.

This explains the story that immediately follows, about Adam, Eve, the serpent, and the forbidden fruit. What the fruit was, why the serpent spoke, and what was the nature of the first sin – all these are secondary. The primary point the Torah is making is that, even in paradise, there are limits. There is forbidden fruit. Not everything we can do may we do.

Few moral principles have been forgotten more often and more disastrously. The record of human intervention in the natural order is marked by devastation on a massive scale.[3] Within a thousand years, the first human inhabitants of America had travelled from the Arctic

---

2. Washington, DC, January 20, 1961.
3. Jared Diamond's *Guns, Germs, and Steel* (New York: W. W. Norton, 1997) and *Collapse: How Societies Choose to Fail or Succeed* (New York: Viking Penguin, 2005) are classic texts on the subject.

north to the southernmost tip of Patagonia, making their way through two continents and, on the way, destroying most of the large mammal species then extant, among them mammoths, mastodons, tapirs, camels, horses, lions, cheetahs, and bears.

When the first British colonists arrived in New Zealand in the early nineteenth century, bats were the only native land mammals they found. They discovered, however, traces of a large, ostrich-like bird the Maoris called "moa." Eventually skeletons of a dozen species of this animal came to light, ranging from three to ten feet high. The remains of some twenty-eight other species have been found, among them flightless ducks, coots, and geese together with pelicans, swans, ravens, and eagles. Animals that have not had to face human predators before are easy game, and the Maoris must have found them a relatively effortless source of food.

A similar pattern can be traced almost everywhere human beings have set foot. They have consistently been more mindful of the ability to "subdue" and "rule" than of the responsibility to "serve" and "guard." An ancient midrash sums this up, in a way that deeply resonates with contemporary ecological awareness:

> When God made man, He showed him the panoply of creation and said to him: "See all My works, how beautiful they are. All I have made, I have made for you. Take care, therefore, that you do not destroy My world, for if you do, there will be no one left to mend what you have destroyed."[4]

Environmental responsibility seems to be one of the principles underlying the three great commands of periodic rest: Shabbat, the Sabbatical year, and the Jubilee year. On Shabbat all agricultural work is forbidden, "so that your ox and your donkey may rest" (Ex. 23:12). It sets a limit to our intervention in nature and the pursuit of economic growth. We remind ourselves that we are creations, not just creators. For six days the earth is handed over to us and our labours, but on the seventh we may perform no "work," namely, any act that alters the state of something

4. Ecclesiastes Rabba 7:13.

for human purposes. Shabbat is thus a weekly reminder of the integrity of nature and the limits of human striving.

What Shabbat does for humans and animals, the Sabbatical and Jubilee years do for the land. The earth too is entitled to its periodic rest. The Torah warns that if the Israelites do not respect this, they will suffer exile: "Then shall the land make up for its Sabbatical years throughout the time that it is desolate and you are in the land of your enemies; then shall the land rest and make up for its Sabbath years" (Lev. 26:34). Behind this are two concerns. One is environmental. As Maimonides points out, land which is overexploited eventually erodes and loses its fertility. The Israelites were therefore commanded to conserve the soil by giving it periodic fallow years, not pursuing short-term gain at the cost of long-term desolation.[5] The second, no less significant, is theological: "The land," says God, "is Mine; you are but strangers and temporary residents with Me" (Lev. 25:23). We are guests on earth.

Another set of commands is directed against over-interference with nature. The Torah forbids crossbreeding livestock, planting a field with mixed seeds, and wearing a garment of mixed wool and linen. These rules are called *ḥukkim* or "statutes." Samson Raphael Hirsch (Germany, 1808–1888) in the nineteenth century, like Nahmanides six centuries earlier, understood *ḥukkim* to be *laws that respect the integrity of nature.* They represent the principle that "the same regard which you show to man you must also demonstrate to every lower creature, to the earth which bears and sustains all, and to the world of plants and animals." They are a kind of social justice applied to the natural world: "They ask you to regard all living things as God's property. Destroy none; abuse none; waste nothing; employ all things wisely.... Look upon all creatures as servants in the household of creation."[6]

So it was no accident that Jewish law interpreted the prohibition against cutting down fruit-bearing trees in the course of war as an instance of a more general prohibition against needless destruction, and more generally still, against acts that deplete earth's non-renewable resources, or damage the ecosystem, or lead to the extinction of species.

5. Maimonides, *Guide for the Perplexed,* III:39.
6. Samson Raphael Hirsch, *The Nineteen Letters,* letter 11.

Václav Havel made a fundamental point in *The Art of the Impossible*: "I believe that we have little chance of averting an environmental catastrophe unless we recognise that we are not the masters of Being, but only a part of Being."[7] That is why a religious vision is so important, reminding us that we are not owners of our resources. They belong not to us but to the Eternal and eternity. Hence we may not needlessly destroy. If that applies even in war, how much more so in times of peace. "The earth is the Lord's and all that is in it" (Ps. 24:1). We are its guardians, on behalf of its Creator, for the sake of future generations.

7. Václav Havel, *The Art of the Impossible* (New York: Knopf, 1997), 79.

Ki Tetzeh
כי תצא

With *Ki Tetzeh*, Moses reaches the heart of the detailed provisions of the covenant. The *parasha* contains no fewer than seventy-four commands, more than any other in the Torah. Among them are laws about family dysfunctions, moral and legal obligations towards neighbours and fellow citizens, sexual misdemeanours, moral behaviour in relation to financial matters, and other rules of social responsibility. The *parasha* ends with the command to be eternally vigilant about Amalek, the Torah's paradigm case of hatred and cruelty.

The first of the following essays is about loved and unloved wives and about the relationship between the law and the story of Jacob, Leah, and Rachel. The second is about the logic of the command regarding the "stubborn and rebellious son." The third is about the Torah's approach to animal welfare. The fourth essay is about the command not to hate an Egyptian. Why was this important for the Israelites to hear? The fifth is about the rehabilitation of offenders, a principle derived by the sages from a phrase in this *parasha*. The sixth is about Amalek. What does this law tell us about the nature of hatred in general, and anti-Semitism in particular? Are there different kinds of hate, and should they be treated differently?

Love Is Not Enough

In a *parasha* laden with laws, one in particular is fascinating. Here it is:

> If a man has two wives, one loved, the other unloved [*senua*, literally, "hated"], and both the loved and the unloved bear him sons but the firstborn is the son of the unloved wife, then when he wills his property to his sons, he must not give the rights of the firstborn to the son of the beloved wife in preference to his actual firstborn, the son of the unloved wife. He must recognise [the legal rights of] the firstborn of his unloved wife so as to give him a double share of all he has, for he is the first of his father's strength. The birthright is legally his. (Deut. 21:15–17)

The law makes eminent sense. In biblical Israel the firstborn was entitled to a double share in his father's inheritance.[1] What the law tells us is

1. This is already implicit in the story of Jacob, Reuben, and Joseph; on this, see below. The sages also inferred it from the episode of the daughters of Tzlofhad. See Num. 27:7, Bava Batra 118b.

that this is not at the father's discretion. He cannot choose to transfer this privilege from one son to another. In particular he cannot do this by favouring the son of the wife he loves most if, in fact, the firstborn came from another wife.

The *parasha*'s opening three laws – a captive woman taken in the course of war, the above law about the rights of the firstborn, and the "stubborn and rebellious son" – are all about dysfunctions within the family. The sages said that they were given in this order to hint that someone who takes a captive woman will suffer from strife at home, and the result will be a delinquent son (Sanhedrin 107a). In Judaism marriage is seen as the foundation of society. Disorder there leads to disorder elsewhere. So far, so clear.

What is remarkable about it, though, is that it seems to be in sharp conflict with a major narrative in the Torah, namely, Jacob and his two wives, Leah and Rachel. Indeed the Torah, by its use of language, makes unmistakable verbal linkages between the two passages. One is the pair of opposites, *ahuva/senua*, "loved" and "unloved/hated." This is precisely the way the Torah describes Rachel and Leah.

Recall the context. Fleeing from home to his uncle Laban, Jacob fell in love at first sight with Rachel and worked seven years for her hand in marriage. On the night of the wedding, however, Laban substituted his elder daughter Leah. When Jacob complained, "Why have you deceived me?" Laban replied, with intentional irony, "It is not done in our place to give the younger before the elder."[2] Jacob then agreed to work another seven years for Rachel. The second wedding took place a mere week after the first. We then read: "And [Jacob] went in also to Rachel, and he loved also Rachel more than Leah... God saw that Leah was unloved [*senua*] and He opened her womb, but Rachel remained barren" (Gen. 29:30–31).

Leah called her firstborn Reuben, but her hurt at being less loved remained, and we read this about the birth of her second son: "She became pregnant again and had a son. 'God has heard that I was unloved [*senua*],' she said, 'and He also gave me this son.' She named the child Simeon" (Gen. 29:33).

2. Gen. 29:25–26; probably an oblique reference to Jacob buying Esau's birthright and taking his blessing.

The word *senua* appears only four times in the Torah, twice in the passage above about Leah, twice in our *parasha* in connection with the law of the rights of the firstborn.

There is an even stronger connection. The unusual phrase "first of [his father's] strength" appears only twice in the Torah, here ("for he is the first of his father's strength") and in relation to Reuben, Leah's firstborn: "Reuben, you are my firstborn, my might and the first of my strength, first in rank and first in power" (Gen. 49:3).

Because of these substantive and linguistic parallels, the attentive reader cannot but hear in the law in *Parashat Ki Tetzeh* a retrospective commentary on Jacob's conduct vis-à-vis his own sons. Yet that conduct seems to have been the opposite of what is legislated here. Jacob *did* transfer the right of the firstborn from Reuben, his actual firstborn, son of the less-loved Leah, to Joseph, the firstborn of his beloved Rachel. This is what he told Joseph: "Now, the two sons who were born to you in Egypt before I came here shall be considered as mine. Ephraim and Menashe shall be just like Reuben and Simeon to me" (Gen. 48:5).

Reuben should have received a double portion, but instead this went to Joseph. Jacob recognised each of Joseph's two sons as entitled to a full portion in the inheritance. So Ephraim and Menashe each became a tribe in their own right. In other words, we seem to have a clear contradiction between Deuteronomy and Genesis.

How are we to resolve this? It may be that, despite the rabbinic principle that the patriarchs observed the whole Torah before it was given, this is only an approximation. Not every law was precisely the same before and after the covenant at Sinai. For instance, Nahmanides notes that the story of Judah and Tamar seems to describe a slightly different form of levirate marriage from the one set out in Deuteronomy (commentary to Gen. 38:8).

In any case, this is not the only apparent contradiction between Genesis and later law. There are others, not least the very fact that Jacob married two sisters, something categorically forbidden in Leviticus 18:18. Nahmanides' solution – an elegant one, flowing from his radical view about the connection between Jewish law and the land of Israel – is that the patriarchs observed the Torah only while they were living in Israel itself (commentary to Gen. 26:5). Jacob married Leah and Rachel outside Israel, in the house of Laban in Haran (situated in today's Turkey).

Abrabanel gives a quite different explanation. The reason Jacob transferred the double portion from Reuben to Joseph was that God told him to do so. The law in Deuteronomy is therefore stated to make clear that the case of Joseph was an exception, not a precedent.

Sforno suggests that the Deuteronomy prohibition applies only when the transfer of the firstborn's rights happens because the father favours one wife over another. It does not apply when the firstborn has been guilty of a sin that would warrant forfeiting his legal privilege. That is what Jacob meant when, on his deathbed, he said to Reuben: "Unstable as water, you will no longer be first, for you went up onto your father's bed, onto my couch and defiled it" (Gen. 49:4). This is stated explicitly in the book of Chronicles which says that "Reuben ... was the firstborn, but when he defiled his father's marriage bed, his rights as firstborn were given to the sons of Joseph son of Israel" (I Chr. 5:1).

It is not impossible, though, that there is another kind of explanation altogether. What makes the Torah unique is that it is a book about both law (the primary meaning of "Torah") and history. Elsewhere these are quite different genres. Law is an answer to the question, "What may we or may not do?" History is an answer to the question, "What happened?" There is no obvious relationship between these two at all.

Not so in Judaism. In many cases, especially in *mishpat,* civil law, there is a connection between law and history, between what happened and what we should or should not do.[3] Much of biblical law, for example, emerges directly from the Israelites' experience of slavery in Egypt, as if to say: This is what our ancestors suffered in Egypt; therefore do not do likewise. Do not oppress your workers. Do not turn an Israelite into a lifelong slave. Do not leave your servants or employees without a weekly day of rest. And so on.

3. This is the subject of a famous essay by Robert Cover, "Nomos and Narrative," Foreword to the Supreme Court 1982 Term, Yale Faculty Scholarship Series, Paper 2705, 1983; the paper can be found at http://digitalcommons.law.yale.edu/fss_papers/2705. Cover's view was that "no set of legal institutions or prescriptions exists apart from the narratives that locate it and give it meaning. For every constitution there is an epic, for each decalogue a scripture."

Not all biblical law is like this, but some is. It represents *truth learned through experience,* justice as it takes shape through the lessons of history. The Torah takes the past as a guide to the future – often positively but sometimes also negatively. Genesis tells us, among other things, that Jacob's favouritism towards Rachel over Leah, and Rachel's firstborn Joseph over Leah's firstborn, Reuben, was a cause of lingering strife within the family. It almost led the brothers to kill Joseph. It led to their selling him as a slave. According to Ibn Ezra, the resentment felt by the descendants of Reuben endured for several generations, which is why Datan and Aviram, both Reubenites, became key figures in the Korah rebellion (Ibn Ezra to Num. 16:1).

Jacob did what he did as an expression of love. His feeling for Rachel was overwhelming, as it was for Joseph, her elder son. Love is central to Judaism – not just love between husband and wife, parent and child, but also love for God, for neighbour and stranger. But love is not enough. There must also be justice and the impartial application of the law. People must feel that law is on the side of fairness. You cannot build a society on love alone. Love unites but it also divides. It leaves the less loved feeling abandoned, neglected, disregarded, "hated." It can leave in its wake strife, envy, and a vortex of violence and revenge.

That is what the Torah is telling us when it uses verbal association to link the law in this *parasha* with the story of Jacob and his sons in Genesis. It is teaching us that law is not arbitrary. It is rooted in the experience of history. Law is itself a *tikkun,* a way of putting right what went wrong in the past. We must learn to love; but we must also know the limits of love, and the importance of justice-as-fairness in families as in society.

Stubborn and Rebellious Sons

The law of the stubborn and rebellious son is one that generated considerable debate among the sages. What was its logic? How was it to be applied? Was it, in fact, ever applied? What does it teach us about the nature of justice, human and divine? Here is the law as it appears in *Parashat Ki Tetzeh*:

> If a man has a stubborn and rebellious son who does not obey his father and mother and will not listen to them when they discipline him, his father and mother shall take hold of him and bring him to the elders at the gate of his town. They shall say to the elders, "This son of ours is stubborn and rebellious. He will not obey us. He is a profligate and a drunkard." Then all the men of his town shall stone him to death. You must purge the evil from among you. All Israel will hear of it and be afraid. (Deut. 21:18–21)

The apparent harshness of the law led R. Shimon b. Yoḥai to conclude that "there never was nor ever will be a stubborn and rebellious son. Why then was it written? So that we should expound the law and receive reward" (Sanhedrin 71a). The law was, in his view, a matter of theory rather than practice – a way of signalling the gravity of the case rather than specifying action to be taken. (Perhaps the law was meant to be recited to such a child in order to persuade him to mend his ways.)

In fact, the whole tendency of rabbinic interpretation was so restrictive as to make it difficult if not impossible for such a case to arise. The child must be within three months of attaining maturity. He must have stolen money from his parents, used it to buy a specific measure of meat and Italian wine, eaten and drunk his purchases in one go in a place other than his parents' house, and so on (Sanhedrin 68b–71a). The conditions that had to be satisfied for the law to be applied were so stringent that they could almost never have been met. Indeed, some sages suggested conditions that in practice would never be fulfilled. For example, R. Yehuda held that "if his mother is not like his father in voice, appearance, and stature, he does not become a rebellious son. Why? Because the Torah states, He will not obey our voice, and since they must be alike in voice, they must be alike in appearance and stature also" (Sanhedrin 71a).

Nevertheless, there were those who held that the law was intended to be, and actually was, applied. What, according to them, was the logic of the law? R. Yose the Galilean said:

> The Torah foresaw the ultimate destiny of the stubborn and rebellious son. Having dissipated his father's wealth, he would seek to satisfy his wants and be unable to do so. He would then go to a crossroad and rob. Therefore the Torah ordained: Let him die innocent rather than die guilty – for the death of the wicked benefits both themselves and the world. (Sanhedrin 71b)

On this view, the law of the stubborn and rebellious son is a form of preemptive punishment. He is deemed worthy of punishment not for what he has done but for what he is likely to do in the future. The equivalent nowadays would be preventive detention, that is to say, putting someone in prison because he or she is judged to be a danger to society. There is a concept in secular law of *punishment as deterrence*, not just punishment as retribution. That, according to R. Yose, is the logic of this law. Not only is the child himself sentenced, but the aim is also that "all Israel will hear of it and be afraid" – in other words, that other potential criminals will be discouraged by seeing the fate of this one. One explanation of the disagreement between R. Shimon b. Yoḥai and R. Yose is therefore that they differ as to whether punishment-as-deterrence is part of the Torah's view of justice.

One of the most significant post-Enlightenment arguments about the nature of ethics was between Kantians and Benthamites. For Kant, ethics was a matter of duty. For Bentham it was a matter of consequences. Kant believed in justice as retribution. If a wrong had been done, it had to be set right by wrong being done to the wrongdoer. Justice thus restores moral balance to the world. Bentham, by contrast, developed the theory known as utilitarianism. An act is right if it produces the best consequences for society as a whole: the greatest happiness for the greatest number. On this view, justice looks less to the past than to the future. If it deters wrongdoing and leads to less crime it is justified.

This leads to significant differences in practice. According to Bentham, a punishment might be justified even if it is out of proportion to the crime, so long as it deters others (an "exemplary punishment"). A Kantian would disagree. If a punishment is disproportionate to the crime[1] it is unjust, and no utilitarian benefits can justify injustice. Conversely, Kant considered the hypothetical case of a man who had committed murder on a desert island where the remaining inhabitants were about to leave. Should they sentence him to death and carry out the punishment? There is no deterrence in such a case. There would be no one else on the island to murder. Nonetheless, said Kant, the sentence should be carried out, for if it were not, a past wrong would remain unrequited. There would be a failure of justice.

Some such disagreement seems to lie between R. Shimon and R. Yose. R. Yose believed that the Torah sometimes prescribes punishment-as-deterrence in order to protect society and reduce the incidence of serious crimes. R. Shimon held that it does not, for punishment-as-deterrence contravenes the principle of retributive justice. One should not commit an injustice, even if lives will be lost in future as a result.

1. A Jewish principle; see Maimonides, *Guide for the Perplexed*, III:41.

Thus far, the halakhic debate. However, the Torah is a rich and complex document and does not confine itself to legal provisions alone. It also contains narrative. One narrative in particular has a bearing on the question of the stubborn and rebellious son – namely, the story of Ishmael. Ishmael was the son of Abraham and Sarah's handmaid Hagar, by whom Sarah proposed that Abraham have a child (what is nowadays called "surrogate motherhood").

When Sarah eventually had a child of her own, Isaac, she saw Ishmael *metzaḥek* (Gen. 21:9). Literally, this means "mocking"; Rashi interprets it to mean "guilty of cardinal sins." Whatever Ishmael was doing, it was enough to convince Sarah that he was not fit company for her own son (God Himself had told Hagar that her son would be "a wild donkey of a man; his hand against everyone, and everyone's hand against him" [Gen. 16:12]). Hagar and the young Ishmael were sent out into the desert in the blazing sun. Their water ran out, and Hagar put the child under a bush, saying, "I cannot watch the boy die" (Gen. 21:16). We then read:

> God heard the boy crying, and the angel of God called to Hagar from heaven and said to her, "What is the matter, Hagar? Do not be afraid; God has heard the voice of the lad there where he is. Lift the boy up and take him by the hand, for I will make him into a great nation." Then God opened her eyes and she saw a well of water. So she went and filled the skin with water and gave the boy a drink. (Gen. 21:17–19)

The Midrash adds the following commentary:

> R. Shimon said, The ministering angels immediately began accusing him, saying, "Lord of the universe, will You bring up a well for an individual who will one day slay Your children with thirst?" God said to them, "At this moment, what is he?" "Righteous," they replied. "I judge man only as he is at the moment."[2]

2. Genesis Rabba 54:13.

Similarly the Talmud states: "Individuals are judged only according to their acts at the time, as it says, 'God has heard the voice of the lad there where he is'" (Rosh HaShana 16b).

Ishmael was the first stubborn and rebellious son, rejected by his parents (father Abraham and stepmother Sarah) for what he might become ("a wild donkey of a man; his hand against everyone, and everyone's hand against him"). Yet the Torah, as interpreted by the midrash, rejects the argument of R. Yose in favour of the logic of R. Shimon. Punishment as deterrence against future crimes is not divine justice. God does not judge people for what they might become. He judges them as they are now.

Beneath this principle of justice is a deeper idea still: human freedom. Only the certainty that a juvenile delinquent will grow into a murderer can justify punishing him now to prevent acts he may commit in the future. But because we are free, and because even the most hardened criminal can repent and change, there can be no such certainty in human affairs. A stubborn and rebellious child may grow into a responsible adult. (Indeed, according to the Talmud, Ishmael repented in the lifetime of Abraham [Bava Batra 16b].)

The story of Ishmael in Genesis is an important commentary on the law in Deuteronomy, and incidentally tells us something not only about the nature of biblical justice but also about why the Torah contains narrative as well as law. Law deals in generalities. Narrative focuses on particularities: this person, that family, this time, that place. Without law, society becomes chaos. But without narrative, law itself loses contact with the realities of human life. It becomes impersonal and at times inhuman.[3]

It is one thing to discuss justice-as-deterrence in the abstract; it is quite another to do so with the image of the young Ishmael about to die of thirst before us. When R. Shimon b. Yoḥai stated that "there never was nor ever will be a stubborn and rebellious son," he was articulating one of the deepest instincts of biblical justice. We do not condemn people for what they may become. We judge them for what they are.

3. See, on this, Martha Nussbaum, *Poetic Justice* (Boston: Beacon Press, 1995).

The story of Ishmael tells us something profound: that God never abandons us or gives up on us, because He never ceases to believe that, whatever wrong we may have done in the past, we can mend and transcend in the future. More than we have faith in God, God has faith in us. The law of the stubborn and rebellious son was never applied in practice, said R. Shimon bar Yoḥai, because we are never judged for what we might become, only for what we are now. We are free. We can change. We are not held captive by our past. That is justice combined with hope.

Animal Welfare

K*i Tetzeh* is about relationships: between men and women, parents and children, employers and employees, lenders and borrowers. Strikingly, though, it is also about relationships between humans and animals.

Descartes thought that animals lacked souls. Therefore you could do with them as you pleased.[1] Judaism does not believe that animals lack souls – "The righteous person cares about the *nefesh* of his animal," says the book of Proverbs (12:10). To be sure, *nefesh* here probably means "life" rather than "soul" (*neshama* in Hebrew). But Tanakh does regard animals as sentient beings. They may not think or speak, but they do feel. They are capable of distress. Therefore there is such a thing as animal distress, *tzaar baalei ḥayim*, and as far as possible it should be avoided.

So we read in *Parashat Ki Tetzeh*: "Do not muzzle an ox when it is treading grain" (Deut. 25:4). What is striking about this law is that it parallels provisions for human beings as well: "When you come [to

1. See Tom Regan and Peter Singer, eds., *Animal Rights and Human Obligations* (Englewood Cliffs, NJ: Prentice Hall, 1989), 13–19.

work] in your neighbour's vineyard, you may eat as many grapes as you desire to satisfy your hunger.... When you come [to work] in your neighbour's standing grain, you may take the ears with your hand" (Deut. 23:25–26). The principle is the same in both cases: it is cruel to prevent those working with food from eating some of it. The parallel is instructive. Animals, not just humans, have feelings and they must be respected.

Another law is: "Do not plough with an ox and donkey together" (Deut. 22:10). The ox is stronger than a donkey, so expecting the donkey to do the work of an ox is cruel. Each animal species has its integrity, its role, its niche in the scheme of creation that we must respect.

The most fascinating animal legislation in this *parasha* is the law of "sending the mother bird away":

> If you come across a bird's nest beside the road, either in a tree or on the ground, and the mother is sitting on the young or on the eggs, do not take the mother with the young. You may take the young, but be sure to let the mother go, so that it may go well with you and you may have a long life. (Deut. 22:6–7)

Much has been written on this command. Here I discuss only the analysis given by Moses Maimonides, fascinating in its complexity. There is a law that appears twice in the Mishna, stating that if a leader of prayer says, "Your mercies extend even to a bird's nest," he is to be silenced.[2] The Talmud offers two possible explanations, of which one is that such a prayer "makes it seem as the attributes of God are an expression of compassion, whereas in fact they are mere decrees."

In both his commentary to the Mishna and his law code,[3] Maimonides adopts this view. He adds: If the reason for sending the mother bird away were divine compassion towards animals then, in consistency, God should have forbidden killing animals for food. The law therefore should be understood as a decree (*gezerat hakatuv*), and has nothing to do with compassion, human or divine.

---

2. Mishna Berakhot 5:3; Mishna Megilla 4:9.
3. Maimonides, *Mishneh Torah, Hilkhot Tefilla* 9:7.

In *Guide for the Perplexed*, however, Maimonides adopts the opposite approach. There he rejects the very idea that there are commands that have no reason. The reason it is permitted to kill animals for food is, he says, because meat eating is necessary for human health. *Sheḥita* (ritual slaughter), however, has been ordained because it is the most painless way to kill an animal. He continues:

> It is also prohibited to kill an animal with its young on the same day, in order that people should be restrained and prevented from killing the two together in such a manner that the young is killed in the sight of the mother, for the pain of the animals under such circumstances is very great. *There is no difference in this case between the pain of human beings and the pain of other living beings, since the love and tenderness of the mother for her young ones is not produced by reasoning but by imagination, and this faculty exists not only in man but also in most living beings*.... The same reason applies to the law which enjoins that we should let the mother bird fly away when we take the young.[4]

So Maimonides, contrary to the position he takes in his law code, here states that the law *does* have compassion as its logic. Moreover, what it seeks to avoid is not physical pain to the animal but psychological distress. Maimonides' view of animals has been confirmed by recent findings in biology that suggest that many species do indeed resemble humans in their ability to form groups, engage in reciprocal altruism, and display a range of emotions.[5] In most animal species, it is the mother that forms an ongoing bond with the young. Among animals, fatherhood is usually far less developed. So Maimonides' explanation in *The Guide* is empirically well founded.

---

4. Maimonides, *Guide for the Perplexed*, III:48.
5. See on this the many works of primatologist Frans de Waal, including *Good Natured* (Cambridge, MA: Harvard University Press, 1997); *Chimpanzee Politics* (Baltimore, MD: John Hopkins University Press, 2007); *The Age of Empathy* (London: Souvenir, 2011); *The Bonobo and the Atheist* (New York: W. W. Norton and Co., 2014); and *Are We Smart Enough to Know How Smart Animals Are?* (New York: W. W. Norton and Co., 2017).

However, elsewhere in *The Guide*,[6] Maimonides takes yet a third position. Divine providence, he says, extends to individuals only among humans. Amongst animals, it applies solely to a species as a whole. So the reason we must not cause animals pain or distress is not because the Torah is concerned about animals but because it is concerned about humans. We should not be cruel:

> There is a rule laid down by our sages that it is directly prohibited in the Torah to cause pain to an animal. This rule is based on the words [of the angel to Balaam], "Why have you beaten your donkey?" (Num. 22:32). The object of this rule is to make us perfect, that we should not assume cruel habits, and that we should not uselessly cause pain to others – that on the contrary, we should be prepared to show pity and mercy to all living creatures except when necessity demands the contrary.

In this view, we are forbidden to cause needless suffering to animals because this will desensitise us and lead us eventually to be cruel to human beings.

Maimonides thus seems to embrace three sharply conflicting views:

1. The law of the mother bird is a divine decree with no reason.
2. It is intended to spare the mother bird emotional pain.
3. It is intended to have an effect on us, not the animal, by training us not to be cruel.

In fact all three are true, because they answer different questions.

The first view explains why we have the laws we have. The Torah forbids certain acts that are cruel to animals but not others. Why these and not those? Because that is the law. Laws will always seem arbitrary. Why, for example, is one permitted to drive at thirty miles an hour in a city, but not thirty-one? Why not set the bar at twenty-nine? The reason for the law is obvious: to avoid accidents. But we observe the law because

6. *Guide for the Perplexed*, III:17.

it is the law, even though, under certain circumstances, driving at forty miles an hour would be safe, and at others, driving at twenty would be dangerous. The second view explains the immediate logic of the law. It exists to prevent needless suffering to animals, because they too feel physical pain and sometimes emotional distress as well. The third view sets the law in a larger perspective. Cruelty to animals is wrong, not because animals have *rights* but because we have *duties*. The duty not to be cruel is intended to promote virtue, and the primary context of virtue is the relationship between human beings. But virtues are indivisible. Those who are cruel to animals often become cruel to people. Hence we have a duty not to cause needless pain to animals, because of its effect on us. Hence the third proposition. Interestingly, Maimonides' analysis was repeated almost exactly, six centuries later, by the greatest philosopher of modern times, Immanuel Kant.[7]

This is a subtle and nuanced approach. Animals are part of God's creation. They have their own integrity in the scheme of things. We now know that they are far closer to human beings than philosophers like Descartes thought. This would not have been news to the heroes of the Bible. Abraham, Moses, and David were all shepherds who lived their formative years watching over and caring for animals. That was their first tutorial in leadership, and they knew that this was one way of understanding God Himself ("The Lord is my shepherd" [Ps. 23:1]).

Judaism also reminds us of what we sometimes forget: that the moral life is too complex to summarise in a single concept like "rights." Alongside rights, there are duties, and there can be duties without corresponding rights. Animals do not have rights, but we have duties towards them. As several laws in *Parashat Ki Tetzeh* and elsewhere make clear, we must not cause them unnecessary pain or emotional distress.

As we saw in the case of environmental legislation in *Shofetim*, Genesis 1 gives us the mandate to "subdue" and "rule" creation, including animals, but Genesis 2 gives us the responsibility to "serve" and "guard." Animals may not have rights but they have feelings, and we must respect them if we are to honour our role as God's partners in creation.

---

7. Immanuel Kant, *Lectures on Ethics* (London: Methuen, 1930).

Letting Go

> Darkness cannot drive out darkness; only light can do that. Hate cannot drive out hate; only love can do that. Hate multiplies hate, violence multiplies violence, and toughness multiplies toughness...[1]

> I imagine one of the reasons people cling to their hates so stubbornly is because they sense, once hate is gone, they will be forced to deal with pain.[2]

There is a verse in *Ki Tetzeh* that is momentous in its implications. It is easy to miss, appearing as it does in the midst of a series of miscellaneous laws about inheritance, rebellious sons, overladen oxen, marriage violations, and escaping slaves. Without any special emphasis or preamble, Moses delivers a command so counter-intuitive that we have to read it twice to make sure we have heard it correctly: "Do not hate an Edomite, because he is your brother. Do not hate an Egyptian, because you were a stranger in his land" (Deut. 23:8).

1. Martin Luther King Jr., *Strength to Love* (Minneapolis, MN: Fortress Press, 2010), 47.
2. James Arthur Baldwin, *Collected Essays* (New York: Library of America, 1998), 75.

What does this mean in its biblical context? The Egyptians of Moses' day had enslaved the Israelites, "embittered their lives" (Ex. 1:14), subjected them to a ruthless regime of hard labour, and forced them to eat the bread of affliction. They had embarked on a programme of attempted genocide, Pharaoh commanding his people to throw "every male [Israelite] child born into the river" (1:22).

Now, forty years later, Moses speaks as if none of this had happened, as if the Israelites owed the Egyptians a debt of gratitude for their hospitality. Yet he and the people were where they were only because they were escaping from Egyptian persecution. Nor did he want the people to forget it. To the contrary, he told them to recite the story of the Exodus every year, as we still do on Passover, re-enacting it with bitter herbs and unleavened bread so that the memory is passed on to all future generations. If you want to preserve freedom, he implies, never forget what it feels like to lose it. Yet here, on the banks of the Jordan, addressing the next generation, he tells the people, "Do not hate an Egyptian." What is going on in this verse?

To be free, you have to let go of hate. That is what Moses is saying. If they continued to hate their erstwhile enemies, Moses would have taken the Israelites out of Egypt, but he would not have taken Egypt out of the Israelites. Mentally, they would still be there, slaves to the past. They would still be in chains, not of metal but of the mind[3] – and chains of the mind are the most constricting of all.

You cannot create a free society on the basis of hate. Resentment, rage, humiliation, a sense of injustice, the desire to restore honour by inflicting injury on your former persecutors – these are conditions of a profound lack of freedom. You must live *with* the past, implies Moses, but not *in* the past. Those who are held captive by anger against their former persecutors are captive still. Those who let their enemies define who they are have not yet achieved liberty.

The Mosaic books refer time and again to the Exodus and the imperative of memory: "You shall remember that you were slaves in

3. William Blake, in his poem "London" (originally published in *Songs of Experience* in 1794; found in *Songs of Innocence and Experience* [New York: Dover, 1992], 41), spoke of "mind-forg'd manacles."

Egypt." Yet never is this invoked as a reason for hatred, retaliation, or revenge. Always it appears as part of the logic of the just and compassionate society the Israelites are commanded to create: the alternative order, the antithesis of Egypt. The implicit message is: Limit slavery, at least as far as your own people are concerned. Do not subject them to hard labour. Give them rest and freedom every seventh day. Release them every seventh year. Recognise them as like you, not ontologically inferior. No one is born to be a slave.

Give generously to the poor. Let them eat from the leftovers of the harvest. Leave them a corner of the field. Share your blessings with others. Do not deprive people of their livelihood. The entire structure of biblical law is rooted in the experience of slavery in Egypt, as if to say: You know in your heart what it feels like to be the victim of persecution; therefore do not persecute others.

Biblical ethics is based on repeated acts of role reversal, using memory as a moral force. In Exodus and Deuteronomy, we are commanded to use memory not to preserve hate but to conquer it by recalling what it feels like to be its victim. "Remember" – not to live in the past but to prevent a repetition of the past.

Only thus can we understand an otherwise inexplicable detail in the Exodus story itself. In Moses' first encounter with God at the burning bush, he is charged with the mission of bringing the people out to freedom. God adds a strange rider:

> I will make the Egyptians favourably disposed towards this people, so that when you leave you will not go empty-handed. Every woman is to ask her neighbour and any woman living in her house for articles of silver and gold and for clothing, which you will put on your sons and daughters. (Ex. 3:21–22)

The point is twice repeated in later chapters (Ex. 11:2; 12:35). Yet it runs utterly against the grain of biblical narrative. From Genesis (14:23) to the book of Esther (9:10, 15, 16), taking booty, spoil, plunder from enemies is frowned on. In the case of idolaters it is strictly forbidden: their property is *ḥerem*, taboo, to be destroyed, not possessed (Deut. 7:25; 13:16). When, in the days of Joshua, Achan took spoil from the ruins of

Jericho, the whole nation was punished (Josh. 7). And what happened to the gold? The Israelites eventually used it to make the Golden Calf. Why then was it important – commanded – that on this one occasion the Israelites should ask for gifts from the Egyptians?

The Torah itself provides the answer in a later law of Deuteronomy about the release of slaves:

> If a fellow Hebrew, a man or a woman, sells himself to you and serves you six years, in the seventh year you must let him go free. When you release him, do not send him away empty-handed. Supply him liberally from your flock, your threshing floor, and your winepress. Give to him as the Lord your God has blessed you. Remember that you were slaves in Egypt and the Lord your God redeemed you. That is why I give you this command today. (Deut. 15:12–15)

Slavery needs "narrative closure." To acquire freedom, a slave must be able to leave without feelings of antagonism to his former master. He must not depart laden with a sense of grievance or anger, humiliation or slight. Were he to do so, he would have been released but not liberated. Physically free, mentally he would still be a slave. The insistence on parting gifts represents the Bible's psychological insight into the lingering injury of servitude. There must be an act of generosity on the part of the master if the slave is to leave without ill will. Slavery leaves a scar on the soul that must be healed.

When God told Moses to tell the Israelites to take parting gifts from the Egyptians, it is as if He were saying: Yes, the Egyptians enslaved you, but that is about to become the past. Precisely because I want you to remember the past, it is essential that you do so without hate or desire for revenge. What you are to recall is the pain of being a slave, not the anger you feel towards your slave-masters. There must be an act of symbolic closure.

This cannot be justice in the fullest sense of the word: such justice is a chimera, and the desire for it insatiable and self-destructive.[4] There

4. Thomas Sowell's *The Quest for Cosmic Justice* (New York: Free Press, 2002) is an interesting book on this theme.

is no way of restoring the dead to life, or of recovering the lost years of liberty denied. But neither can a people deny the past, deleting it from the database of memory. If they try to do so it will eventually come back – Freud's "return of the repressed" – and claim a terrible price in the form of high-minded, altruistic vengeance. Therefore the former slave-owner must give the former slave a gift, acknowledging him as a free human being who has contributed, albeit without choice, to his welfare. This is not a squaring of accounts. It is, rather, a minimal form of restitution, of what today is called "restorative justice."

Hatred and liberty cannot coexist. A free people does not hate its former enemies; if it does, it is not yet ready for freedom. To create a non-persecuting society out of people who have been persecuted, you have to break the chains of the past; rob memory of its sting; sublimate pain into constructive energy and the determination to build a different future.

Freedom involves the abandonment of hate, because hate is the abdication of freedom. It is the projection of our conflicts onto an external force whom we can then blame, but only at the cost of denying responsibility. That was Moses' message to those who were about to enter the Promised Land: that a free society can be built only by people who accept the responsibility of freedom, subjects who refuse to see themselves as objects, people who define themselves by love of God, not hatred of the other.

"Do not hate an Egyptian, because you were a stranger in his land," said Moses, meaning: to be free, you have to let go of hate.

Rehabilitation of Offenders

P*arashat Ki Tetzeh* provides us with a fine example of the humanity of Jewish law – as well as the way the sages interpreted the Torah. Our point of departure is this passage:

> When people have a dispute, they shall take it to court and the judges will decide the case, acquitting the innocent and condemning the guilty. If the guilty person deserves to be beaten, the judge shall make him lean over and have him flogged in his presence with the number of lashes his crime deserves, but he must not give him more than forty lashes. If he is flogged more than that, your brother will be degraded in your eyes. (Deut. 25:1–3)

Our focus in this essay will be on the last phrase: "Your brother will be degraded in your eyes."

The sages derived from this a fundamental principle, namely, *the rehabilitation of an offender* once he has served his punishment. In the earlier part of the passage the offender is called *harasha*, translated here as "the guilty" but which literally means "the wicked." At the end, however, he is called "your brother." From this, the sages drew the conclusion that "once he has been beaten, he becomes [again] your brother."[1]

This has both a specific and more general application. The specific rule applies to offences that carried with them the severe punishment of *karet,* literally, "being cut off" from one's people. In many cases this was interpreted as a divine rather than human punishment; the human punishment was to receive lashes. The principle that "once he has been beaten, he becomes [again] your brother" was taken to mean that the human punishment cancels the divine punishment. Once the offender has been beaten, there is no residual guilt (Mishna Makkot 3:15).

In addition, however, the sages inferred the far wider principle that when the guilty has received the punishment his offence deserved, he is restored to his earlier status. For example, he is permitted to be a witness, and his testimony is not invalidated by the fact that previously he had been found guilty of an offence. The stain on his character is temporary, not permanent. Offenders are to be rehabilitated.

This led to a specific enactment by the sages, known as *takkanat hashavim,* a rule designed to remove obstacles to penitence. The Mishna teaches that "if a beam which was acquired by robbery has been built into a building, restitution for it may be made in money so as not to put obstacles in the way of penitents" (Mishna Gittin 5:5).

The rule is that in the case of robbery, the guilty party must return what he has taken to its rightful owner ("He shall restore that which he took by robbery" [Lev. 5:23]). This makes obvious sense. If a robber were allowed merely to make monetary compensation rather than return the stolen object, the law would, in effect, allow someone to acquire an object – albeit at a price – by violence. That must be wrong.

Yet this rule was suspended in a case in which returning the object would involve massive loss for the robber. The situation envisaged by the Mishna is one in which, having stolen a beam, the robber has used it to build a house. Restoring the beam would involve tearing down the house. A sense of guilt at the original crime might induce remorse in

1. Sifrei, *Ki Tetzeh* 286.

the robber and an effort on his part to return objects he has wrongly taken. But if this would involve disproportionate loss for him – not just returning the stolen object, but also having to dismantle what he has built using it – he might decide that restitution was just too costly, and decide against giving the object back.

One might ask: So what? The man is a robber. What matters is the right of the innocent – the original owner of the beam – not the right of the guilty. Surely the robber, by breaking the law, has forfeited any claim on the court's clemency. Yet Jewish law ruled otherwise. To be sure, the owner must be compensated for his loss. Without this, he will have suffered an injustice. But we must have concern for the offender also, in the sense that we must clear away any obstacles in the path of his return to law-abidingness. The sages fully understood that this was not part of Torah law. It required a positive enactment, *takkanat hashavim,* on their part. But the sages would not have made this enactment if they did not feel that it was in the spirit of Torah law.

The sages went further still. We find in the Talmud this remarkable principle: "If robbers or usurers [repent, and of their own accord] are prepared to restore what they have wrongly taken, it is not right to accept it from them, and one who does so is not acting with the approval of the sages" (Bava Kamma 94b). The Talmud explains how this teaching emerged from an actual case.

In the time of R. Yehuda HaNasi, head of the Jewish community in the early third century, a robber decided to end his life of crime and restore everything he had wrongly taken to its owners. His wife said to him: "Fool. If you give back everything you have taken, you will not be left with even the belt you are wearing." The rule was then instituted that those who had been robbed should not insist on the return of their property (Bava Kamma 94b).

Needless to say, this does not apply to a robber who has been brought to court – only to one who has, without any prompting other than his own conscience, decided to confess his guilt and make amends. It does not apply if the robber still has the stolen objects in his possession. Nor is it a legal requirement. The rightful owner may still take the robber to court if he so chooses. Some go so far as to say that this was never intended as a permanent enactment, for it is all too easily exploitable: robbers could steal and then pretend to be penitent.[2] Yet despite all this, Maimonides writes: "Even though robbing someone is like taking their life...we must help [a robber who repents of his own accord] and pardon him in order to bring him back to the right path of penitents."[3]

Another principle the sages articulated, this time on the basis of a biblical command, was that one should not make reference to a penitent's past. One should not say to someone who committed a crime but has now served his sentence and expressed remorse, "Remember the crime you committed." To do so is to be guilty of "verbal oppression," which is forbidden by the verse "You shall not oppress one another, but you shall fear your God; I am the Lord your God" (Lev. 25:17).[4] In the tenth century, Rabbenu Gershom instituted a rule that one who made public mention of a penitent's earlier deeds was to be excommunicated.[5]

The rules of rehabilitation are complex, and I make no attempt to summarise them here. Yet it is clear that from earliest times the sages tempered their concern for justice with a desire to help criminals and wrongdoers find their way back to honesty and society. What mandated them to do so was the teaching of the prophet Ezekiel:

> Son of man, say to the house of Israel: This is what you have been saying, "Our offences and sins weigh heavily on us, and we are sick at heart because of them. How can we survive?" Say to them, "As surely as I live, declares the Sovereign Lord, I take no pleasure in the death of the wicked, but rather that they turn from their ways and live." (Ezek. 33:10–12)

Not only were these teachings many centuries ahead of their time; they also have much to teach us today. Retributive justice is not incompatible with a sense of human dignity and freedom. To the contrary, it is

2. See the *Maggid Mishneh* to Maimonides, *Mishneh Torah, Hilkhot Gezela* 1:13.
3. Maimonides, *Mishneh Torah, Hilkhot Gezela* 1:13.
4. Maimonides, *Mishneh Torah, Hilkhot Teshuva* 7:8.
5. *Teshuvot Ḥakhmei Tzarfat* 21.

based on them. Jewish law is concerned not only with protecting the rights of those who have been wronged, but also helping wrongdoers rebuild their future. Guilt, in Judaism, is about acts, not persons. It is the act, not the person, that is condemned. Once the criminal has served his punishment and repented of his crime, he becomes, once more, "your brother."

Hate: Curable and Incurable

It is by any standards a strange, almost incomprehensible law. Here it is in the form it appears in *Parashat Ki Tetzeh*:

> Remember what the Amalekites did to you along the way when you came out of Egypt. When you were weary and worn out, they met you on your journey and attacked all who were lagging behind; they had no fear of God. When the Lord your God gives you rest from all the enemies around you in the land He is giving you to possess as an inheritance, you shall blot out the name of Amalek from under heaven. Do not forget. (Deut. 25:17–19)

The Israelites had two enemies in the days of Moses: the Egyptians and the Amalekites. The Egyptians enslaved the Israelites. They turned them into a forced labour colony. They oppressed them. Pharaoh commanded them to drown every male Israelite child. It was attempted genocide. Yet about them, as we saw, Moses commands: "Do not hate an Egyptian, because you were a stranger in his land" (Deut. 23:8).

The Amalekites did no more than attack the Israelites once,[1] an attack that was successfully repelled (Ex. 17:13). Yet Moses commands: "Remember." "Do not forget." "Blot out the name." In Exodus the Torah says that "God shall be at war with Amalek for all generations" (17:16). Why the difference? Why did Moses tell the Israelites, in effect, to forgive the Egyptians but not the Amalekites?

The answer is to be found as a corollary of a teaching in the Mishna:

> Whenever love depends on a cause and the cause passes away, then the love passes away too. But if love does not depend on a cause then the love will never pass away. What is an example of the love which depended upon a cause? That of Amnon for Tamar. And what is an example of the love which did not depend on a cause? That of David and Jonathan. (Mishna Avot 5:19)

When love is conditional, it lasts as long as the condition lasts but no longer. Amnon loved, or rather lusted for, Tamar because she was forbidden to him. She was his half-sister. Once he had had his way with her, "Then Amnon hated her with intense hatred. In fact, he hated her more than he had loved her" (II Sam. 13:15). But when love is unconditional and irrational, it never ceases. In the words of Dylan Thomas: "Though lovers be lost, love shall not, and death shall have no dominion."[2]

The same applies to hate. When hate is rational, based on some fear or disapproval that – justified or not – has some logic to it, then it can be reasoned with and brought to an end. But unconditional, irrational hatred cannot be reasoned with. There is nothing one can do to address it and end it. It persists.

That was the difference between the Amalekites and the Egyptians. The Egyptians' hatred and fear of the Israelites was not irrational. Pharaoh said to his people: "The Israelites are becoming too numerous

1. According to a midrashic explanation cited by Rashi on Num. 21:1 and by *Tosafot* in Rosh HaShana 3a, there was a second attack in the fortieth year of the Exodus.
2. "And Death Shall Have No Dominion," in *The Poems of Dylan Thomas*, ed. John Goodby (New York: New Directions, 2003), 55.

and strong for us. We must deal wisely with them. Otherwise, they may increase so much, that if there is war, they will join our enemies and fight against us, driving [us] from the land" (Ex. 1:9–10). The Egyptians feared the Israelites because they were numerous. They constituted a potential threat to the native population. Historians tell us that this was not groundless. Egypt had already suffered from one invasion of outsiders, the Hyksos, an Asiatic people with Canaanite names and beliefs, who took over the Nile delta during the Second Intermediate Period of the Egypt of the pharaohs. Eventually they were expelled from Egypt and all traces of their occupation were erased. But the memory persisted. It was not irrational for the Egyptians to fear that the Hebrews were another such population. They feared the Israelites because they were strong.

To be sure, there is a difference between "rational" and "justified." The fear of the Egyptians was in this case certainly unjustified. The Israelites did not want to take over Egypt. To the contrary, they would have preferred to leave. Not every rational emotion is justified. It is not irrational to feel fear of flying after the report of a major air disaster, despite the fact that statistically it is more dangerous to drive a car than to be a passenger in a plane. The point is simply that rational but unjustified emotion can, in principle, be cured through reasoning.

Precisely the opposite was true of the Amalekites. They attacked the Israelites when they were "weary and worn out." They focused their assault on those who were "lagging behind." Those who are weak and lagging behind pose no danger. This was irrational, groundless hate.

With rational hate – like that displayed by the Egyptians – it is possible to reason. Moreover, there was no reason for the Egyptians to fear the Israelites any more. They had left. They were no longer a threat. But with irrational hate – like that of the Amalekites – it is impossible to reason. It has no cause, no logic. Therefore it may never go away. Irrational hate is as durable and persistent as irrational love. The hatred symbolised by Amalek lasts "for all generations" (Ex. 17:16). All one can do is to remember and not forget, to be constantly vigilant, and to fight it whenever and wherever it appears.

There is such a thing as rational xenophobia: fear and hate of the foreigner, the stranger, the one not like us. In the hunter-gatherer stage of humanity, it was vital to distinguish between members of your tribe and those of another tribe. There was competition for food and territory. It was not an age of liberalism and tolerance. The other tribe was likely to kill you or oust you, given the chance.

The ancient Greeks were xenophobic, regarding all non-Greeks as barbarians.[3] So still are many native populations. Even people as tolerant as the British and Americans were distrustful of immigrants, be they Jews, Irish, Italian, or Puerto Rican. What happens, though, is that within two or three generations the newcomers acculturate and integrate. They are seen as contributing to the national economy and adding richness and variety to its culture. When an emotion like fear of immigrants is rational but unjustified, eventually it declines and disappears. So far is the United States from persistent hostility to Jews in fact that, as a result of recent research, Harvard sociologist Robert Putnam has shown that Americans have warmer feelings towards Jews than to the members of any other faith.[4]

Anti-Semitism is different from xenophobia. It is the paradigm case of irrational hatred. In the Middle Ages, Jews were accused of poisoning wells, spreading the plague, and in one of the most absurd claims ever – the blood libel – they were suspected of killing Christian children to use their blood to make matzot for Passover. This was self-evidently impossible, but that did not stop people believing it.

The European Enlightenment, with its worship of science and reason, was expected to end all such hatred. Instead it gave rise to a new version of it, racial anti-Semitism. In the nineteenth century, Jews were hated because they were rich and because they were poor; because they were capitalists and because they were communists; because they were exclusive and kept to themselves and because they infiltrated everywhere; because they were believers in an ancient, superstitious faith and because they were rootless cosmopolitans who believed nothing.

Anti-Semitism was the supreme irrationality of the age of reason. It gave rise to a new myth, *The Protocols of the Elders of Zion*, a literary forgery produced by members of Czarist Russia's secret police towards

3. See Benjamin Isaac, *The Invention of Racism in Classical Antiquity* (Princeton, NJ: Princeton University Press, 2006).
4. Robert Putnam, *American Grace* (New York: Simon and Schuster, 2010), 550.

the end of the nineteenth century. It held that Jews had power over the whole of Europe – this at the time of the Russian pogroms of 1881 and the anti-Semitic May Laws of 1882, which sent some three million Jews, powerless and impoverished, into flight from Russia to the West.

The situation in which Jews found themselves at the end of what was supposed to be the century of enlightenment and emancipation was stated eloquently by Theodor Herzl in 1897:

> We have honestly endeavored everywhere to merge ourselves in the social life of surrounding communities and to preserve the faith of our fathers. We are not permitted to do so. In vain are we loyal patriots, our loyalty in some places running to extremes; in vain do we make the same sacrifices of life and property as our fellow-citizens; in vain do we strive to increase the fame of our native land in science and art, or her wealth by trade and commerce. In countries where we have lived for centuries we are still cried down as strangers, and often by those whose ancestors were not yet domiciled in the land where Jews had already had experience of suffering.... If we could only be left in peace.... But I think we shall not be left in peace.[5]

This was deeply shocking to Herzl. No less shocking has been the return of anti-Semitism to parts of the Middle East and even Europe today, within living memory of the Holocaust. Yet the Torah intimates why. Irrational hate does not die.

Not all hostility to Jews, or to Israel as a Jewish state, is irrational, and where it is not, it can be reasoned with. But some of it is irrational. Some of it, even today, is a repeat of the myths of the past, from the blood libel to the *Protocols*. All we can do is remember and not forget, confront it and defend ourselves against it.

Amalek does not die. But neither does the Jewish people. Attacked so many times over the centuries, it still lives, giving testimony to the victory of the God of love over the myths and madness of hate.

---

5. Theodor Herzl, *A Jewish State* (New York: Dover, 1988), 76.

Ki Tavo
כי תבוא

In *Parashat Ki Tavo* Moses reaches the end of the detailed provisions of the covenant, with commands about bringing first fruits to the central Sanctuary, as well as allocating the various tithes. He closes this section with a reminder of what the covenant is: a mutual pledge between the people and God. The people are to give God their total loyalty. God, in turn, will hold the people in special regard.

The text then turns to the next feature of ancient covenants: the blessings and curses that will attend faithfulness on the one hand, disloyalty on the other. Given that Israel's entire existence as a nation is predicated on the covenant, it means that their fate will be an ongoing commentary on their relationship with God and the ideals, both sacred and social, to which the people have dedicated themselves as "a holy people to the Lord your God" (Deut. 7:6). The *parasha* ends with Moses summoning the people, at the end of their forty-year journey and in sight of the Promised Land, to renew the covenant their parents made with God at Mount Sinai.

The first of the following essays is about the declaration to be made on bringing first fruits, a unique institution that illustrates the connection between memory and identity. The second takes up the theme, noted in earlier essays, about the importance of the verb "to listen" in Deuteronomy, and the absence from biblical Hebrew of a verb meaning "to obey." Here I argue that a proper understanding of the many meanings of *shema* refutes the arguments made by Immanuel Kant against religious ethics. Judaism embodies not only a system of morality but also, and no less importantly, of moral *growth*, not unlike those articulated in modern times by Jean Piaget and Lawrence Kohlberg. The third essay is about the curses in the Torah. Do they mean that Jewish suffering during the many centuries of exile was divine punishment? The fourth essay is about the difference between the curses in Leviticus and those in *Ki Tavo*. Leviticus spoke about the Israelites rejecting the covenant, whereas here Moses merely speaks about their failure to serve God with joy. Why should this be so serious? The last essay is about the nature of the covenant itself, and why language is so sacred in Judaism.

History and Memory

The late Sir Isaiah Berlin was one of the great sages of post-war Britain, a brilliant philosopher and historian of ideas, of whom Noel Annan once wrote that he "seems to me to have offered the truest and most moving interpretation of life that my own generation made."[1] He did more than most to define the liberalism that took shape in his lifetime, and his lecture "Two Concepts of Liberty" became one of the most famous essays on politics in the twentieth century.

I came to know him late in his life, and in 1997 I asked him whether he would be kind enough to read the book I had just published, *The Politics of Hope*,[2] and give me his impressions. In it I developed a somewhat different account of the nature of freedom, not because I disagreed with Berlin, but because I felt that times had changed, and the threat to liberty was not what it had been forty years before, when he delivered his lecture. Then, the perceived threat was from communism and the Soviet Union. By 1997, the Soviet Union had collapsed, the

1. Henry Hardy, ed., *The Book of Isaiah: Personal Impressions of Isaiah Berlin* (Woodbridge: Boydell Press, 2009), 15.
2. London: Jonathan Cape, 1997.

Berlin Wall had fallen, and the Cold War was at an end. I believed that the new threat had to do with the loss, in the West, of a shared moral code. Without morality, societies eventually disintegrate. Individualism becomes so strong that people no longer work for the common good. They lose the sense of collective responsibility, and they can no longer muster the energies needed to defend their way of life.

He agreed, and I sent him the book. Months passed and I did not hear from him, so I phoned his home, just outside Oxford, and his wife, Lady Aline, answered. To my surprise, she said, "Isaiah has just been talking about you." "In what context?" I asked, knowing that rabbis were not his usual topic of conversation. "He wants to ask you," she said, "to officiate at his funeral." I rapidly changed the subject, thinking this was far too morbid. Clearly, though, he knew his end was near. Four days later, he died, and I did officiate at his funeral.

In the course of the eulogy, I said that his work had been an ongoing commentary to the story of the Exodus. I knew that Isaiah, though in many respects a secular Jew, was always punctilious in holding a Seder and telling the story. As a child in Riga, he had lived through the Russian Revolution, which is what brought his family to Britain. He knew what totalitarianism could look like, and he had experienced his own personal exodus. He knew also that Judaism was born in the journey from slavery to freedom, and that this was something every Jewish child knew, because of the Seder night and the Haggada.

In one of his relatively few statements about Jewish identity, he wrote this:

> All Jews who are at all conscious of their identity as Jews are steeped in history. They have longer memories, they are aware of a longer continuity as a community than any other which has survived.... Whatever other factors may have entered into the unique amalgam which, if not always Jews themselves, at any rate the rest of the world instantly recognizes as the Jewish people, historical consciousness – sense of continuity with the past – is among the most powerful.[3]

3. Isaiah Berlin, *Against the Current* (Princeton, NJ: Princeton University Press, 2013), 317.

This is surely true, but it elides an important distinction. The best way of seeing this is by way of a paradox. Jews were the first people to find God in history. They were the first to think in historical terms – of time as an arena of change as opposed to cyclical time in which the seasons rotate, people are born and die, but nothing really changes. Jews were the first people to write history – many centuries before Herodotus and Thucydides, often wrongly described as the first historians. Yet biblical Hebrew has no word that means "history" (the closest equivalent is *divrei hayamim*, "chronicles"). Instead it uses the root *zakhor*, meaning "memory."

Twenty-one times in Deuteronomy, Moses uses the verb Z-KH-R, to remember. Fourteen times he warns the people not to forget. There is a fundamental difference between history and memory. History is "his story,"[4] an account of events that occurred sometime else to someone else. Memory is "my story." It is the past internalised and made part of my identity. History is an answer to the question, "What happened?" Memory is an answer to the question, "Who am I?" We are what we remember. As with an individual suffering from dementia, so with a culture as a whole: the loss of memory is experienced as a loss of identity.

That is why a passage in *Parashat Ki Tavo* is so important. It describes the bringing of first fruits to the Temple. This was a dramatic occasion. A mishna in Bikkurim (3:4) describes the joyous scene as people converged on Jerusalem from across the country, bringing their first fruits to the accompaniment of music and celebration. Merely bringing the fruits, though, was not enough. Each person had to make a declaration. That declaration has become one of the best-known passages in the Torah because, though it was originally said on Shavuot, the festival of first fruits, it later[5] became a central text expounded in the Haggada on Seder night:

> My father was a wandering Aramean, and he went down into Egypt and lived there, few in number, there becoming a great

4. This is a simple reminder, not an etymology. *Historia* is a Greek word meaning inquiry. The same word came to mean, in Latin, a narrative of past events.
5. Some scholars believe that this happened already in Second Temple times.

> nation, powerful and numerous. But the Egyptians ill-treated us and made us suffer, subjecting us to harsh labour. Then we cried out to the Lord, the God of our ancestors, and the Lord heard our voice and saw our misery, toil, and oppression. So the Lord brought us out of Egypt with a mighty hand and an outstretched arm, with great terror and with signs and wonders. (Deut. 26:5–8)

Here for the first time *the retelling of the nation's past became an obligation for every citizen of the nation.* But this passage, known as *vidui bikkurim*, "the confession made over first fruits," was nothing like epic history engraved in stone on the walls of temples or national monuments. Nor was it the neutral, detailed account of events of the kind that the early Greek historians pioneered. It was simple, elemental. It was to be spoken, not read. It is, compressed into the shortest possible space, the entire history of the nation in summary form. In a few short sentences, it outlines

> the patriarchal origins in Mesopotamia, the emergence of the Hebrew nation in the midst of history rather than in mythic prehistory, slavery in Egypt and liberation therefrom, the climactic acquisition of the land of Israel, and throughout – the acknowledgement of God as lord of history.[6]

Most importantly, it is written in the first person: "*My* father.... The Lord brought *us* out of Egypt." This is history transformed into memory. This is not a detached tale of some disembodied past. It is the story of where I came from and who I am. It is history internalised. It is what led the sages of the Mishna to say, "In each generation, every person should see himself as if he personally came out of Egypt" (Mishna Pesaḥim 10:5).

It is impossible to overestimate the impact this had on the Jewish people from then to now. Identity is not just a matter of who my parents were. It is also a matter of *what they remembered and handed on to me.*

---

6. Yosef Hayim Yerushalmi, *Zakhor: Jewish History and Jewish Memory* (Seattle: University of Washington Press, 1982), 12.

Personal identity is shaped by individual memory. Group identity is formed by collective memory.[7] The mere act of telling the story, regularly, as a religious duty, sustained Jewish identity across the centuries, even in the absence of all the normal accompaniments of nationhood – land, geographical proximity, independence, self-determination – and never allowed the people to forget its ideals, its aspirations, its collective project of building a society that would be the opposite of Egypt, a place of freedom and justice and human dignity, in which no human being is sovereign, where God alone is king.

In our time, it has been the philosopher Alasdair MacIntyre who has emphasised the importance of narrative to the moral life. "Man," he writes, "is in his actions and practice, as well as in his fictions, essentially a story-telling animal." It is through narratives that we begin to learn who we are and how we are called on to behave. "Deprive children of stories and you leave them unscripted, anxious stutterers in their actions as in their words."[8] To know who we are is in large part to understand of which story or stories we are a part. Moses wanted the people never to forget of which story they are a part.

Jews have told the story of who we are for longer and more devotedly than any other people on the face of the earth. That is what makes Jewish identity so rich and resonant. In an age in which computer and smartphone memories have grown from kilobytes to megabytes to gigabytes, while human memories have become foreshortened, this remains an important message, not just to Jews but also to humanity as a whole. You can delegate history to computers, looking it up when you need it. But you cannot delegate memory. Memory is inherently, inescapably personal. It is what makes us who we are. If you seek to sustain identity, you have to renew memory regularly and teach it to the next generation. That is what Moses taught the Israelites, and what we have done ever since.

---

7. The classic works on group memory and identity are Maurice Halbwachs's *On Collective Memory* (Chicago: University of Chicago Press, 1992) and Jacques le Goff's *History and Memory* (New York: Columbia University Press, 1992).
8. Alasdair MacIntyre, *After Virtue* (Notre Dame, IN: University of Notre Dame Press, 1981).

The gift of collective memory is precious. Winston Churchill once said: "The longer you can look back, the further you can see forward."[9] Those who tell the story of their past have already begun to build their children's future.

9. Chris Wrigley, *Winston Churchill: A Biographical Companion* (Santa Barbara: ABC-CLIO, 2002), xxiv.

Listening and Moral Growth

From Deuteronomy 5 to 26 Moses has set out, in their full panoply, the laws of the covenant, the basic structure of a society under the sovereignty of God, from the most general outline to the most detailed specifics. Beginning with chapter 27, he now turns to the great choice between the blessing and the curse, the blessing if the people stay faithful to the covenant, the curse if they do not.

But before he does so, he, together with the priests, turns to the people and with a touch of drama says: "*Be silent, Israel, and listen!* You have now become the people of the Lord your God. *Listen* to the Lord your God and follow His commands and decrees that I give you today" (Deut. 27:9–10).

What exactly is Moses saying here? In a previous essay, I pointed to the strange fact that biblical Judaism, a religion of 613 commands, contains no word that means "obey." Instead, it uses the word *shema*, which means, to hear, to listen, to attend, to understand, to internalise, and to respond. *Shema* is a key word of the book of Deuteronomy, occurring no less than ninety-two times. What it means is fundamental to an understanding of Judaism. An extremely subtle point is being made.

To understand it we have to think our way into the great movement of Western rationalism, the eighteenth-century Enlightenment. It was then that that distinguished philosopher of modern times, Immanuel Kant, mounted a double challenge to religious ethics.

The first had to do with a distinction he made between *hypothetical* and *categorical* imperatives. A hypothetical imperative has the form, "If…then": "If you want to be happy, this is how to behave"; "If you want to avoid punishment, this is what you should not do." Categorical imperatives come with no "if"s: "Do not lie"; "Do not cheat"; "Do not kill." They apply regardless of what you want. Morality, said Kant, is about categorical imperatives, not hypothetical ones.

That is a direct challenge to the arguments put forward by Moses in Deuteronomy. He keeps telling the people: If you want the blessing, not the curse, then obey God. Keep His laws and you will have prosperity and peace. Otherwise there will be famine and war. These are hypothetical imperatives, and Kant would say that they do not constitute a morality. To obey God for the sake of reward or to avoid punishment may be sensible and pragmatic, but it is not being moral. We are moral when we do things that are right *because* they are right, not for the sake of reward or punishment.

The second has to do with his distinction between *heteronomy* and *autonomy*. Heteronomy means a law imposed by someone else. Autonomy means a law imposed by ourselves. And, said Kant, to be moral is to be autonomous – to do right because we have decided that it is the right thing to do, not because someone else – even God – has said so. The Hebrew Bible is the classic example of a heteronomous system. It is God, not we, who decides what is permitted and what is forbidden. Therefore to obey the Bible is not to be moral.

This, in its day, was a huge challenge to all forms of religious morality, but especially to Judaism. Kant believed in reason, not revelation. He was saying, in so many words, not only do we not *need* to be religious to be moral; being religious is a bar to being moral, because it means obeying someone else, not our own conscience.

In this, I believe, Kant was simply wrong – and not just because the Torah says otherwise but because the facts are otherwise. We now know, through the pioneering work of developmental psychologists like Jean Piaget (1896–1980) and Lawrence Kohlberg (1927–1987), that the distinctions made by Kant are not either/or. Rather, they represent developmental stages. We begin, in childhood, by doing things to receive reward or avoid punishment, and because someone else, usually a parent, has told us what to do or not do. Eventually, though, we develop our own internalised conscience, and learn that right and wrong do not depend on punishment or reward.

Maimonides makes precisely this developmental case in his *Commentary to the Mishna* (to Sanhedrin 10:1), and states in his law code that those who serve God in love "do what is right because it is right,"[1] and not for the sake of reward.

What Moses is doing in Deuteronomy is something very subtle. He is speaking at different levels to people at different stages in their moral and spiritual development. At the most basic level he is speaking to a nation still in its childhood. The people he is addressing are the children of those he led out of Egypt. They are more used to freedom than their parents, who were slaves. But they have not yet entered the land, or created a society, or been forced to work for a living. For forty years they have had their needs supplied by God. So he speaks to them in very simple terms. Follow God and be blessed, or follow your own inclinations and be cursed. This is the way one might speak to a child. As he himself says in this *parasha*: "To this day the Lord has not given you a mind that understands or eyes that see or ears that hear" (Deut. 29:3).

But interwoven in his speeches is an appeal to a much deeper level of understanding. So, for example, in this *parasha* he says, "The Lord will establish you as His holy people, as He swore to you, if you obey the Lord's commands and walk in His ways" (Deut. 28:9). "Walk in His ways" means, says Maimonides, not just *obeying* God, but rather, *imitating* God,[2] internalising the values and virtues by which God relates to humanity. The pinnacle of the moral life, to which we should all aspire, is precisely to do what is right because it is right, because that is what it is to walk in God's ways.

1. Maimonides, *Mishneh Torah, Hilkhot Teshuva* 10:2.
2. Maimonides, *Sefer HaMitzvot*, positive command 8; idem, *Mishneh Torah, Hilkhot Deot* 1:5.

That is why the key word of Deuteronomy is *shema,* the word that is untranslatable precisely because it covers this multiplicity of senses from simple obedience to deep internalisation. As we grow and mature, we move from thinking of commands as hypothetical imperatives to thinking of them as categorical, and we move from heteronomy to autonomy, because we have made God's will our will.[3]

The Torah lacks a word that means simple, blind obedience because that is the relation between a slave-owner and a slave: the slave-owner orders and the slave obeys. There is no active thought process involved. The connection between the word of the master and the deed of the slave is one of action and reaction, stimulus and response. For practical purposes, the slave has no mind of his own.

That is not how the Torah conceives the relationship between God and us. God, who created us in His image, giving us freedom and the power to think, wants us to *understand* His commands. Gersonides (Rabbi Levi ben Gershom or Ralbag, 1288–1344) argues that it is precisely this that makes the Torah different:

> Behold our Torah is unique among all the other doctrines and religions that other nations have had, in that our Torah contains nothing that does not originate in equity and reason. Therefore this divine law attracts people in virtue of its essence, so that they behave in accordance with it. The laws and religions of other nations are not like this: they do not conform to equity and wisdom, but are foreign to the nature of man, and people obey them because of compulsion, out of fear of the threat of punishment but not because of their essence.[4]

Along similar lines the modern scholar David Weiss Halivni speaks of "the Jewish predilection for justified law," and contrasts this with other cultures in the ancient world:

3. See Mishna Avot 2:4.
4. Gersonides, commentary to *Va'etḥanan,* par. 14.

> Ancient law in general is apodictic, without justification and without persuasion. It style is categorical, demanding, and commanding.... Ancient Near Eastern law in particular is devoid of any trace of desire to convince or to win hearts. It enjoins, prescribes, and orders, expecting to be heeded solely on the strength of being an official decree. It solicits no consent (through justification) from those to whom it is directed.[5]

For the most part, Torah is not written this way. It uses three devices to show that Jewish law is not arbitrary, a mere decree. First, evident throughout the book of Deuteronomy, is the giving of *reasons for the commands*. Often, though not always, the reason has to do with the experience of the Israelites in Egypt. They know what it feels like to be oppressed, a stranger, an outsider. I want you to create a different kind of society, says God through Moses, where slavery is more limited, where everyone is free one day a week, where the poor do not go hungry and the powerless are not denied justice.

The second is *the juxtaposition of narrative and law*, as if to say, the law is best understood against the backdrop of history and the experience of the Israelites in their formative years. So, for instance, the law of the red heifer – purification from contact with the dead – occurs just before the death of Miriam and Aaron, as if to say: Bereavement and grief interfere with our contact with God but this does not last forever. We can become pure again. The story explains the law, and the law illuminates the story.

The third is *the connection between law and the underlying order of the cosmos*. There is a strong link between Genesis 1, the story of creation, and the laws of *kedusha*, holiness. Both belong to *Torat Kohanim*, the priestly voice, and both are about order and the maintenance of boundaries. The laws against mixing meat and milk, wool and linen, and so on, are about respecting the deep structure of nature as described in the opening chapter of the Torah.

5. David Weiss Halivni, *Midrash, Mishnah, Gemara: The Jewish Predilection for Justified Law* (Cambridge, MA: Harvard University Press, 1986), 5.

Throughout Deuteronomy, Moses becomes an educator, explaining to the next generation that the laws God has given them are not just divine decrees. They make sense in human terms. They constitute the architectonics of a free and just society. They respect human dignity. They honour the integrity of nature. They give the land the chance to rest and recuperate. They protect Israel against the otherwise inexorable laws of the decline and fall of nations.

That is why Moses, consistently throughout Deuteronomy, uses the verb SH-M-A. He wants the Israelites to obey God, but not blindly or through fear alone. God did not give the Torah to Israel for His sake but for theirs. As Weiss Halivni puts it: the Torah "invites the receiver of the law to join in grasping the beneficent effect of the law, thereby bestowing dignity upon him and giving him a sense that he is a partner in the law."[6]

That is the meaning of Moses' great words: "Be silent, Israel, and listen" (Deut. 27:9). Keeping the commands involves an act of listening, not just submission and blind obedience – in all of listening's multiple senses of attending, meditating, and reflecting. It means understanding our limits and imperfections as human beings and remembering what it felt like to be a slave in Egypt. It involves humility and memory and gratitude. But it does not involve abdication of the intellect or silencing of the questioning mind.

God is not a tyrant (Avoda Zara 3a) but a teacher.[7] He seeks not just our obedience but also our understanding. All nations have laws, and laws are there to be obeyed. But few nations other than Israel set it as their highest task to understand *why* the law is as it is. *Shema* is the Torah's call to moral growth.

---

6. Ibid., 14.
7. *Tanḥuma* (Buber), *Yitro*, 16.

The Blessing and the Curse

The *parasha* of *Ki Tavo* contains one of the most terrifying passages in the Hebrew Bible, rivalled only by the parallel text in Leviticus 26. Both are known to tradition as *tokhaḥa*, "reprimand" or "rebuke." Essentially they are warnings of the terrible fate that will overtake Jews if they neglect or abandon their covenant with God. Reading them in the context of our time, after the Holocaust, they sound like horrific prefigurations of what in fact occurred. If much of Deuteronomy is a prophetic vision or dream, the *tokhaḥa* is the nightmare.

The passage raises the most fundamental questions. Is God a God of anger and retribution? What about the sufferings of the innocent? Is every bad thing that happens to human beings an instance of divine justice? Do the victims always deserve their fate? Did not Abraham say, "Will you sweep away the innocent along with the guilty? What if there should be fifty innocent people within the city?... Shall not the Judge of all the earth deal justly?" (Gen. 18:25). Did not Moses say, "Shall one man sin and will You be angry with the whole congregation?" (Num. 16:22).

The question is most acute in relation to the Holocaust itself. Why did God not stop the slaughter? To put the dilemma in its sharpest form:

Either God could not have prevented Auschwitz, or He could have but chose not to. If He could not, how then can He be all-powerful? If He could but did not, how can He be all good?

These are difficult questions. No tradition has wrestled with them longer or with greater courage than Judaism. For us, these are not doubts raised by unbelievers. They were raised by some of the greatest believers of all time – by Abraham, Moses, Jeremiah, and Job, by the sages of the Babylonian Talmud and the writers of the medieval *kinot* (elegies).

There is no answer that will resolve all doubts. The Talmud itself states that God answered every question Moses asked of Him except one: Why do bad things happen to good people? (Berakhot 7a). There is profound wisdom in the knowledge that there are some things that will always lie beyond the horizons of human understanding. "If I could understand God," said one Jewish sage, "I would be God."

In his essay *Kol Dodi Dofek*, the late Rabbi Joseph Soloveitchik compared our understanding of providence to seeing a Persian carpet from underneath.[1] Seen upside down, it looks like a mass of disconnected threads without pattern or purpose. Only when we view it the right way up do we see its intricate design. So it is with history. We are on the ground looking up. We cannot see things from the point of view of God looking down. We are human, not divine.

This essay, therefore, should not be taken as more than a speculation – one among many in the Jewish tradition. When one speaks of such things one should do so with fear and trembling, for they are among the deepest mysteries of faith. If these words do not speak to you, please ignore them and turn to some among the many other writings on the subject.

The blessings and curses in the Bible are both supernatural and natural. It is one of the essential aspects of the book, as the sages and Maimonides noted, that it can be read at many levels. On the one hand, the entire vision of the Torah is dedicated to the proposition that Israel's destiny depends on divine intervention in history. In that sense it is supernatural. On the other hand, reading it more deeply, there is a sense that there is something natural at work also. Not by chance

1. *Kol Dodi Dofek: Listen – My Beloved Knocks* (New York: Yeshiva University, 2006).

are the children of Israel and the land of Israel exemplars of the relationship between humanity and God. The people of Israel will always be small: "You are the fewest of all peoples" (Deut. 7:7). The land of Israel will always be vulnerable, occupying as it does a strategic location between three continents – Europe, Africa, and Asia – and two ancient birthplaces of empire, the Nile and Tigris-Euphrates valleys. Only by almost superhuman achievements of national unity and moral purpose will Israel survive as a nation in its land. So it was in biblical times; so it is today.

The geography of Israel is also significant. Lacking as it does a constant, predictable water supply, its people will constantly find themselves looking up to the heavens for rain. They will know also that there will be times of drought and famine when the poor and small farmers will be dependent on the generosity of others. The strength of the social bond – *tzedaka,* the charity which is also justice – will be constantly tested. Any age in which the rich fail to support those less well off, or in which sellers exploit buyers, will be full of danger because the nation can survive only through a strong sense of collective responsibility.

For these reasons, the external fate of Israel dramatically mirrors its internal faith. In good times it will seem to record almost miraculous achievements, outperforming nations far larger and more powerful. In bad times it will suffer grievously as the surrounding empires take vengeance on its mere existence as an independent nation whose laws and beliefs are different from theirs.

You do not have to be Jewish to sense the presence, in Israel's history, of something larger than merely human. As Pascal put it in his *Pensées*:

> It is certain that in certain parts of the world we can see a peculiar people, separated from the other peoples of the world, and this is called the Jewish people.... This people is not only of remarkable antiquity but has also lasted for a singularly long time.... For whereas the peoples of Greece and Italy, of Sparta, Athens and Rome, and others who came so much later have perished so long ago, these still exist, despite the efforts of so many powerful

> kings who have tried a hundred times to wipe them out.... My encounter with this people amazes me...[2]

Israel's history mirrors the unique feature that its existence is predicated on a covenant with God Himself. Its successes will seem to point to a force greater than itself. Likewise, its collapse will be dramatic. It will happen because the unity of God is no longer reflected in the unity of the people. Some will be faithful, others will not. The institutions of power will become corrupt. Strains will develop in the social fabric. Prophets will warn of this, but their words will not be heeded.

The result will be catastrophe. The nation that once seemed invincible will be defeated. Worse, it will sometimes seem (as it did to Josephus, witnessing the disastrous revolt against Rome) as if Jews were more intent on fighting other Jews than the enemy at the gates. The people who once seemed to be under the special protection of God will now seem to be abandoned by God. As Moses puts it in the *tokhaḥa*: "You will become a consternation, a proverb and a byword among all the peoples to which the Lord will drive you" (Deut. 28:37).

Israel will find itself in exile. The significance of exile is not merely geographical. It is political and spiritual as well. Jews will no longer be under the unmediated, direct sovereignty of God. They will be under the sovereignty of the rulers in whose lands they live. Their fate will depend on the whim of a king or the shifting winds of popular opinion. In this sense *galut*, exile, is a metaphysical dislocation – a lack of freedom in every sense of the word. The Torah calls this the "hiding of the face" of God.

This means that *what happens to the Jewish people in exile is not the work of God but of human beings*. Exile is precisely the loss of the protection of God and subjection, instead, to human powers. This is how Moses puts it in the name of God:

> On that day I will become angry with them and forsake them; I will hide My face from them, and they will be destroyed. Many

2. Blaise Pascal, *Pensées*, trans. Alban John Krailsheimer (Harmondsworth: Penguin, 1968), 171, 176–77.

> disasters and difficulties will come upon them, and on that day they will ask, "Have not these disasters come upon us because our God is not with us?" And I will certainly hide My face on that day… (Deut. 31:17–18)

The major Jewish thinkers of the Middle Ages – Judah Halevi, Maimonides, and Nahmanides – all agreed on this: that divine providence governs the affairs of Israel only when they exist as a sovereign people in their own land. Then there is reward and punishment, prophecy and a correlation between what happens to the people and what they do. But exile, *galut*, dispersion, means being removed from the mercy of God and being placed at the mercy of the nations. Exilic history is not providence but the loss of providence, what Maimonides calls "being left to chance."[3]

This has immense consequences. Gersonides points this out in his commentary to the episode in the book of Judges (7:1) that tells of how the Israelites were defeated at Ai with the loss of thirty-six men. The problem is this: The people killed in battle were not guilty of a sin. It was the sin of someone else (Achan the son of Zerah) that brought about the defeat. How could it happen that the guilty survived while the innocent died?

Gersonides draws a fundamental distinction between a tragedy which is the work of providence (for example, the destruction of Sodom and Gomorrah) and a tragedy that comes about because of a *withdrawal* of providence (as happened at Ai). When God destroys, He destroys only the guilty. When God withdraws and *man* destroys, the innocent suffer as well.

Abrabanel (to Josh. 7:1) makes essentially the same point:

> There is a distinction between punishment which comes about by a divine action and punishment which comes about through removal of providence. When God punishes by direct action, He does not punish the person who has not sinned on account of him who has.... Not so the punishment which comes about by

3. Maimonides, *Guide for the Perplexed*, III:17.

> chance as a result of God's withdrawing His providence. For this befalls the community in its entirety in that, because there are sinners among them, God hides His face from them all.... All of them become exposed to the workings of chance and accident, so that occasionally a person who has not sinned is also smitten when he is exposed to danger, and the sinner, who may not have been there, escapes unharmed.

In rabbinic times and throughout the Middle Ages there were great catastrophes of which Jews were the victims: the Hadrian persecutions, the massacres of Jews in the Crusades, the blood libels, the Inquisition, the pogroms. All were faithfully recorded in Jewish memory, written down and recited in elegies that we say to this day. In each case the rabbis and poets tried to find religious meaning in tragedy. But rarely did they find that meaning in terms of sin and punishment. The poets of catastrophe during the Crusades compared their sufferings to the binding of Isaac, the tragedy of Job, and the suffering servant of Isaiah – all the cases in the Bible where suffering is not related to sin.

The Holocaust does not tell us about God but about man. It tells us not about divine justice but about human injustice. The question raised by Auschwitz is not "Where was God?" but "Where was man? Where was humanity?" This is not radical post-Holocaust theology but a view already adopted by Judaism's greatest exponents in the eleventh to fifteenth centuries.

Nor is it accidental that the rise of anti-Semitism in Europe in the second half of the nineteenth century led to the birth of Zionism, the desire of Jews to return to their land and recover their sovereignty as a people. This too was foreseen by Moses:

> When all these blessings and curses I have set before you come upon you and you take them to heart wherever the Lord your God disperses you among the nations, and when you and your children return to the Lord your God and obey Him with all your heart and with all your soul according to everything I command you today, then the Lord your God will restore your fortunes and have compassion on you and gather you again from all the

> nations where He scattered you. Even if you have been banished to the most distant land under the heavens, from there the Lord your God will gather you and bring you back. (Deut. 30:1–4)

The story of the Jewish people is an extraordinary interweaving of history and prophecy, of the natural and supernatural, of the choices of human beings and the overarching tutelage of God. The suffering of Jews in the Diaspora is not divine punishment but rather a consequence of exile itself – the loss of providence, the hiding of the face of God, and being "left to chance." The idea that there is one answer to the problem of evil and the sufferings of the innocent, true at all times, is simply wrong. There are different historical eras, and these represent different relationships between Israel and God.

The return of Jews to Israel marks the start of an old-new era in the life of the people of the covenant. Once again, as in the days of Joshua, Jews are faced with the challenge and opportunity of constructing a society on the principles of the covenant: an arena of justice and compassion, liberty and the rule of law, respect for life and for human dignity. It was never easy. Now, as then, Jews face enemies outside and tensions within. Now, as then, there have been moments when the people must have come close to despair. Yet one principle has always been engraved on the Jewish heart, allowing it to emerge from tragedy with hope intact. It is the principle of "the blessing and the curse" of which Moses spoke so eloquently. When Jews have suffered, their first reaction is not to blame others but to examine themselves. That is why bad times – the times spoken of in the *tokhaḥa* – have always led to national renewal, and the worse the times, the greater the renewal. A people capable of seeing suffering as a call from God to return to the covenant, choosing and sanctifying life, is one that cannot be defeated because it can never lose hope.

The Greatest Challenge

Twice in the Torah – once in *Parashat Beḥukkotai,* the second time in *Parashat Ki Tavo* – Moses gives voice to a series of prophecies of the sufferings that will befall the Jewish people if they fail to honour their mission as the people of God. They are terrifying passages. To this day we read them so quietly that they are hardly audible. Each, as we saw, is known as *tokhaḥa,* literally, "remonstration," and that is how we should understand them.

They are not to be interpreted in the manner of a fire-and-brimstone sermon: do this or else bad things will happen to you. That is not how God or Moses spoke. They did not want the Israelites to pursue their vocation out of fear, but in love. Rather, the passages are a form of passionate pleading. They represent a future that neither God nor Moses wants to happen. But such is the risk of Israel's mission – a small people amid mighty empires, a radical faith in the midst of reactionary forces, a commitment to challenge the idols of the age – that bad things will happen if Israel fails to keep to its script. It is as if Israel's history is more like a rocket launch than a car drive – what might be a minor malfunction were it to occur on earth becomes a major tragedy if it happens in space.

There are many differences between the two *tokhaḥot*. The first is the reported speech of God, the second the direct speech of Moses. The first is directed to the Israelites as a whole: it uses the second-person plural. The second is addressed to individuals as individuals: it speaks in the singular. The first ends on a note of consolation. Despite the bad things that will happen, God will not abandon the Jewish people. He will remember His covenant with their ancestors. The Jewish people will survive. The second ends bleakly with no consolation. The people will be forced back to Egypt where they will try to sell themselves as slaves but no one will buy them. According to Nahmanides, the first *tokhaḥa* refers to events surrounding the destruction of the First Temple while the second is about the Second Temple and the sufferings of Jews under the Romans. There is, however, a further difference – and here one can only be awestruck at the reach of Moses' prophetic vision.

In *Beḥukkotai*, God had spoken of a fundamental breach between Israel and its Redeemer. The language is harsh: "If you reject My decrees and abhor My laws" (Lev. 26:15); "If you continue to be hostile to Me" (26:21). What is at stake is an active rebellion of the Israelites against God. In *Ki Tavo*, the language is entirely different. It does not speak of a wilful, petulant nation deliberately spurning God. It speaks of something that hardly sounds like a sin at all. Why would Israel suffer? "Because you did not serve God your Lord with joy and gladness in the midst of the abundance of all" (Deut. 28:47).

Moses here reaches the climax of the paradoxical message he has communicated throughout his speeches in the book of Deuteronomy. If we were to try to summarise it, it would be this: For forty years you and your parents wandered in the wilderness. They were hard times, years without a home, when only by a series of miracles did you have anything to eat or drink. Now you have reached the brink of the Promised Land. You think this will be the end of all your challenges. But it will not be. To the contrary, it is here that the challenge will begin – and it will be the hardest of all because it will not look like a challenge:

> When you eat and are satisfied, when you build fine houses and settle down, and when your herds and flocks grow large and

> your silver and gold increase and all you have is multiplied, then your heart will become proud and you will forget the Lord your God, who brought you out of Egypt, out of the land of slavery. (Deut. 8:12–14)

Here Moses gives voice to his urgent but counter-intuitive message – a message that came true. The paradox is that when we have most to thank God for, we are in the greatest danger of not thanking – or even thinking of – God at all.

And so it came to pass. Throughout the almost unbearable centuries of exile, wanderings, expulsions, forced conversions and autos-da-fé, ghettoes and pogroms, Jews prayed to God, studied His word, kept His commands, handed on His message to their children, and held fast to their identity as Jews. They were a "God-intoxicated" people. It was only when equality beckoned, society opened its doors and Jews were no longer considered a "pariah people," that, in large numbers, they abandoned their faith.

How did Moses know this? The fact is that he did know it, and 3,300 years later we know it, too. As we discussed earlier,[1] the greatest challenge comes when we are least conscious of the presence of a challenge. In this context we can understand the full depth of the first of the priestly blessings: "May God bless you and protect you" (Num. 6:24). It is when we are most blessed that we are most in need of protection – and the protection for which we pray is that the blessing remain a blessing and not turn into a curse – the curse of forgetting from where the blessings come.

That is the story of our time. At the very moment that Jews have reached the heights of affluence and achievement, they are abandoning Judaism in unprecedented numbers. That is what Moses foresaw in the *tokhaḥa* in *Parashat Ki Tavo*. It is almost as if Jews need suffering to survive.

It is not so – so Moses pleads with all the eloquence at his disposal. This faith I have communicated to you from heaven, he says, is not a religion of tragedy, a melody scored in the minor key, a story written

1. See "The Politics of Memory."

in tears, a lament. It is a celebration of life. Time and again he emphasises: "These are the commands you shall do and live by them" (Lev. 18:5); "All of you who hold fast to God are alive today" (Deut. 4:4); "I have set before you life and death, blessing and curse. Therefore choose life" (Deut. 30:19).

This is not marginal to Judaism but of its essence. The Torah begins by God bringing a universe into being and "seeing that it is good." God is found in the goodness of the world, not in its pain. This is anything but self-evident in the history of the spirit. Eastern mysticisms teach the individual to rise above the sufferings and vicissitudes of the world into a private nirvana of the soul. Manichaeism and Gnosticism held that the physical world was created by an evil force; finding the true God means abandoning the world. The natural response to such a way of seeing reality is asceticism, the principled denial of pleasure.

At the opposite extreme philosophers like Epicurus (from whom rabbinic Hebrew derived its word for "heretic," *epikoros*) argued that since the only reality is material, one should devote oneself to the principled pursuit of pleasure. These views have appealed to great numbers of people throughout history. The Jewish view, by contrast, is unusual.

God is to be found in life. His blessings are material as well as spiritual – good crops, fine harvests, a land of plenty, and a politics of peace. The God of revelation and redemption is also the God of creation – meaning that to be close to God is to go with, not against, the grain of nature. Judaism embraces neither asceticism nor hedonism. Asceticism is the *denial* of pleasure, hedonism is the *worship* of it. Judaism is the sanctification of pleasure: food, by the laws of *kashrut* and pronouncing blessings over enjoyment; drink through Kiddush at sacred times; sex through the disciplines of marriage and *taharat hamishpaḥa*. To be a Jew is to celebrate life, to see God in life, and to make a blessing over life. It is to find joy in family and community, to find meaning through constant study of Torah, and to share one's blessings with others.

It is precisely this capacity to sanctify pleasure by enjoying it in and through the disciplines of *kedusha* (sanctification) that has made Judaism immune to the one tendency that has destroyed other civilisations, namely, affluence as a prelude to decadence. In Judaism pleasure is never mere pleasure, because first, it is dedicated to God; second, it is shared with others; third, it is seen as God's blessing, not something we made ourselves.

What a tragedy it would be – Moses seems to be saying throughout Deuteronomy – if you came through the trials and torments of Egyptian slavery and the long years of wandering through the desert and then lost your way within sight of the destination. When you have everything to thank God for, do not forget to thank Him.

There is a rabbinic aphorism that "God creates the remedy before the disease" (Megilla 13b). Prior to the *tokhaḥa,* Moses outlined the law of bringing first fruits, in celebration, to the Temple. The Torah concludes the passage with the following words: "And you and the Levites and the strangers among you shall rejoice in all the good things the Lord your God has given to you and your household" (Deut. 26:11).

Judaism is a religion of rejoicing; of remembering where we came from, and therefore not taking our blessings for granted; of recalling the source of the good, and therefore not forgetting the larger truth that it comes to us from the hand of God; of knowing that what we have, God has placed in our trust, to be used for the good of all, not just ourselves. I know of no more sane, wise way of seeing reality steadily and seeing it whole.

The beauty of Judaism is that it did not become traumatised by tragedy. Despite their suffering, Jews did not let themselves become defined by it. They mourned on Tisha B'Av and the other specified fasts but did not allow the rest of their days to be darkened by grief. They set limits to sadness. During the rest of the week they might be toiling, but on Shabbat they ate as if at the royal table. During the rest of the year they might be in exile but on festivals they rejoiced.

It is that central affirmation – that we find God in the midst of life and its blessings – that we must not lose. Moses, more than three millennia ago, understood our contemporary situation better than we understand it ourselves. When affluence leads to forgetfulness, and prosperity to religious indifference, we are in the midst of Judaism's greatest challenge: to make a blessing over life, turning material satisfactions into spiritual affirmations.

Covenant and Conversation

In two sentences in *Parashat Ki Tavo*, the Torah summarises the entire relationship between God and the people of Israel:

> You have affirmed [*he'emarta*] this day that the Lord is your God, that you will walk in His ways, that you will observe His laws and commandments and rules, and that you will obey Him. And the Lord has affirmed [*he'emirkha*] this day that you are, as He promised you, His treasured people who shall observe all His commandments. (Deut. 26:17–18)

Here, set out with disarming simplicity, is the dual relationship, the reciprocity, at the heart of the covenant. It is an idea made famous in the form of two jingles: the first, that of William Norman Ewer, "How odd/of God/to choose/the Jews"; the second, the Jewish riposte, "Not quite/so odd – /the Jews/chose God."

Between God and the people is a mutual bond of love. The Israelites pledge themselves to be faithful to God and His commands. God pledges Himself to cherish the people as His treasure – for though He is the God of all humanity, He holds a special place in His affection (to speak anthropomorphically) for the descendants of those who first heard and heeded His call. This is the whole of Tanakh, the Hebrew Bible. The rest is commentary.

The English translation, above, is that of the Jewish Publication Society (1985). Any translation, however, tends to conceal the difficulty in the key verb in both sentences: *lehaamir*. What is strange is that, on the one hand, it is a form of one of the most common of all biblical verbs, *leimor*, "to say." On the other, the specific form used here – the *hifil*, or causative, form – is unique. Nowhere else does it appear in this form in the Bible, and its meaning is, as a result, obscure.

In place of the JPS translation, "affirmed," Aryeh Kaplan in *The Living Torah* reads it as "declared allegiance to."[1] Robert Alter renders it: "proclaimed."[2] Other interpretations include "separated to yourself" (Rashi), "chosen" (Septuagint), "recognised" (Saadia Gaon), "raised" (Radak, Sforno), "betrothed" (Malbim), "given fame to" (Ibn Janah), "exchanged everything else for" (Hizkuni), "accepted the uniqueness of" (Rashi to Ḥagiga 3a), and "caused God to declare" (Judah Halevi, cited by Ibn Ezra).

Among non-Jewish translations, the King James Version has: "Thou hast *avouched* the Lord this day to be thy God." The New International Version reads: "You have *declared* this day that the Lord is your God." Others have "agreed," "acknowledged," "said," "lifted up," "announced," "obtained the agreement," "distinguished," and "caused to promise."

What is the significance of this unique form of the verb "to say"? Why is it used here? The use of language in the Torah is not vague, accidental, or imprecise. In general, in the Mosaic books, style mirrors substance. The *way* something is said is often connected to *what* is being said. So it is here.

What we have before us is a proposition of far-reaching consequence for the two most fundamental questions humanity can ask itself. The first is: What is the nature of the bond between human beings and

1. Aryeh Kaplan, *The Living Torah: The Five Books of Moses and the Haftarot* (Brooklyn, NY: Moznaim, 1981), ad loc.
2. Robert Alter, *The Five Books of Moses: A Translation with Commentary* (W. W. Norton, 2008), ad loc.

God? How can the finite relate to the Infinite? The second – I have argued that this is the key question to which the Torah is the answer – is: How, in human affairs, can we achieve both *freedom* and *order*? The world before the Flood, "filled with violence," was a world of freedom without order: chaos. The Egypt the Israelites left was a world of order without freedom: slavery. How can we achieve both?

The profound answer given by the Torah to the first question is *language, speech, words*. Hence the importance, in this definitive statement of Jewish faith, of the verb meaning "to say, declare, affirm." Since the days of Socrates, philosophers have tended to concentrate on just one function of language: its use to describe, or state facts. This gave rise to the key questions of philosophy and science: Is this statement true? Does it correspond to the facts? It is consistent with other facts? Can I be sure? What evidence do I have? What warrant do I have for believing what I believe? Language is the medium we use to describe what is.

We owe to the later work of Wittgenstein, developed further by John L. Austin and John Rogers Searle,[3] the realisation that language has many other functions besides. We use language to classify, evaluate, express emotion, question, command, hypothesise, and imagine. There are literary genres like fiction and poetry which use language in complex ways to extend our imaginative engagement with reality. Sometimes we use it simply to establish a relationship. Malinowski called this *phatic communion*, where what matters is not what we say but the mere fact that we are talking to one another.[4] The philosophical-scientific mindset that sees the sole significant function of language as stating facts – taken to an absurd extreme in the early-twentieth-century movement known as "logical positivism" – is a kind of tone-deafness to the rich variety of speech.

---

3. Ludwig Wittgenstein, *Philosophical Investigations* (Hoboken: John Wiley & Sons, 2010); John L. Austin, *How to Do Things with Words* (Oxford: Clarendon Press, 1962); John R. Searle, *Speech Acts* (Cambridge, UK: Cambridge University Press, 2012).
4. Bronislaw Malinowski, "The Problem of Meaning in Primitive Languages," in Charles K. Ogden and Ian A. Richards, *The Meaning of Meaning* (London: Kegan Paul, 1923), 296–336. More recently, Robin Dunbar has argued that human speech had its origins in "grooming behaviour." See his *Grooming, Gossip, and the Evolution of Language* (Cambridge, MA: Harvard University Press, 1997).

The Mosaic books are, among other things, a deep set of reflections on the nature and power of language. This may have to do with the fact that the Israelites of Moses' day would have encountered the first alphabet, the Proto-Semitic script from which all subsequent alphabets are directly or indirectly derived. Judaism marks the world's first transition on a national scale from an oral to a literate culture. Hence the unique significance it attaches to the spoken and written word.

There is a radical statement of this at the very beginning of the Torah. God *spoke* and the world came into being. Unlike every ancient myth about the beginning of things, there was no struggle, no use of force. Instead, the key verb is simply *leimor*, "God *said* [*vayomer*], Let there be . . . and there was." This is the use of language to create worlds.

That, of course, is divine – not human – speech. However, there is a human counterpart. There are things we can create with words when we use them in a special way. Austin called this use of speech *performative utterance*.[5] So, for example, when a judge says, "This court is now in session," he or she is not *describing* something but *doing* something. When a groom says to his bride under the wedding canopy, "Behold you are betrothed to me by this ring according to the laws of Moses and Israel," he is not *stating* a fact but *creating* a fact.

The most basic type of performative utterance is *making a promise*. This involves the use of language to *create an obligation*. Some promises are unilateral, but others are mutual. Some are highly specific, others are open-ended. The supreme example of an open-ended mutual pledge between human beings is marriage. The supreme example of an open-ended mutual pledge between human beings and God is a covenant. That is what our two verses state: that God and the people of Israel pledged themselves to one another by making a covenant, a relationship brought into existence by words and sustained by honouring those words.

Hence the radical proposition at the heart of the Hebrew Bible. *What is supremely holy is language*, when used to create a moral bond between two parties. This answers the first question: How can the finite relate to the Infinite? The answer is: by words. It happens when God

5. See earlier, "The World We Make with Words."

speaks and we listen (revelation), and when we speak and God listens (prayer).

It also answers the second question: How can there be, in the human situation, both freedom and order? It happens when we freely make a promise and undertake obligations, as happened in the covenant ceremony at Mount Sinai, the covenant Moses was about to renew with the next generation. This mutual pledge between the people and God was a relationship based not on power but on freely given consent.

Thus, the use of language to create a mutually binding relationship is what links God and humankind. The two verses mean: "Today, by an act of speech, you have made God your God, and God has made you His people." Words, language, an act of saying, have created an open-ended, eternally binding relationship.

Hence the name I have given to my series of Torah commentaries: *Covenant and Conversation*. Judaism is a covenant, a marriage between God and a people. The Torah is its written record. It is Israel's marriage contract as God's bride. Conversation – speaking and listening – is what makes covenant possible. Hence the dual form of Torah: the Written Torah, through which God speaks to us, and the Oral Torah, through which we speak to God by way of interpreting His word. *Judaism is the open-ended, mutually binding, conversation between Heaven and earth.*

Despite the deep influence of Judaism on two later faiths, Christianity and Islam, neither fully adopted this idea.[6] There are no conversations between God and human beings in either the New Testament or the Koran that echo the dialogues in Tanakh between God and Abraham, Moses, Elijah, Hosea, Jeremiah, Jonah, Habakkuk, and Job. Judaism, the religion of sacred dialogue between Heaven and earth, remains unique in its profound focus on the use of language – through covenant on the one hand, conversation on the other – to create a moral bond between the Infinite and the finite.

That is what is set out simply in these two verses: *Speaking a relationship into being, lehaamir,* is what makes God our God, and us His people.

6. To be sure, some Christian theologians speak of covenant, but a different kind of covenant, more unilateral than reciprocal.

Nitzavim
נצבים

In dramatic fashion, Moses assembles the people, *all* the people – leaders, tribes, elders, officials, children, wives, and strangers in the camp, from woodcutter to water-drawer – to renew the covenant prior to their entry into the land. He warns them solemnly that their future depends on their faithfulness to it. If they break it, they will suffer defeat, devastation, and exile. Yet even then, the covenant and its promise would remain. Even in the midst of dispersion and dislocation, if the people return to God He will return to them and cause them to return to their land. The choice will always be theirs. Therefore, "Choose life, that you and your children may live" (Deut. 30:19).

In the first of the following essays, I look at the phrase in which Moses says that he is making the covenant not only with the Israelites of his day but with all future generations of Jews. How can a covenant be binding on people not yet born? The second essay focuses on *teshuva*, "repentance" or "return." Nahmanides derives the concept from *Parashat Nitzavim*, while Maimonides gives it a different source and understands it differently. I show how the two approaches came together in the post-biblical era. The third and fourth essays are about Moses' statement that the Torah is "not in heaven" (Deut. 30:12) nor is it "across the sea" (30:13). The former gave rise to a radical rabbinic reading about the authority given to the sages of each generation to interpret the Torah. The latter, I argue, is a warning against the recurring Jewish temptation to seek salvation outside Judaism. The final essay is about choice itself, which turns out to be the fourteenth principle of Jewish faith.

Why Be Jewish?

In the last days of his life Moses renews the covenant between God and Israel. The entire book of Deuteronomy has been an account of the covenant – how it came about, what its terms and conditions are, why it is the core of Israel's identity as an *am kadosh*, a holy people, and so on. Now comes the moment of renewal itself, a national rededication to the terms of its existence as a holy people under the sovereignty of God Himself.

Moses, however, is careful not to limit his words to those who are actually present. About to die, he wants to ensure that no future generation can say, "Moses made a covenant with our ancestors but not with us. We did not give our consent. We are not bound." To preclude this he says these words: "It is *not with you alone* that I am making this sworn covenant, but with whoever is standing here with us today before the Lord our God, and *with whoever is not here* with us today" (Deut. 29:13–14).

As the commentators point out, the phrase "whoever is not here" cannot refer to Israelites alive at the time who happened to be somewhere else. That cannot be, since the entire nation was assembled there. It can only mean "generations not yet born." The covenant bound all Jews from that day to this. As the Talmud says: We are all *mushba ve'omed meHar Sinai,* "foresworn from Sinai."[1] By agreeing to be God's people, subject to God's laws, our ancestors obligated us.

Hence one of the most fundamental facts about Judaism. Converts excepted, we do not choose to be Jews. We are born as Jews. We become legal adults, subject to the commands and responsible for our actions, at the age of twelve for girls, thirteen for boys. But we are part of the covenant from birth. A bat or bar mitzva is not a "confirmation." It involves no voluntary acceptance of Jewish identity. That choice took place more than three thousand years ago when Moses said, "It is *not with you alone* that I am making this sworn covenant, but with...*whoever is not here* with us today," meaning all future generations including us.

But how can this be so? A fundamental principle of Judaism is that *there is no obligation without consent.* How can we be bound by an agreement to which we were not parties? How can we be subject to a covenant on the basis of a decision taken long ago and far away by our distant ancestors?

The sages, after all, raised a similar question about the wilderness generation in the days of Moses who were actually there and did give their assent. The Talmud suggests that they were not entirely free to say no. "The Holy One, Blessed Be He, suspended the mountain over them like a barrel and said: If you say yes, all will be well, but if you say no, this will be your burial place" (Shabbat 88b). On this, R. Aḥa b. Yaakov said: "This constitutes a fundamental challenge to the legitimacy of the covenant." The Talmud replies that even though the agreement may not have been entirely free at the time, Jews asserted their identity voluntarily in the days of Ahasuerus, as suggested by the book of Esther.

This is not the place to discuss this particular passage, but the essential point is clear. The sages believed with great force that an agreement must be free to be binding. Yet we did not agree to be Jews. We were, most of us, born Jews. We were not there in Moses' day when the agreement was made. We did not yet exist. How then can we be bound by the covenant?

1. Yoma 73b; Nedarim 8a.

This is not a small question. It is the question on which all others turn. How can Jewish identity be passed on from parent to child? If Jewish identity were merely racial or ethnic, we could understand it. We inherit many things from our parents – most obviously our genes. But being Jewish is not a genetic endowment; it is a set of religious obligations. There is a halakhic principle: *Zakhin le'adam shelo befanav,* "You can confer a benefit on someone else without their knowledge or consent" (Ketubbot 11a). And though it is doubtless a benefit to be a Jew, it is also in some sense a liability, a restriction on our range of legitimate choices. Had we not been Jewish, we could have worked on Shabbat, eaten non-kosher food, and so on. You can confer a benefit, *but not a liability,* on someone without their consent (Ketubbot 11a).

In short, this is the question of questions of Jewish identity. How can we be bound by Jewish law, without our choice, merely because our ancestors agreed on our behalf?

In my book *Radical Then, Radical Now*[2] (published in America as *A Letter in the Scroll*[3]) I pointed out how fascinating it is to trace exactly when and where this question was asked. Despite the fact that everything else depends on it, it was not asked often. For the most part, Jews did not ask the question, Why be Jewish? The answer was obvious. My parents are Jewish. My grandparents were Jewish. So I am Jewish. Identity is something most people in most ages take for granted.

It did, however, become an issue during the Babylonian exile. The prophet Ezekiel says, "What is in your mind shall never happen – the thought, 'Let us be like the nations, like the tribes of the countries, and worship wood and stone'" (Ezek. 20:32). This is the first reference to Jews actively seeking to abandon their identity.

It happened again in rabbinic times. We know that in the second century BCE there were Jews who Hellenised, seeking to become Greek rather than Jewish. There were others who, under Roman rule, sought to become Roman. Some even underwent an operation known as *epispasm*

2. London: HarperCollins, 2000.
3. New York: Free Press, 2000.

to reverse the effects of circumcision (in Hebrew they were known as *meshukhim*) to hide the fact that they were Jews.[4]

The third time was in Spain in the fifteenth century. That is where we find two Bible commentators, Rabbi Isaac Arama and Rabbi Isaac Abrabanel, raising precisely the question we have raised about how the covenant can bind Jews today. The reason they ask it while earlier commentators did not was that in their time – between 1391 and 1492 – there was immense pressure on Spanish Jews to convert to Christianity, and as many as a third may have done so (they were known in Hebrew as the *anusim*, in Spanish as the conversos, and derogatively as Marranos, "swine"). The question "Why stay Jewish?" was real.

The answers given were different at different times. Ezekiel's answer was blunt: "As I live, declares the Lord God, surely with a mighty hand and an outstretched arm and with wrath poured out I will be king over you" (Ezek. 20:33). In other words, Jews might try to escape their destiny but they would fail. Even against their will they would be known as Jews. That, tragically, is what happened during the two great ages of assimilation, in fifteenth-century Spain and in Europe in the nineteenth and early twentieth centuries. In both cases, racial anti-Semitism persisted, and Jews continued to be persecuted.

The sages answered the question mystically. They said that even the souls of Jews not yet born were present at Sinai and ratified the covenant.[5] Every Jew, in other words, *did* give his or her consent in the days of Moses even though he or she had not yet been born. Demystifying this, perhaps the sages meant that in his or her innermost heart even the most assimilated Jew knew that he or she was still a Jew. That seems to have been the case with figures like Heinrich Heine and Benjamin Disraeli, who lived as Christians but often wrote and thought as Jews.

The fifteenth-century Spanish commentators found this answer problematic. As Arama said, we are each of us both body and soul. How then is it sufficient to say that our soul was present at Sinai? How can the soul obligate the body? Of course the soul agrees to the covenant.

4. This is what R. Elazar of Modiin means in Mishna Avot 3:15 when he refers to one who "nullifies the covenant of our father Abraham."

5. Exodus Rabba 28:6.

Spiritually, to be a Jew is a privilege, and you can confer a privilege on someone without their consent. But for the body, the covenant is a burden. It involves all sorts of restrictions on physical pleasures. Therefore if the souls of future generations were present but not their bodies, this would not constitute consent.

Radical Then, Radical Now is my answer to this question. But perhaps there is a simpler one. Not every obligation that binds us is one to which we have freely given our assent. There are obligations that come with birth. The classic example is a crown prince. To be the heir to a throne involves a set of duties and a life of service to others. It is possible to neglect these duties. In extreme circumstances it is possible for even a king to abdicate. But no one chooses to be royal. That is a fate and destiny that comes with birth.

The people of whom God Himself said "My child, My firstborn, Israel" (Ex. 4:22) knows itself to be royalty. That may be a privilege. It may be a burden. It is almost certainly both. It is a peculiar post-Enlightenment delusion to think that the only significant things about us are those we choose. The truth is that some of the most important facts about us we did not choose. We did not choose to be born. We did not choose our parents. We did not choose the time and place of our birth. Yet each of these affects who we are and what we are called on to do.

We are part of a story that began long before we were born and will continue long after we are no longer here, and the question for all of us is: Will we continue the story? The hopes of a hundred generations of our ancestors rest on our willingness to do so. Deep in our collective memory the words of Moses continue to resonate. "It is *not with you alone* that I am making this sworn covenant, but with...*whoever is not here* with us today." We are part of that story. We can live it. We can abandon it. But it is a choice we cannot avoid and it has immense consequences. The future of the covenant rests with us.

Two Concepts of Teshuva

The *parasha* of *Nitzavim* is always read on the Shabbat before Rosh HaShana, when our thoughts are directed towards *teshuva* – the great mitzva of the ten days that begin with Rosh HaShana and culminate on Yom Kippur. Where, though, in the Torah itself do we find the mitzva of *teshuva*? On this, two of the greatest sages of the Middle Ages, Maimonides and Nahmanides, differed fundamentally.

Here is Maimonides' account:

> With regard to all the precepts of the Torah, positive and negative, if a person transgressed any one of them, either wilfully or in error, and repents and turns away from his sin, he is under a duty to confess before God, Blessed Be He, as it is said, "When a man or a woman shall commit any sin that men commit, to do a trespass against the Lord, and that person be guilty, then they shall confess their sin which they have done" (Num. 5:6–7). This means *confess in words*, and this confession is a positive command. How does one confess? The penitent says, "I beseech you, O Lord, I have sinned, I have acted perversely, I have transgressed before You and have done such and such, and I repent and am ashamed

> of my deeds, and I will never do this again." This constitutes the essence of confession. The fuller and more detailed the confession one makes, the more praiseworthy he is.[1]

According to Maimonides, *teshuva* has its origin in the Temple and its sacrifices, specifically those brought for transgressions (sin offering, guilt offering, etc.). Part of the rite for such offerings was a verbal confession – *vidui* – on the part of the wrongdoer. The *conditions for the sincerity* of such confessions were (a) an acknowledgement that one did wrong, (b) remorse or shame, and (c) a determination not to repeat the offence in future. These are the fundamental elements of *teshuva*.

There are obvious questions. If *teshuva* is linked to the sacrificial order, what happened to it once the Temple was destroyed and the sacrificial system came to an end? What of *teshuva* outside Israel and outside the confines of the Temple? Maimonides answers these questions in his *Sefer HaMitzvot*[2] by reference to the *Mekhilta*. The *Mekhilta* uses various textual warrants to show that confession is in fact a separate command in its own right, and applies with or without a sacrifice, in and outside the land of Israel. Verbal confession, *vidui*, is the outer act; *teshuva* is its internal correlate.

Nahmanides locates *teshuva* in a completely different source, namely, *Parashat Nitzavim* (commentary to Deut. 30:11). Moses, having set out the terms of the covenant and its attendant blessings and curses, then says this:

> When all these blessings and curses I have set before you come upon you and *you take them to heart* wherever the Lord your God disperses you among the nations, and when you and your children *return* to the Lord your God and obey Him with all your heart and with all your soul according to everything I command you today, then the Lord your God will *restore your fortunes* and have compassion on you and gather you *again* from all the nations where He scattered you. Even if you have been banished to the most distant

1. Maimonides, *Mishneh Torah, Hilkhot Teshuva* 1:1.
2. *Sefer HaMitzvot*, positive command 73.

> land under the heavens, from there the Lord your God will gather you and bring you back. He will bring you to the land that belonged to your fathers, and you will take possession of it. He will make you more prosperous and numerous than your fathers.... You will *again* obey the Lord and follow all His commands that I am giving you today. Then the Lord your God will make you prosperous in all the work of your hands and in the fruit of your womb, the young of your livestock and crops of your land. The Lord will *again* delight in you and make you prosperous, just as He delighted in your fathers, if you obey the Lord your God and keep His commands and decrees that are written in this book of the law and *turn* to the Lord your God with all your heart and with all your soul. (Deut. 30:1–10)

The next verse continues, "For *this command* which I am commanding you today is not too difficult for you or beyond your reach." Which command? Nahmanides says: the command of *teshuva*. Why so?

The most striking feature of the passage above is that it is a set of variations on the Hebrew verb *lashuv*, the root of the noun *teshuva*. This is almost entirely lost in English translation. All the italicised phrases – "take to heart," "restore your fortunes," "again," and "turn" – are, in the Hebrew text, forms of this verb. The Torah often repeats a word several times to emphasise its significance as a key word: sometimes three or five times, but usually seven, as in the present instance (taking "restore your fortunes," *veshav et shevutekha*, as one composite phrase). Thus Nahmanides is quite right to see the subject of the passage as *teshuva*. What, though, *is teshuva* in this context?

In the Torah sin is something more than a transaction in the soul, or even an act of wrongdoing narrowly conceived. It is *an act in the wrong place*. It disturbs the moral order of the world. The words for sin – *ḥet* and *avera* – both have this significance. *Ḥet* comes from the same verb as "to miss a target." *Avera*, like the English word "transgression," means "to cross a boundary, to enter forbidden territory, to be in a place one should not be."

Only when we understand this does it become clear why the deepest punishment for sin in the Torah is exile. Adam and Eve were exiled from Eden. Cain was condemned to be an eternal wanderer. We say in our prayers, "Because of our sins we were exiled from our land." Because a sin is an act in the wrong place, its consequence is that the one who performs it finds himself in the wrong place – in exile, meaning, not at home. Sin *alienates*; it distances us from God, and the result is that we are distanced from where we ought to be, where we belong. We become aliens, strangers.

Hence the double meaning of *teshuva*, most clearly expressed in this *parasha*, but found throughout the entire prophetic literature. It has both a physical and spiritual dimension, and the two are inseparable as if bonded by superglue: it means *the physical return to the land* and *the spiritual return to God. Teshuva* is a double homecoming.

We can now see how deeply different are the approaches of Maimonides and Nahmanides. For Maimonides sin and repentance are part of the world of the priest (*Torat Kohanim*). They belonged initially to the Temple and its service. When an individual or group sinned in biblical times, they brought a sacrifice and, as a token of their contrition, confessed their wrong. The supreme example of this was the service of the high priest on Yom Kippur, when he made atonement "for himself, his household, and the whole community of Israel" (Lev. 16:17).

For Nahmanides, sin and repentance are part of the broader sweep of Jewish history. They belong to the world not of the priest but of the prophet (*Torat Nevi'im*), the figure who heard the voice of God in history, warned the people that public wrongdoing would lead to defeat and exile, and who, when the exile eventually occurred, summoned the people back to their vocation as a prelude to their return to the land.

Every individual act of *teshuva* recapitulates, in some way, this larger pattern of return. *Teshuva* in this sense is less *atonement* than *homecoming* – a subtle difference, but a difference nonetheless. It has nothing to do with the Temple and everything to do with a sense of the divine call ("Where are you?") within the events that happen to us, whether individually as personal fate or collectively as Jewish history.

The primary feeling of sin in priestly consciousness is *guilt*; in prophetic consciousness it is a sense of *alienation*.[3] For the priest, *teshuva*

3. *Alienation* became a key word in both Marxism and existentialism – for the former as a symptom of the capitalist system in the industrial age, for the latter as the mark of "inauthentic" existence; Judaism, more ethically, links it with bad conscience, the knowledge that we have not acted as we should.

is integrally linked with sacrifice. For the prophet, it is associated with behavioural change (*teshuva* as "returning" to the right way) and leads to healing and restoration. For the priest, the key words are atonement (*kappara*) and purification (*tahara*). For the prophet they are return (the verb *lashuv*) and healing (*refua*). Both priest and prophet use the verb S-L-Ḥ (pardon, forgive), but the priest always uses the passive (*venislaḥ*, "it will be forgiven"), while the prophet uses the active (*eslaḥ*, *vesalaḥti*, "I [God] will forgive"). For the priest, atonement relates primarily to individuals, whereas for the prophet (as in the words of Moses above) the reference is often to the people as a whole. It is individuals who sin and repent; it is the nation that undergoes exile and return.

How does Maimonides interpret the passage in *Parashat Nitzavim* that Nahmanides takes as the source for the mitzva of *teshuva*? He reads it, simply, not as a *command* but as a *prophecy and promise*:

> All the prophets charged the people concerning *teshuva*. Only through *teshuva* will Israel be redeemed, and the Torah has already *given the assurance that Israel will, at the end of its exile, finally repent and then be immediately redeemed*, as it is said, "When all these blessings and curses I have set before you come upon you and you take them to heart…then the Lord your God will restore your fortunes and have compassion on you and gather you again from all the nations where He scattered you…"[4]

This difference of interpretation goes back to the geonic period, three centuries earlier, when Rabbi Hefetz read the passage as did Nahmanides, and Rabbi Samuel ben Hofni like Maimonides.[5]

There is no doubt that Maimonides and Nahmanides were both right. Priest and prophet were not in conflict: they were two voices in a single conversation, two perspectives on a complex reality. When the Second Temple was destroyed and both priesthood and prophecy came to an end as functioning institutions, both traditions merged into the institution of *teshuva* as we have it today.

4. Maimonides, *Mishneh Torah, Hilkhot Teshuva* 7:5.
5. *Otzar HaGeonim*, Sanhedrin, 514.

On the one hand, Yom Kippur retains strong links with the service of the high priest in Temple times. We read the details of that service during *Musaf*. We perform *vidui*, confession, in various ways. We make a point of giving *tzedaka* (financial sacrifice substituting for animal sacrifice). On the other hand, during the morning we read one of the greatest of all prophetic calls to repentance (Is. 57–58), with its insistence that fasting is nothing – a mere ritual – without ethical conduct: "Is this not the kind of fasting I have chosen," says God:

> To loose the chains of injustice and untie the cords of the yoke,
> To set the oppressed free and break every yoke?
> Is it not to share your food with the hungry and to provide the poor wanderer with shelter? (Is. 58:6–7)

In the afternoon, we read another example of a prophetic call to *teshuva*, that of Jonah. *Ne'ila*, the closing service, ends with the words, repeated seven times, "The Lord He is God" (I Kings 18:39) – the climax of one of the great prophetic confrontations, between Elijah and the prophets of Baal on Mount Carmel, when the people publicly abandoned idolatry and proclaimed the kingship of God. It is wondrous how these two strands, priestly and prophetic, have been woven together so seamlessly in our liturgy.

So *teshuva* is two things: a religious-metaphysical experience of sin and atonement (Maimonides), and an ethical-historical drama of exile and return (Nahmanides). For nearly two thousand years, the former predominated while the latter was no more than a distant memory and a pious hope. The Temple was gone, and so too were the prophets. But whereas there was a substitute for the Temple (the synagogue as *mikdash me'at*, "a temple-in-microcosm"), there was no real substitute for Israel as a nation-among-nations in the arena of history.

In the course of the twentieth century, that changed. Jews returned. The State of Israel was reborn. The promise of the prophets, millennia ago, came true. It follows that a great challenge remains. There has been a *physical* homecoming to the land, but not yet a full spiritual homecoming to the faith. Among a section of the population, yes; among the people as a whole, no. That challenge rests with us and our children.

The words of the prophets, never less than inspiring, have acquired a new salience. *How* it will happen, we do not know, but we have faith *that* it will happen, for we have God's promise, that the faith of Israel will be reborn just as its land and state have been.

The Jewish people has come home to the land. Heaven is calling us now to come home to the faith.

Not in Heaven

In *Nitzavim,* Moses' eloquence reaches its most sublime heights. Even before the Israelites have entered their land he already foresees that the day will come when once again they will suffer exile. There they will reflect on the strange vicissitudes of history and will realise that their national purpose is not land or power, sovereignty or independence, but faithfulness to their covenant with God. When they return to Him, He will return to them and bring them back to their land.

Moses brings his peroration to an end with four magnificent verses:

> Now what I am commanding you today is not too difficult for you or beyond your reach. It is not in heaven, so that you have to ask, "Who will ascend into heaven to get it and proclaim it to us so we may obey it?" Nor is it beyond the sea, so that you have to ask, "Who will cross the sea to get it and proclaim it to us so we may obey it?" No, the word is very near you; it is in your mouth and in your heart so you may obey it. (Deut. 30:11–14)

At the simplest level Moses is telling the Israelites: Your religion is unlike the religion of others. It is not esoteric, difficult, beyond the comprehension of ordinary minds. It is not a religion of mysteries that need oracles, adepts, or religious virtuosi to decode. "The Torah speaks in the language of human beings," said the sages (Berakhot 31b). This is fundamental.

Almost every culture has placed a premium on forms of knowledge available only to an elite.[1] Egypt had its "decipherers of hieroglyphics." Ancient Greece had the Delphic oracle. Until the Reformation, literacy was confined largely to priests. Latin was the language of scholars, beyond the reach of the masses. Modern French and German philosophical works were mostly written in such a way as to be virtually unintelligible to non-specialists. Post-modernists use an even more opaque way of speaking. This is not the Jewish way (which may be why neither Jewish philosophy nor Jewish mysticism – both of which sometimes use difficult, opaque language – ever became mainstream, although they are certainly part of our tradition).

In Judaism, if something can be said, it can be said simply. God says about Moses: "With him I speak face-to-face, clearly and not in riddles" (Num. 12:8). The prophets spoke the language of the people. When Ezra read the Torah to the exiles who had returned from Babylon, he made sure that there were instructors available to clarify anything the people did not understand (Neh. 8:7–8). Knowledge must be accessible if it is to be the common property of the people – if it is to become the basis of a society in which everyone has equal dignity as citizens of the community of faith under the sovereignty of God.

This can never be taken for granted. Knowledge is power; power confers privilege; therefore those who have knowledge will try to hide it from the masses. They will speak in such a way that they can only be understood by fellow initiates, professional colleagues, or other members of the elite. Such a view, according to Judaism, must always be challenged. Knowledge – even divine knowledge – is "not in heaven" nor is it "beyond the sea." In these great words we hear the democratic sensibility in its true depth. Democracy in Judaism is less a matter of one person, one vote; it is more a matter of education and culture. Everyone must

1. See Amos Funkenstein and Adin Steinsaltz, *The Sociology of Ignorance* [Hebrew] (Tel Aviv: Ministry of Defence, 1988).

be articulate in the literature of citizenship (i.e., the Torah). Everyone must understand the way of life they are called on to lead.

But the phrase "not in heaven" took on an extraordinary life of its own in the rabbinic era. It gave rise to a justly famous passage in the Talmud, one of the most radical in all religious literature:

> We learned: If a stove is taken apart and sand strewed between the sections, R. Eliezer declares it is clean, the sages that it is unclean.
>
> It has been taught: On that day R. Eliezer brought all the proof in the world, but they did not accept it from him.
>
> Then he said to them: "If the law agrees with me, this locust tree shall prove it." The locust tree was flung a hundred ells out of the soil where it was rooted; others say four hundred ells.
>
> They said to him: "One cannot bring a proof from a locust tree."
>
> Then he spoke to them again: "If the law agrees with me, this stream of water shall prove it." The stream began to flow uphill.
>
> They said to him: "One cannot bring a proof from a stream."
>
> Then he spoke to them again: "If the law agrees with me, the walls of the house of study shall prove it." The walls of the house of study leaned over, as though they were about to fall.
>
> Then R. Yehoshua cried out to them, saying: "Is it any concern of yours if scholars argue with one another about the law?" So they did not fall, out of respect for R. Yehoshua's honour, nor did they straighten up, out of respect for R. Eliezer's honour. To this day they remain leaning.
>
> Then he spoke to them again: "If the law agrees with me, heaven itself shall prove it." A voice came from heaven, saying: "Why do you dispute with R. Eliezer, seeing that the law agrees with him in every case?"
>
> Then R. Yehoshua arose and said: "It is not in heaven."
>
> What did he mean by "not in heaven"? R. Yirmiyahu says: The Torah was given on Mount Sinai. Thereafter, the voice from heaven does not concern us. For it was written in the Torah on Mount Sinai: "After the majority one must incline." (Bava Metzia 59a)

The subject under dispute is ritual purity. An earthenware vessel that becomes unclean can only be purified by being broken. What then is the law in the case of a vessel – in this case an earthenware stove – that is composed of several parts? Does dismantling it constitute "breaking"? R. Eliezer says no. The sages say yes. Thus far this is a standard disagreement of a type recorded in thousands of places in the Mishna.

The passage suddenly shifts, however, into a metaphysical drama about the nature of halakhic disagreement and determination. R. Eliezer (b. Hyrcanus) proceeds to perform a number of miracles. He acts, in other words, like a prophet who produces signs and wonders to establish his credentials. Irrelevant, say the sages. What matters is whether you are right or wrong. Stick to the argument. Stop producing signs.

R. Eliezer then invokes heaven itself. A *bat kol* (literally, "the daughter of a voice," a heavenly echo) declares that the law is usually in accord with the view of R. Eliezer. This too, says R. Yehoshua, is irrelevant, and he cites as proof the phrase from *Parashat Nitzavim*: "It is not in heaven." At this point the Talmud interpolates an explanation given by R. Yirmiyahu. "The Torah has already been given. We therefore must use the rule: 'After the majority one must incline'" – meaning: the majority of sages disagree with R. Eliezer. The law is therefore not in accord with his view, even though he seems to be supported by heaven itself.

Several things are going on here. First is a rejection of supernatural authority when it comes to determining the law. We cannot be sure of the historical context in which this passage is set. It may be an early anti-Christian polemic. It may be more generally directed against the visionaries and apocalyptics of whom there were many in the years surrounding the destruction of the Second Temple. From time to time within Jewry charismatic leaders arose who claimed to have the authority – sometimes authenticated by performing miracles, as R. Eliezer did – to overturn the law. That is not, said the sages, how Judaism works.

Even the classic prophets did not claim the authority to make changes in Judaism. They recalled the people to their mission. They reminded them of their duties. They spoke out against corruption and injustice within society. They were social critics, not innovators.

The Torah itself contains a warning against prophetic innovation:

> If a prophet ... appears among you and announces to you a miraculous sign or wonder, and if the sign or wonder of which he has spoken takes place, and he says, "Let us follow other gods – gods you have not known – and let us worship them," you must not listen to the words of that prophet or dreamer. (Deut. 13:2–4)

The Torah does not dispute the miracles wrought by visionaries. The case it speaks of is one where "the sign or wonder of which he has spoken *takes place*." The prophet *does* work wonders, but that fact is irrelevant. In Judaism what is primary is the covenant between Israel and God. A prophet who seeks to change the covenant or lead the people in a different direction must not be heeded.

Thus R. Eliezer's contemporaries were following biblical precedent. The Torah is "not in heaven," which is to say, its meaning must be determined rationally, in accordance with exegetical principles. Once the Torah has been given, no further miracle or supernatural revelation can change it. The prophets spoke the word of God for their time, but the Torah is the word of God for all time. The prophets summoned the people to *return* to the Torah, not to turn to a new Torah.

The second issue at stake, however, was the self-understanding of the sages at a time of crisis. The dialogue between R. Eliezer and the sages is set in one of the most traumatic moments in Jewish history. The Temple had been destroyed. There was no king, no high priest, no sacrificial order. Jews had lost every base of national existence except one – the Torah. "From the day the Temple was destroyed," they said in one of their most poignant yet defiant remarks, "the Holy One, Blessed Be He, has only one thing left in the world – the four cubits of halakha" (Berakhot 8a). Jews had lost all the physical preconditions of nationhood. All they had left was their spiritual bond with God, and it was enough. It sustained Jews through the longest exile ever suffered by a people. If biblical history was full of wonders, post-biblical history is itself an extended wonder, that a people so afflicted and dispersed could survive, their identity intact.

One thing made the destruction of the Second Temple even more painful than the first. This time there were no prophets – or rather, there were too many of them. The Dead Sea Scrolls tell us of a sect that imminently expected a messianic figure they called "the teacher of righteousness." We know from Josephus that there were many quasi-messianic figures in the years leading up to the destruction. Nor was this true only then. Moses Maimonides, in his *Epistle to Yemen* (1172), mentions four messianic figures close to his time, as well as a fifth who had appeared in Yemen in his day.

What we glimpse in the dialogue between R. Eliezer and the sages is the extraordinary transition that took place in Judaism after the destruction. It is summed up in a single sentence from that era: "A sage is greater than a prophet" (Bava Batra 12a).

The prophets *spoke* the word of God. The sages *interpreted* the word of God. We might think that the former was greater. But the sages saw things differently. The very process of interpretation meant, in effect, that God had vested authority in the sages. He trusted them. He empowered them. In so doing, He granted them the highest religious dignity. They had dignity *because they were human*; because they used the human mind and human intelligence to interpret and apply the word of God. The Torah is *from* heaven but not *in* heaven. It was given by God and handed over to the care of Israel, the community of those who study, debate, and decipher His word.

This idea is a constant feature of the rabbinic literature. Thus for example:

> R. Yehuda said in the name of Shmuel: Three thousand traditional laws were forgotten during the period of mourning for Moses. They [the Israelites] said to Joshua: "Ask." He replied: "It is not in heaven." (Temura 16a)

The people told Joshua to ask God what the law was. He refused to do so. Once God has given us the Torah, he implied, it is our duty to interpret it without recourse to further revelation. Maimonides makes a similar point in the introduction to his *Commentary to the Mishna*:

> Know that prophecy does not help in-depth study of the meanings of the Torah or the derivation of laws by the "thirteen principles" of interpretation. What Joshua and Pinhas did [after the

> death of Moses] by way of study and determining the law is what Ravina and R. Ashi [the compilers of the Babylonian Talmud] also did...
>
> When it comes to the study, determination, and investigation of the Torah, a prophet is no different from the sages who were not prophets. If a prophet gives one interpretation and a sage who is not a prophet gives a different interpretation, and if the prophet says, "God has told me that my interpretation is correct," we do not listen to him. Indeed if 1,000 prophets – each of the stature of Elijah and Elisha – were to give one interpretation, and 1,001 sages gave another interpretation, we follow the majority and rule in accordance with the 1,001 sages, and not like the 1,000 distinguished prophets.

Here *divine respect for human intelligence* reaches heights never surpassed. God empowers His children. He gives them His greatest gift: His will as encoded in His word. That is enough. The dialectic between *revelation* and *interpretation*, between "Torah from heaven" and "not in heaven," is the endless conversation between Israel and God.

With this we return to the plain sense of the passage with which we began. The Torah is "not in heaven," meaning that it is intelligible to all. Each member of the covenantal community has something to contribute to the totality of its meaning. As Maharsha (Rabbi Samuel Eliezer Edels, 1555–1631) put it: There are 600,000 possible interpretations of the Torah, which is why the Torah was given to 600,000 Israelites, so that the revelation would include all possible interpretations.[2]

We all have a share in the Torah. We are all part of its meaning, voices in the endless conversation between heaven and earth. We are each – in the lovely phrase of the Baal Shem Tov (Rabbi Israel ben Eliezer, c. 1698–1760) – "letters in the scroll" written by God.

---

2. Maharsha, novellae to Berakhot 58a.

Not Beyond the Sea

When I was a student at university in the late 1960s – the era of student protests, psychedelic drugs, and the Beatles meditating with the Maharishi Mahesh Yogi – a story went the rounds. An American Jewish woman in her sixties travelled to north India to see a celebrated guru. There were huge crowds waiting to see the holy man, but she pushed through, saying that she needed to see him urgently. Eventually, after weaving through the swaying throng, she entered the tent and stood in the presence of the master himself. What she said that day has entered the realm of legend. She said, "Marvin, listen to your mother. Enough already. Come home."

Starting in the sixties Jews made their way into many religions and cultures with one notable exception: their own. Yet Judaism has historically had its mystics and meditators, its poets and philosophers, its holy men and women, its visionaries and prophets. It has often seemed as if the longing we have for spiritual enlightenment is in direct proportion to its distance, its foreignness, its unfamiliarity. We prefer the far to the near.

Moses already foresaw this possibility:

> Now what I am commanding you today is not too difficult for you or beyond your reach. It is not in heaven, so that you have to

> ask, "Who will ascend into heaven to get it and proclaim it to us so we may obey it?" Nor is it beyond the sea, so that you have to ask, "Who will cross the sea to get it and proclaim it to us so we may obey it?" No, the word is very near you; it is in your mouth and in your heart so you may obey it. (Deut. 30:11–14)

Moses sensed prophetically that in the future Jews would say that to find inspiration we have to ascend to heaven or cross the sea. It is anywhere but here. So it was for much of Israel's history during the First and Second Temple periods. First came the era in which the people were tempted by the gods of the people around them: the Canaanite Baal, the Moabite Chemosh, or Marduk and Astarte in Babylon. Later, in Second Temple times, they were attracted to Hellenism in its Greek or Roman forms. It is a strange phenomenon, best expressed in the memorable line of Groucho Marx: "I don't want to belong to any club that would have me as a member." Jews have long had a tendency to fall in love with people who do not love them and pursue almost any spiritual path so long as it is not their own. But it is very debilitating.

When great minds leave Judaism, Judaism loses great minds. When those in search of spirituality go elsewhere, Jewish spirituality suffers. And this tends to happen in precisely the paradoxical way that Moses describes several times in Deuteronomy. It occurs in ages of affluence, not poverty, in eras of freedom, not slavery. When we seem to have little to thank God for, we thank God. When we have much to be grateful for, we forget.

The eras in which Jews worshipped idols or became Hellenised were Temple times when Jews lived in their land, enjoying either sovereignty or autonomy. The age in which, in Europe, they abandoned Judaism was the period of Emancipation, from the late eighteenth to the early twentieth centuries, when for the first time they enjoyed civil rights.

The surrounding culture in most of these cases was hostile to Jews and Judaism. Yet Jews often preferred to adopt the culture that rejected them rather than embrace the one that was theirs by birth and inheritance, where they had the chance of feeling at home. The results were often tragic.

Becoming Baal worshippers did not lead to Israelites being welcomed by the Canaanites. Becoming Hellenised did not endear Jews to either the Greeks or the Romans. Abandoning Judaism in the nineteenth century did not end anti-Semitism; it inflamed it. Hence the power of Moses' insistence: to find truth, beauty, and spirituality, you do not have to go elsewhere. "The word is very near you; it is in your mouth and in your heart so you may obey it."

The result was that Jews enriched other cultures more than their own. Part of Mahler's Eighth Symphony is a Catholic mass. Irving Berlin, son of a *ḥazan*, wrote "White Christmas." Felix Mendelssohn, grandson of one of the first "enlightened" Jews, Moses Mendelssohn, composed church music and rehabilitated Bach's long-neglected St Matthew Passion. Simone Weil, one of the deepest Christian thinkers of the twentieth century – described by Albert Camus as "the only great spirit of our times" – was born to Jewish parents. So was Edith Stein, celebrated by the Catholic Church as a saint and martyr, but murdered in Auschwitz because to the Nazis she was a Jew. And so on.

Was it the failure of Europe to accept the Jewishness of Jews and Judaism? Was it Judaism's failure to confront the challenge? The phenomenon is so complex it defies any simple explanation. But in the process, we lost great art, great intellect, great spirits and minds.

To some extent the situation has changed both in Israel and in the Diaspora. There has been much new Jewish music and a revival of Jewish mysticism. There have been important Jewish writers and thinkers. But we still spiritually underachieve. The deepest roots of spirituality come from within: from within a culture, a tradition, a sensibility. They come from the syntax and semantics of the native language of the soul: "The word is very near you; it is in your mouth and in your heart so you may obey it."

The beauty of Jewish spirituality is precisely that in Judaism God is close. You do not need to climb a mountain or enter an ashram to find the Divine Presence. It is there around the table at a Shabbat meal, in the light of the candles and the simple holiness of the Kiddush wine and the *ḥallot*, in the praise of the *Eshet Ḥayil* and the blessing of children, in the peace of mind that comes when you leave the world to look after itself for a day while you celebrate the good things that come not from working but resting, not from buying but enjoying – the gifts you have had all along but did not have time to appreciate.

In Judaism, God is close. He is there in the poetry of the psalms, the greatest literature of the soul ever written. He is there listening in to our debates as we study a page of the Talmud or offer new interpretations of ancient texts. He is there in the joy of the festivals, the tears of Tisha B'Av, the echoes of the shofar of Rosh HaShana, and the contrition of Yom Kippur. He is there in the very air of the land of Israel and the stones of Jerusalem, where the oldest of the old and the newest of the new mingle together like close friends.

God is near. That is the overwhelming feeling I get from a lifetime of engaging with the faith of our ancestors. Judaism needed no cathedrals, no monasteries, no abstruse theologies, no metaphysical ingenuities – beautiful though all these are – because for us God is the God of everyone and everywhere, who has time for each of us, and who meets us where we are, if we are willing to open our soul to Him.

I am a rabbi. For many years I was a chief rabbi. But in the end I think it was we, the rabbis, who did not do enough to help people open their doors, their minds, and their feelings to the Presence-beyond-the-universe-who-created-us-in-love that our ancestors knew so well and loved so much. We were afraid – of the intellectual challenges of an aggressively secular culture, of the social challenges of being *in* yet not entirely *of* the world, of the emotional challenge of finding Jews or Judaism or the State of Israel criticised and condemned. So we retreated behind a high wall, thinking that made us safe. High walls never make you safe; they only make you fearful.[1] What makes you safe is confronting the challenges without fear and inspiring others to do likewise.

What Moses meant in those extraordinary words, "It is not in heaven … nor is it beyond the sea," was: *Kinderlach*, your parents trembled when they heard the voice of God at Sinai. They were overwhelmed. They said: If we hear any more we will die. So God found ways in which you could meet Him without being overwhelmed. Yes, He is creator, sovereign, supreme power, first cause, mover of the planets and the

1. See Rashi to Num. 13:18.

stars. But He is also parent, partner, lover, friend. He is *Shekhina,* from *shakhen,* meaning, the neighbour next door.

So thank Him every morning for the gift of life. Say the *Shema* twice daily for the gift of love. Join your voice to others in prayer so that His spirit may flow through you, giving you the strength and courage to change the world. When you cannot see Him, it is because you are looking in the wrong direction. When He seems absent, He is there just behind you, but you have to turn to meet Him.

Do not treat Him like a stranger. He loves you. He believes in you. He wants your success. To find Him you do not have to climb to heaven or cross the sea. His is the voice you hear in the silence of the soul. His is the light you see when you open your eyes to wonder. His is the hand you touch in the pit of despair. His is the breath that gives you life.

The Fourteenth Principle of Faith

Ask anyone how many principles of Jewish faith there are, and the answer is almost certain to be thirteen.[1] That is a mark of the influence of Moses Maimonides, who was the first to formulate the Jewish creed in this way. The principles are taken from his *Commentary to the Mishna*, in his introduction to chapter 10 of Tractate Sanhedrin. A later formulation (*Ani Maamin*) is found in many siddurim. The most famous version is to be found in the liturgical poem *Yigdal*, often said at the beginning or end of services. In their briefest form, the principles are:

1. God's existence
2. God's unity
3. God's incorporeality
4. God's existence before and after time
5. God alone may be worshipped
6. Prophecy
7. The special nature of Moses' prophecy
8. Torah from Heaven
9. The eternity of the Torah
10. God's knowledge

1. I owe the argument of this essay to my teacher, Rabbi Nahum Rabinovitch.

11. Reward and punishment
12. The Messiah
13. Resurrection

However, this is not the full story.

To understand this, we must first know that Maimonides was not only the supreme commentator and codifier of Jewish law. He also took immense care in the construction of his work. Nothing he wrote was accidental, especially the *structure* of his literary works. Maimonides was a trained logician and philosopher. He devoted special attention to first principles. He left detailed explanations of why he wrote a particular work in one style rather than another, one language rather than another. For example, he wrote the *Mishneh Torah* in rabbinic Hebrew, unlike most of his other works, which were written in Arabic. The *Mishneh Torah* itself is one of the most lucid books ever written in Hebrew, quite unlike *Guide for the Perplexed*, which is written (as he explains in the introduction) to be deliberately opaque. He cared about the architectonics, the literary shape, of his works.

It is with some surprise, therefore, that we discover that in all his major works, he used fourteen, not thirteen, as his organising principle. The most famous example is the *Mishneh Torah* itself, commonly called the *Yad* ("Hand") because it is composed of fourteen books (the numerical value of the Hebrew word *yad* is fourteen). The books are:

1. Knowledge (*Madda*)
2. Love (*Ahava*)
3. Times (*Zemanim*)
4. Women (*Nashim*)
5. Sanctity (*Kedusha*)
6. Expression (*Haflaa*)
7. Seeds (*Zera'im*)
8. Service (*Avoda*)
9. Sacrifices (*Korbanot*)
10. Purity (*Tahara*)
11. Damages (*Nezikin*)

12. Acquisition (*Kinyan*)
13. Judgement (*Mishpatim*)
14. Judges (*Shofetim*)

In his introduction to *Sefer HaMitzvot,* where he lists the 613 commands, he sets out *fourteen principles* by which to decide whether a biblical passage is to count as a command or not. The book itself is divided into two (positive and negative commands), each of which is subdivided into fourteen groups:

Positive commands		Negative commands	
1	God (1–9)	1	God (1)
2	Torah and prayer (10–19)	2	Idolatry (2–66)
3	Sanctuary and priests (20–38)	3	Sanctuary and priests (67–88)
4	Offerings (39–93)	4	Offerings (89–154)
5	Vows (94–95)	5	Vows (155–57)
6	Purity and impurity (96–113)	6	Impurity (158–71)
7	Agriculture (114–45)	7	Prohibited food (172–209)
8	Food regulations (146–52)	8	Cultivation of land (210–31)
9	Holy days (153–71)	9	Duties to fellow man (232–72)
10	State functions (172–93)	10	Administration of justice (273–300)
11	Duties to fellow man (194–208)	11	Public order (301–19)
12	Family life (209–23)	12	Holy days (320–29)
13	Punishments (224–31)	13	Sexual regulations (330–61)
14	Property regulations (232–48)	14	State affairs (362–65)

In the third part of *Guide for the Perplexed,* Maimonides gives a general account of the reasons for the commands. He divides the commandments into basic groups, differentiated by their purpose. Again, the number he chooses is fourteen. These are the types:

1. Fundamental opinions
2. Idolatry
3. Ethical qualities
4. Giving of alms and bestowing of gifts
5. Other wrongdoing and aggression
6. Punishments
7. Mutual property transactions
8. Days on which work is forbidden
9. Other general practices of worship
10. Sanctuary
11. Sacrifices
12. Clean and unclean
13. Forbidden food and related matters
14. Prohibited sexual unions

What is fascinating is that none of these lists is related to the others. The way Maimonides divides the commands in his law code is different from the way he does so in *Sefer HaMitzvot* and different again from the classification in the *Guide*. Nor is any related to the fourteen rules for counting the number of the commands. It seems, simply, that for Maimonides the number fourteen (2 x 7) was his favoured organising principle.[2]

If, therefore, we knew nothing of Maimonides' principles of faith and had to guess, on the basis of everything else we know about his writings, how many there were, the answer would be not thirteen but fourteen. Does Maimonides in fact believe in a fourteenth principle of faith? The answer is: he does. Here is how he sets it out:

> Free will is bestowed on every human being. If one desires to turn towards the good way and be righteous, he has the power to do so. If one wishes to turn towards the evil way and be wicked, he is at liberty to do so.... This doctrine is an important principle, the

2. Note too that his birthday was 14 Nisan 4895 (1135).

> pillar of the law and the commandment.... If God had decreed that a person should either be righteous or wicked...what room could there be for the whole of the Torah? By what right or justice could God punish the wicked or reward the righteous?[3]

Maimonides leaves us in no doubt that free will is one of the fundamental principles of faith, without which Judaism would not make sense. If we lacked freedom, there would be no point in God commanding us, "Do this. Do not do that." Nor would there be any logic in reward and punishment, both of which presuppose human responsibility for our actions. *Free will is the fourteenth principle of Jewish faith.*

Why then did we assume otherwise? Why, in his *Commentary to the Mishna*, does Maimonides list thirteen principles, not fourteen? The answer lies in the context. Maimonides is commenting on a mishna which speaks about those who "have no share in the World to Come." He is listing, in other words, those principles whose denial places one outside the community of faith. What they have in common is that they are beliefs about God. *The fourteenth principle is not a belief about God but about humanity.* The first thirteen summarise our faith in God. The fourteenth – the fact that God has granted us the freedom to choose how to behave – represents God's faith in humankind.

The prooftext for the fourteenth principle comes from *Parashat Nitzavim*. It appears at the climax of Moses' great challenge to the next generation: "This day I call heaven and earth as witnesses against you that I have set before you life and death, the blessing and the curse. Therefore choose life, that you and your children may live" (Deut. 30:19).

Judaism is a religion of freedom and responsibility. Against all the many determinisms in the history of thought – astrological, philosophical, Spinozist, Marxist, Freudian, neo-Darwinian – Judaism insists that we are masters of our fate. We are neither programmed nor predestined. We can choose. That is the fourteenth principle of Jewish faith.

3. Maimonides, *Mishneh Torah, Hilkhot Teshuva* 5:1–6.

Vayelekh
וילך

Vayelekh is the shortest of all *parashot*, a mere thirty verses long. Poignantly, Moses tells the people, "I am now a hundred and twenty years old, and I can no longer go forth and come in" (Deut. 31:2). He will not lead them across the Jordan into the Promised Land. He summons his successor Joshua and, in the presence of the people, gives him words of encouragement. He instructs the people to gather every seven years to hear a public reading of the Torah. God appears to Moses and Joshua, warning them that the Israelites may eventually stray from the covenant. He instructs them to write down the Torah and teach it to the people, as permanent testimony of the covenant itself. He then encourages Joshua, assuring him that He will be with him as he leads the people.

The first essay is about a subtle difference in the words Moses, and then God, say to Joshua, indicating two different styles of leadership. The second is about the national gathering every seven years to hear the Torah proclaimed in a covenant renewal ceremony. The third is about the 613th command, to write a *sefer Torah*, and what it tells us about the relationship between the people and the Book. The fourth is about the use of the word "song" in this command to describe the Torah. In what sense is the Torah a song?

Leadership: Consensus or Command?

The great transition was about to take place. Moses' career as a leader was coming to an end. Joshua's leadership was about to begin. Moses blessed his successor. Then God did. But if we listen carefully to the text, we note a subtle difference in what they said.

Moses said this: "Be strong and courageous, for you must *go with* this people into the land that the Lord swore to their ancestors to give them, and you must divide it among them as their inheritance" (Deut. 31:7).

And this is what God said: "Be strong and courageous, for you will *bring* the Israelites into the land I promised them on oath, and I Myself will be with you" (Deut. 31:23).

The difference in Hebrew is even subtler than it is in English. Moses used the verb *tavo*, "go with." God used the verb *tavi*, "bring." It is the slightest of nuances, but Rashi explains how the words are worlds apart in their significance. They refer to two quite different styles of leadership. Here is Rashi's comment:

> Moses said to Joshua, "Make sure that the elders of the generation are with you. Always act according to their opinion

> and advice." However, the Holy One, Blessed Be He, said to Joshua, "For you will bring the Israelites into the land I promised them" – meaning, "Bring them even against their will. It all depends on you. If necessary, take a stick and beat them over the head. There is only one leader for a generation, not two." (Rashi to Deut. 31:7)

Moses advised his successor to lead by consultation and consensus. God told Joshua to lead firmly and with authority. Even if people do not agree with you, you must lead from the front. Be clear. Be decisive. Be forceful. Be strong.

These are both strange comments in the light of what we learn elsewhere about the leadership styles, respectively, of God and Moses. This is what Rashi has to say about the words of God immediately prior to the creation of humanity: "Let us make man in our image after our likeness" (Gen. 1:26). Who are the "us"? To whom is God speaking and why? Rashi says:

> From here we learn the humility of God. Since man was [created] in the image of the angels they were jealous of him. He therefore consulted them. Similarly, when He judges kings, He consults His heavenly court.... Though they [the angels] did not help in His creation and [the wording of the verse] may give the heretics an opportunity to rebel, [nevertheless,] Scripture does not refrain from teaching courtesy and the attribute of humility, that the greater should consult and ask permission of the smaller. (Rashi to Gen. 1:26)

This is a remarkable statement. Rashi is saying that before creating man God consulted with the angels. He did so not because He needed their help; clearly He did not. Nor was it because He needed their advice; He had already resolved to create humankind. It was to show them respect, to pre-empt their jealousy of man, to avoid their resentment at not being consulted on so fateful a decision, and to show us, the readers, the fundamental truth that greatness goes hand in hand with humility. So it was

God who acted according to the advice Moses gave Joshua: "Make sure that others are with you. Consult. Take their advice."

On the other hand, Moses acted the way God advised Joshua to do: "If necessary, take a stick and beat them over the head." Is that not figuratively what Moses did at Kadesh, when he hit the people with his words and the rock with his staff (Num. 20:1–12), for which he was condemned by God not to enter the Promised Land?

So we seem to have God saying words we associate with Moses' type of leadership – firm, strong, decisive – and Moses advocating the kind of leadership – consensual, consultative – that Rashi associates with God. Surely it should have been the other way around.

However, perhaps Rashi is telling us something profound. At the end of his life, Moses recognised one great failure of his leadership. He had taken the Israelites out of Egypt, but he had not taken Egypt out of the Israelites. He had changed his people's fate, but he had not changed their character. He now realised that for this to happen there would have to be a different kind of leadership, one that handed back responsibility to the people as a whole, and to the elders in particular.

So long as there was a Moses performing miracles, the people did not have to accept responsibility for themselves. In order for them to grow, Joshua would have to engage in participative leadership, encouraging diverse views and listening to them, even if that meant going more slowly. That is transformative leadership and it requires the leader to engage in what the kabbalists called *tzimtzum*, self-effacement. Or as Rashi puts it: "Make sure that the elders of the generation are with you. Always act according to their opinion and advice."

As for God, He was not changing His mind. He was not suggesting that Joshua should become, in general, an authoritarian leader. He was suggesting that Joshua needed to do this just once. Listen carefully to the verse: "For you will bring the Israelites into the land." Recall that there was one occasion that condemned an entire generation to die in the wilderness, the episode of the spies, in which the people lacked the faith and courage to enter and take possession of the land. It was then that two men, Joshua and Caleb, stood firm, insisting against the other ten spies that they could conquer the land and defeat their enemies.

God was saying to Joshua that there will be one trial in which he must stand firm, even against the majority, and that will come when they are about to cross the Jordan. That is when the people will be in danger of giving way to fear. That is when Joshua's leadership will consist, not of consultation and consensus, but of allowing no dissent. That is when "It will all depend on you.... There is only one leader for a generation, not two." Sometimes even the most consensual leaders must lead from the front, bringing the people with them.

There is a time to discuss and a time to act, a time to seek agreement and a time to move ahead without waiting for agreement. That is what both God and Moses were telling Joshua in their different ways.

A leader must have the courage to lead, the patience to consult, and the wisdom to know when the time is right for each.

To Renew Our Days

Moses' life was nearing its close. But there were two more commands he had to give the people. The last is the subject of the next essay. Here I focus on the penultimate command. The Israelites were about to cross the Jordan, and enter and take possession of the Promised Land. There they would begin life as a self-governing nation under the sovereignty of God.

With his prophetic eye turned to the furthermost horizon of the future, Moses had been warning the people throughout Deuteronomy, as we have noted time and again, that the real dangers would be the ones they least suspected. They would not be war or famine or poverty or natural disaster. They would be ease and affluence and freedom and prosperity. That is when a nation is in danger of forgetting its past and its mission. It becomes complacent; it may become corrupt. The rich neglect the poor. Those in power afflict the powerless. The people begin to think that what they have achieved, they achieved by and for themselves. They forget their dependence on God. At the very height of its powers, Israelite society might develop fault-lines that would eventually lead to disaster.

No one has set out the terms of the survival of a civilisation more starkly than Moses in Deuteronomy. Nations face their greatest danger at the point of their greatest success. Affluence leads to overconfidence which begets forgetfulness which leads to decadence which results in lack of social solidarity which leads in the end to demoralisation – the prelude to defeat. As historian Will Durant wrote: "A great civilization is not conquered from without until it has destroyed itself from within."[1]

Israel's very existence, said Moses, would depend on memory, mission, and morality – remembering where it came from, what it is called on to do, and how it is called on to do it. Hence the great 612th command, known as *hak'hel*, or national assembly:

> At the end of every seven years, in the year for cancelling debts, during the Feast of Tabernacles, when all Israel comes to appear before the Lord your God at the place He will choose, you shall read this law before them in their hearing. Assemble the people – men, women, and children, and the strangers living in your towns – so they can listen and learn to fear the Lord your God and follow carefully all the words of this law. Their children, who do not know this law, must hear it and learn to fear the Lord your God as long as you live in the land you are crossing the Jordan to possess. (Deut. 31:10–13)

Once every seven years, on the second day of Sukkot in the year after the Sabbatical year, the king was to gather the people together in the Temple courtyard and read to them from the Torah – specifically, selections from Deuteronomy itself.[2] *Hak'hel* was a re-enactment of the covenant ceremony at Mount Sinai.[3] It was intended to remind the people of their history, the laws they are called on to keep, and the principles they must live by. It was to be a ceremony of national rededication – a renewal of their inherited and chosen destiny, a reminder of the duties

---

1. *Caesar and Christ: A History of Roman Civilization and of Christianity from Their Beginnings to A.D. 325* (New York: MFJ Books, 1992), 665.
2. The details are set out in Maimonides, *Mishneh Torah, Hilkhot Ḥagiga*, ch. 3.
3. Ibid. 3:6.

they owed to their ancestors, to their descendants not yet born, and, primarily, to God Himself.

We do not know how this command was carried out in practice. Yet one thing is clear from the biblical record. It is what the leaders of the nation did at critical junctures in their history. Joshua did so at the end of his life (Josh. 24). King Josiah did so when the Torah was rediscovered during a restoration of the Temple:

> Then the king called together all the elders of Judah and Jerusalem. He went up to the Temple of the Lord with the men of Judah, the people of Jerusalem, the priests and the prophets – all the people from the least to the greatest. He read in their hearing all the words of the Book of the Covenant, which had been found in the Temple of the Lord. The king stood by the pillar and renewed the covenant in the presence of the Lord – to follow the Lord and keep His commands, regulations, and decrees with all his heart and all his soul, thus confirming the words of the covenant written in this book. Then all the people pledged themselves to the covenant. (II Kings 23:1–3)

Some two centuries later, Ezra did so, laying the foundations for a nation reborn after the Babylonian conquest and exile:

> So on the first day of the seventh month Ezra the priest brought the Law before the assembly, which was made up of men and women and all who were able to understand. He read it aloud from daybreak till noon as he faced the square before the Water Gate in the presence of the men, women, and others who could understand. And all the people listened attentively to the Book of the Law. (Neh. 8:2–3)

Hak'hel has a significance that goes far beyond its specific details. It belongs to a unique form of politics – covenantal politics. Philip Selznick, in *The Moral Commonwealth*, explains:

> The compact creates a self-conscious moral order. Most vividly at Sinai, the agreement with God is an agreement to uphold a

> code of responsible conduct. God's commands are obeyed by fulfilling obligations to family and community; a social ethic is the linchpin of the covenant.[4]

Covenantal politics are moral politics. They involve ideas of duty and obligation. They are interwoven with a particular view of the history of the nation, whose fate is seen as a reflection of its success or failure in honouring the terms laid down by its founders.

One nation in particular has constructed its politics in terms of a covenant, namely, the United States, whose Puritan founding fathers were saturated by the ideas of Deuteronomy, and which has continued, to the present day, to see itself in these terms.[5] President Ronald Reagan, speaking at the bicentennial celebration of the American Constitution in 1987, described the constitution as a kind of "covenant we've made not only with ourselves but with all of mankind.... It's a human covenant; yes, and beyond that, a covenant with the Supreme Being to whom our founding fathers did constantly appeal for assistance." America's duty, he said, is "to constantly renew their covenant with humanity... to complete the work begun 200 years ago, that grand noble work that is America's particular calling – the triumph of human freedom, the triumph of human freedom under God."[6]

One consequence of this is that American presidential inaugural addresses are the closest equivalent in the contemporary world to *hak'hel*, a covenant renewal ceremony. Usually, the president recapitulates the nation's history in the light of the principles and ideals of its foundational documents. The most famous example was a speech that was not an inaugural, namely, Lincoln's Gettysburg Address, which began with the words: "Four score and seven years ago our fathers brought forth on this continent, a new nation, conceived in Liberty,

---

4. Philip Selznick, *The Moral Commonwealth* (Berkeley: University of California Press, 1992), 478–79.
5. See Robert Bellah, *Beyond Belief* (Berkeley: University of California Press, 1970); idem, *The Broken Covenant* (Chicago: University of Chicago Press, 1992).
6. *Public Papers of the Presidents of the United States, Ronald Reagan, 1987* (Washington, DC: GPO, 1989), 1040–43.

and dedicated to the proposition that all men are created equal."[7] Covenant societies *are* "dedicated to a proposition." They have ideals, and can be called to account for failing to honour them. And regardless of whether the president is personally religious or not, the speech will be religious in tone, biblical in language, and include, explicitly or implicitly, reference to God.

Here, for example, is Bill Clinton in 1997:

> Our founders taught us that the preservation of our liberty and our union depends upon responsible citizenship.... The challenge of our past remains the challenge of our future – will we be one nation, one people, with one common destiny, or not?... The promise we sought in a new land we will find again in a land of new promise.... The greatest progress we have made, and the greatest progress we have yet to make, is in the human heart. In the end, all the world's wealth and a thousand armies are no match for the strength and decency of the human spirit.[8]

And George W. Bush in 2005:

> America's vital interests and our deepest beliefs are now one. From the day of our Founding, we have proclaimed that every man and woman on this earth has rights, and dignity, and matchless value, because they bear the image of the Maker of Heaven and earth. Across the generations we have proclaimed the imperative of self-government, because no one is fit to be a master, and no one deserves to be a slave. Advancing these ideals is the mission that created our Nation.... History has an ebb and flow of justice, but history also has a visible direction, set by liberty and the Author of Liberty.[9]

7. Abraham Lincoln, "The Gettysburg Address" (Soldiers' National Cemetery in Gettysburg, PA, November 19, 1863).
8. Bill Clinton, Second Inaugural Address (Washington, DC, January 20, 1997).
9. George W. Bush, Inaugural Address (Washington, DC, January 20, 2005).

And Barack Obama in 2009:

> We remain a young nation. But in the words of Scripture, the time has come to set aside childish things. The time has come to reaffirm our enduring spirit; to choose our better history; to carry forward that precious gift, that noble idea passed on from generation to generation: the God-given promise that all are equal, all are free, and all deserve a chance to pursue their full measure of happiness.[10]

The language of covenant is unmistakable: a commitment to the equal dignity of individuals as the image of God; collective responsibility and a sense of "We, the people"; loyalty to founding ideals; accountability to past and future; being a role model to the rest of humanity; and being under the judgement of Heaven. In no other democratic country do political leaders speak in these terms.[11] American presidential inaugurals are best understood as a secular counterpart to the command of *hak'hel*.

There is nothing inevitable about the survival of nations. The pages of history are littered with tales of their decline and fall. Few indeed are those that have defeated this almost inevitable cycle. The fact that Moses saw the problem and provided a remedy makes him the most prophetic political leader of all time. The institution of *hak'hel* was central to this vision.

A civilisation that loses its sense of history and destiny does not survive. It must be kept alive by prophetic voices, taught in schools and homes, rehearsed in prayer, enacted in rituals, and renewed periodically in *hak'hel*-type moments. It must be religious, for if not, it becomes, as the late Yeshayahu Leibowitz constantly warned,[12] a form of idolatry – a nation worshipping itself. It may sound strange, yet I truly believe that finding a contemporary equivalent of *hak'hel* is our most pressing task if the free societies of the West are to survive.

---

10. Barack Obama, Inaugural Address (Washington, DC, January 20, 2009).
11. The closest equivalent was Václav Havel, president of the Czech Republic, 1993–2003.
12. Yeshayahu Leibowitz, *Judaism, Human Values, and the Jewish State* (Cambridge, MA: Harvard University Press, 1995).

The Heart, the Home, the Text

By now Moses had given 612 commands to the Israelites. But there was one further instruction he still had to give, the last of his life, the final mitzva in the Torah: "Now therefore write down for yourselves this song and teach it to the people of Israel. Put it in their mouths, that this song may be My witness against the people of Israel" (Deut. 31:19).

The Oral Tradition understood this to be a command that each Israelite should take part in the writing of a *sefer Torah*. Here is how Maimonides states the law:

> Every male Israelite is commanded to write a Torah scroll for himself, as it says, "Now therefore write down for yourselves this song," meaning, "Write for yourselves [a complete copy of] the Torah that contains this song," since we do not write isolated passages of the Torah [but only a complete scroll]. Even if one has inherited a Torah scroll from his parents, nonetheless it is a mitzva to write one for oneself, and one who does so is as if he had received [the Torah] from Mount Sinai. One who does not know how to write a scroll may engage [a scribe] to do it for

> him, and whoever corrects even one letter is as if he has written a whole scroll.[1]

There is something poetic in the fact that Moses left this law until the last. For it was as if he were saying to the next generation, and all future generations: "Do not think it is enough to be able to say, My ancestors received the Torah from Moses. You must take it and make it new in every generation." And so Jews did.

The Koran calls Jews "the people of the book." That is an understatement. The whole of Judaism is an extended love story between a people and a book – between Jews and the Torah. Never has a people loved and honoured a book more. They read it, studied it, argued with it, lived it. In its presence they stood as if it were a king. On Simḥat Torah, they danced with it as if it were a bride. If, God forbid, it fell, they fasted. If one was no longer fit for use it was buried as if it were a relative who had died.

For a thousand years they wrote commentaries to it in the form of the rest of Tanakh: there were a thousand years between Moses and Malachi, the last of the prophets, and in the very last chapter of the prophetic books Malachi says, "Remember the Torah of My servant Moses, the decrees and laws I gave him at Horeb for all Israel" (Mal. 3:22). Then for another thousand years, between the last of the prophets and the closure of the Babylonian Talmud, they wrote commentaries to the commentaries in the form of the documents – Midrash, Mishna, and Gemara – of the Oral Law. Then for a further thousand years, from the *Geonim* to the *Rishonim* to the *Aḥaronim*, they wrote commentaries to the commentaries to the commentaries, in the form of biblical exegesis, law codes, and works of philosophy. Until the modern age virtually every Jewish text was directly or indirectly a commentary to the Torah.

For a hundred generations it was more than a book. It was God's love letter to the Jewish people, the gift of His word, the pledge of their betrothal, the marriage contract between Heaven and the Jewish people, the bond that God would never break or rescind. It was the story of the people and their written constitution as a nation under God. When they

1. Maimonides, *Mishneh Torah, Hilkhot Tefillin, Mezuza, VeSefer Torah* 7:1.

were exiled from their land it became the documentary evidence of past promise and future hope. In a brilliant phrase the poet Heinrich Heine called the Torah "the portable homeland of the Jew."[2] In George Steiner's gloss, "The text is home; each commentary a return."[3]

Dispersed, scattered, landless, powerless, so long as a Jew had the Torah he or she was at home – if not physically then spiritually. There were times when it was all the Jews had. Hence the lacerating line in the liturgical poem in *Ne'ila* at the end of Yom Kippur, written in the eleventh century by Rabbenu Gershom: "There is nothing left except this Torah." It was all that Jews had. They had no home, no rights, no security, only a book – but it was enough.

It was their world. According to one midrash it was the architecture of creation: "God looked in the Torah and created the universe."[4] According to another tradition, the whole Torah was a single, mystical name of God.[5] It was written, said the sages, in letters of black fire on white fire (Y. Shekalim 6:1). R. Yose b. Kisma, arrested by the Romans for teaching Torah in public, was sentenced to death and wrapped in a Torah scroll that was then set on fire. As he was dying his students asked him what he saw. He replied, "I see the parchment burning but the letters flying [back to heaven]" (Avoda Zara 18a). The Romans might burn the scrolls but the Torah was indestructible.

So there is immense power in the idea that, as Moses reached the end of his life, and the Torah the end of its narrative, the final imperative should be a command to continue to write and study the Torah, teaching it to the people and "putting it in their mouths" so that it would not abandon them, nor they it. God's word would live within them, giving them life.

The Talmud tells an intriguing story about King David, who asked God to tell him how long he would live. God told him that this is something no mortal knows. The most God would disclose to David

2. Heinrich Heine, "Geständnisse," in *Düsselforger Heine Ausgabe* (Hamburg: Hoffman and Campe, 1982), 15:44.
3. George Steiner, "Our Homeland, the Text," in *The New Salmagundi Reader*, ed. Robert Boyers and Peggy Boyers (Syracuse: Syracuse University Press, 1996), 99–121.
4. Genesis Rabba 1:1.
5. This is the thesis of *Sefer Yetzira*, an ancient mystical text of unknown date.

was that he would die on Shabbat. The Talmud then says that every Shabbat, David's "mouth would not cease from learning" during the entire day. When the day came for David to die, the Angel of Death was dispatched, but finding David learning incessantly, was unable to take him – the Torah being a form of undying life. Eventually the angel was forced to devise a stratagem. He caused a rustling noise in a tree in the royal garden. David climbed up a ladder to see what was making the noise. A rung of the ladder broke. David fell, and for a moment ceased learning. In that moment he died (Shabbat 30a–b).

What is this story about? At the simplest level it is the sages' way of re-envisioning King David less as a military hero and Israel's greatest king than as a penitent and Torah scholar (note that several of the psalms, notably 1, 19, and 119, are poems in praise of Torah study). But at a deeper level it seems to be saying more. David here symbolises the Jewish people. So long as the Jewish people never stop learning, it will not die. The national equivalent of the Angel of Death – the law that all nations, however great, eventually decline and fall – does not apply to a people who never cease to study, never forgetting who they are and why.

Hence the Torah ends with the last command: to keep writing and studying Torah. And this is epitomised in the beautiful custom, on Simḥat Torah, to move immediately from reading the end of the Torah to reading the beginning. The last word in the Torah is *Yisrael*; the last letter is a *lamed*. The first word of the Torah is *Bereishit*; the first letter is *beit*. *Lamed* followed by *beit* spells *lev*, "heart." So long as the Jewish people never stop learning, the Jewish heart will never stop beating. Never has a people loved a book more. Never has a book sustained a people longer or lifted it higher.

The Torah as God's Song

At the end of his life, having given the Israelites at God's behest 612 commands, Moses gave them the last, as we saw in the previous essay: "Now therefore write down for yourselves this song and teach it to the people of Israel. Put it in their mouths, that this song may be My witness against the people of Israel" (Deut. 31:19).

According to the plain sense of the verse, God was speaking to Moses and Joshua and was referring to the song in the following chapter, "Listen, O heavens, and I will speak; hear, O earth, the words of my mouth" (Deut. 32:1). As we saw in the previous essay, however, Oral Tradition gave it a different and much wider interpretation, understanding it as a command for every Jew to write, or at least take some part in writing, a *sefer Torah*:

> Said Rabba: Even though our ancestors have left us a scroll of the Torah, it is our religious duty to write one for ourselves, as it is said: "Now therefore write down for yourselves this song and teach it to the people of Israel. Put it in their mouths, that this song may be My witness against the people of Israel." (Sanhedrin 21b)

The logic of the interpretation seems to be, first, that the phrase "write down for yourselves" could be construed as referring to every Israelite (Ibn Ezra), not just Moses and Joshua. Second, the passage goes on to say (Deut. 31:24): "Moses finished writing in the book the words of this law from beginning to end." The Talmud offers a third reason. The verse goes on to say: "That this song may be My witness against the people" – implying the Torah as a whole, not just the song in chapter 32 (Nedarim 38a).

Thus understood, Moses' final message to the Israelites was: "It is not enough that you have received the Torah from me. You must make it new again in every generation." The covenant was not to grow old. It had to be periodically renewed.

So it is to this day that Torah scrolls are still written as in ancient times, by hand, on parchment, using a quill – as were the Dead Sea Scrolls two thousand years ago. In a religion almost devoid of sacred objects (icons, relics), the Torah scroll is the nearest Judaism comes to endowing a physical entity with sanctity.

My earliest memories are of going to my late grandfather's little beit midrash in North London and being given the privilege, as a two- or three-year-old child, of putting the bells on the Torah scroll after it had been lifted, rolled, and rebound in its velvet cover. Even then, I had a sense of the awe in which the scroll was held by the worshippers in that little house of study and prayer. Many of them were refugees. They spoke with heavy accents redolent of worlds they had left, worlds that I later discovered had been destroyed in the Holocaust. There was an air of ineffable sadness about the tunes they sang – always in a minor key. But their love for the parchment scroll was palpable. I later defined it as their equivalent of the rabbinic tradition about the Ark in the wilderness: it carried those who carried it (Rashi to I Chr. 15:26). It was my first intimation that Judaism is the story of a love affair between a people and a book, the Book of books.

What, though – if we take the command to refer to the whole Torah and not just one chapter – is the significance of the word "song" (*shira*): "Now therefore write down for yourselves this song"? The word *shira* appears five times in this passage. It is clearly a key word. Why? On this, two nineteenth-century scholars offered striking explanations.

The Netziv (Rabbi Naftali Zvi Yehuda Berlin, 1816–1893, one of the great yeshiva heads of the nineteenth century) interprets it to mean that the whole Torah should be read as poetry, not prose; the word *shira* in Hebrew means both a song and a poem.

To be sure, most of the Torah is written in prose, but the Netziv argued that it has two characteristics of poetry. First, it is allusive rather than explicit. It leaves unsaid more than is said. Secondly, like poetry, it hints at deeper reservoirs of meaning, sometimes by the use of an unusual word or sentence construction. Descriptive prose carries its meaning on the surface. The Torah, like poetry, does not.[1]

In this brilliant insight, the Netziv anticipates one of the great twentieth-century essays on biblical prose, Erich Auerbach's "Odysseus' Scar."[2] Auerbach contrasts the narrative style of Genesis with that of Homer. Homer uses dazzlingly detailed descriptions so that each scene is set out pictorially as if bathed in sunlight. By contrast, biblical narrative is spare and understated. In the example Auerbach cites – the story of the binding of Isaac – we do not know what the main characters look like, what they are feeling, what they are wearing, what landscapes they are passing through.

> The decisive points of the narrative alone are emphasised, what lies between is non-existent; time and place are undefined and call for interpretation; thoughts and feelings remain unexpressed, only suggested by the silence and the fragmentary speeches; the whole, permeated with the most unrelieved suspense and directed towards a single goal, remains mysterious and "fraught with background."[3]

A completely different aspect is alluded to by Rabbi Yehiel Michel Epstein, author of the halakhic code *Arukh HaShulḥan*.[4] Epstein points out that the rabbinic literature is full of arguments, about which the sages said: "These and those are the words of the living God."[5] This, says Epstein, is one of the reasons the Torah is called "a song" – because a

1. *"Kidmat davar,"* preface to *Haamek Davar*, 3.
2. Erich Auerbach, *Mimesis: The Representation of Reality in Western Literature* (Princeton, NJ: Princeton University Press, 2013), 3–23.
3. Ibid., 12.
4. *Arukh HaShulḥan, Ḥoshen Mishpat,* introduction.
5. Eiruvin 13b; Gittin 6b.

song becomes more beautiful when scored for many voices interwoven in complex harmonies.

I would suggest a third dimension. The 613th command is not simply about the Torah, but about the duty to make the Torah new in each generation. To make the Torah live anew, it is not enough to hand it on cognitively – as mere history and law. It must speak to us affectively, emotionally.

Judaism is a religion of words, and yet whenever the language of Judaism aspires to the spiritual it breaks into song, as if the words themselves sought escape from the gravitational pull of finite meanings. There is something about melody that intimates a reality beyond our grasp, what William Wordsworth called the

> sense sublime
> Of something far more deeply interfused
> Whose dwelling is the light of setting suns
> And the round ocean and the living air.[6]

Words are the language of the mind. Music is the language of the soul.

The 613th command, to make the Torah new in every generation, symbolises the fact that though the Torah was given once, it must be received many times, as each of us, through our study and practice, strives to recapture the pristine voice heard at Mount Sinai. That requires emotion, not just intellect. It means treating Torah not just as words read, but also as a melody sung. The Torah is God's libretto, and we, the Jewish people, are His choir, the performers of His choral symphony. And though when Jews speak they often argue, when they sing, they sing in harmony, as the Israelites did at the Red Sea, because music is the language of the soul, and at the level of the soul Jews enter the unity of the Divine which transcends the oppositions of lower worlds.

The Torah is God's song, and we collectively are its singers.

---

6. Wordsworth, "Lines Composed a Few Miles Above Tintern Abbey, On Revisiting the Banks of the Wye During a Tour, July 13, 1798" (*Favorite Poems* [Mineola, NY: Dover, 1992], 23).

Haazinu
האזינו

Parashat Haazinu consists, for the most part, of the song sung by Moses as his last lesson to the Israelites before blessing them and ascending Mount Nebo to die. It expresses in poetic form the relationship between the God of righteousness and His often recalcitrant people. The basic idea behind the song belongs to the logic of covenant, in which one of the parties can bring a case against the other for non-fulfilment of duties agreed to in the covenant itself. This kind of lawsuit (known in biblical Hebrew as a *riv*) is referred to often by the later prophets, usually an accusation by God against the Israelites but occasionally the opposite.

In post-biblical times this idea came to influence the imagery of the High Holy Days, Rosh HaShana and Yom Kippur, as the time when God sits on the throne of justice and passes judgement on our lives. Here, though, the essentially legal nature of the covenant is transformed into high poetry as Moses speaks not just to the minds of his listeners but also to their emotions and imaginations. The theme, though, remains stark and simple: God is just. It is we humans who are the source of injustice in the world.

The first of the following essays is about the place of song generally in the life of the spirit. The second reflects on the rabbinic understanding of the Torah as rain, fascinating in its insistence on the importance of individuality as well as commonality in Judaism. The third is about an idea present in an early midrash that the existence of the universe and humanity testifies to faith – not our faith in God but God's faith in us. The fourth is about a striking interpretation given by the Netziv of the phrase "a warped and twisted generation." The fifth is about the concept of divine vengeance, a theme of the song. Paradoxically, this is intended to diminish, not legitimate, acts of revenge by human beings.

The Spirituality of Song

With *Haazinu,* we climb to one of the peaks of Jewish spirituality. For a month Moses had taught the people. He had told them their history and destiny, and the laws that would make theirs a unique society of people bound in covenant with one another and with God. He renewed the covenant and then handed the leadership on to his successor and disciple Joshua. His final act would be blessing the people, tribe by tribe. But before that, there was one more thing he had to do. He had to sum up his prophetic message in a way the people would always remember and be inspired by. He knew that the best way of doing so was in music. So the last thing Moses did before giving the people his deathbed blessing was to teach them a song.

There is something profoundly spiritual about music. When language aspires to the transcendent, and the soul longs to break free of the gravitational pull of the earth, it modulates into song. Jewish history is not so much read as sung. The rabbis enumerated ten songs at key moments in the life of the nation. There was the song of the Israelites in Egypt (see Is. 30:29), the song at the Red Sea (Ex. 15), the song at the well (Num. 21), and *Haazinu,* Moses' song at the end of his life. Joshua sang a song (Josh. 10:12–13). So did Deborah (Judges 5), Hannah

(I Sam. 2), and David (II Sam. 22). There was the Song of Solomon, *Shir HaShirim,* about which R. Akiva said, "All songs are holy but the Song of Songs is the holy of holies" (Mishna Yadayim 3:5). The tenth song has not yet been sung. It is the song of the Messiah.[1]

Many biblical texts speak of the power of music to restore the soul. When Saul was depressed, David would play for him and his spirit would be restored (I Sam. 16). David himself was known as the "sweet singer of Israel" (II Sam. 23:1). Elisha called for a harpist to play so that the prophetic spirit could rest upon him (II Kings 3:15). The Levites sang in the Temple. Every day, in Judaism, we preface our morning prayers with *Pesukei DeZimra,* the "Verses of Song," with their magnificent crescendo, Psalm 150, in which instruments and the human voice combine to sing God's praises.

Mystics go further and speak of the song of the universe, what Pythagoras called "the music of the spheres." This is what Psalm 19 means when it says, "The heavens declare the glory of God; the skies proclaim the work of His hands.... There is no speech, there are no words, where their voice is not heard. Their music[2] carries throughout the earth, their words to the end of the world" (Ps. 19:2–5). Beneath the silence, audible only to the inner ear, creation sings to its Creator.

So, when we pray, we do not read; we sing. When we engage with sacred texts, we do not recite; we chant. Every text and every time has, in Judaism, its own specific melody. There are different tunes for Shaḥarit, Minḥa, and Maariv, the morning, afternoon, and evening prayers. There are different melodies and moods for the prayers for a weekday, Shabbat, the three pilgrimage festivals – Passover, Shavuot, and Sukkot (which have much musically in common but also tunes distinctive to each) – and for the High Holy Days, Rosh HaShana and Yom Kippur.

There are different tunes for different texts. There is one kind of cantillation for Torah, another for the *haftara* from the prophetic books, and yet another for *Ketuvim,* the Writings, especially the five megillot. There is a particular chant for studying the texts of the Oral Torah: Mishna and Gemara. So by music alone we can tell what kind of

1. *Tanḥuma, Beshallaḥ* 10; *Shir HaShirim Zuta* 1:1.
2. *Kavam,* literally, "their line," possibly meaning the reverberating string of a musical instrument.

day it is and what kind of text is being used. Jewish texts and times are not colour-coded but music-coded. The map of holy words is written in melodies and songs.

Music has extraordinary power to evoke emotion. The *Kol Nidrei* prayer with which Yom Kippur begins is not really a prayer at all. It is a dry legal formula for the annulment of vows. There can be little doubt that it is its ancient, haunting melody that has given it its hold over the Jewish imagination. It is hard to hear those notes and not feel that you are in the presence of God on the Day of Judgement, standing in the company of Jews of all places and times as they pleaded with heaven for forgiveness. It is the holy of holies of the Jewish soul.[3]

Nor can you sit on Tisha B'Av reading *Eikha*, the book of Lamentations, with its own unique cantillation, and not feel the tears of Jews through the ages as they suffered for their faith and wept as they remembered what they had lost, the pain as fresh as it was the day the Temple was destroyed. Words without music are like a body without a soul.

Beethoven wrote over the manuscript of the third movement of his String Quartet no. 15 in A Minor the words *Neue Kraft fühlend*, "feeling new strength." That is what music expresses and evokes. It is the language of emotion unsicklied by the pale cast of thought. That is what King David meant when he sang to God the words: "You turned my grief into dance; You removed my sackcloth and clothed me with joy, that my heart may sing to You and not be silent" (Ps. 30:12–13). You feel the strength of the human spirit no terror can destroy.

In his book, *Musicophilia*,[4] the late Oliver Sacks (no relative, alas) told the poignant story of Clive Wearing, an eminent musicologist who was struck by a devastating brain infection. The result was acute amnesia. He was unable to remember anything for more than a few seconds. As his wife Deborah put it, "It was as if every waking moment was the first waking moment."[5] Unable to thread experiences together, he was

3. Beethoven came close to it in the opening notes of the sixth movement of the String Quartet no. 14 in C Sharp Minor op. 131, his most sublime and spiritual work.
4. London: Picador, 2018.
5. His wife tells the story in a moving memoir: Deborah Wearing, *Forever Today: A Memoir of Love and Amnesia* (London: Corgi Books, 2005).

caught in an endless present that had no connection with anything that had gone before. One day his wife found him holding a chocolate in one hand and repeatedly covering and uncovering it with the other hand, saying each time, "Look, it's new." "It's the same chocolate," she said. "No," he replied. "Look. It's changed." He had no past at all.

Two things broke through his isolation. One was his love for his wife. The other was music. He could still sing, play the organ, and conduct a choir with all his old skill and verve. What was it about music, Sacks asked, that enabled him, while playing or conducting, to overcome his amnesia? He suggests that when we "remember" a melody, we recall one note at a time, yet each note relates to the whole. He quotes the philosopher of music, Victor Zuckerkandl, who wrote, "Hearing a melody is hearing, having heard, and being about to hear, all at once.... Every melody declares to us that the past can be there without being remembered, the future without being foreknown."[6] Music is a form of sensed continuity that can sometimes break through the most overpowering disconnections in our experience of time.

Faith is more like music than science.[7] Science analyses, music integrates. And as music connects note to note, so faith connects episode to episode, life to life, age to age in a timeless melody that breaks into time. God is the composer and librettist. We are each called on to be voices in the choir, singers of God's song. *Faith is the ability to hear the music beneath the noise.*

So music is a signal of transcendence. The philosopher and musician Roger Scruton writes that it is "an encounter with the pure subject, released from the world of objects, and moving in obedience to the laws of freedom alone."[8] He quotes Rilke: "Words still go softly out towards the unsayable./And music, always new, from palpitating stones/builds

6. Victor Zuckerkandl, *Sound and Symbol: Music and the External World,* trans. Willard R. Trask (Princeton, NJ: Princeton University Press, 1973), 235.
7. I once said to the well-known atheist Richard Dawkins, in the course of a radio conversation, "Richard, religion is music, and you are tone-deaf." He replied, "Yes, it's true, I am tone-deaf, but *there is no music.*"
8. Roger Scruton, *An Intelligent Person's Guide to Philosophy* (London: Duckworth, 1996), 151.

in useless space its godly home."[9] The history of the Jewish spirit is written in its songs.

I once watched a teacher explaining to young children (they were not yet teens) the difference between a physical possession and a spiritual one. He had them build a paper model of Jerusalem. Then (this was in the days of tape recorders) he put on a tape with a song about Jerusalem that he taught to the class. At the end of the session he did something very dramatic. He tore up the model and shredded the tape. He asked the children, "Do we still have the model?" They replied, "No." "Do we still have the song?" They replied, "Yes."

We lose physical possessions, but not spiritual ones. We lost the physical Moses. But we still have the song.

9. Rainer Maria Rilke, *Sonnets to Orpheus,* quoted in Scruton, *Intelligent Person's,* 141.

Let My Teaching Drop as Rain

In the glorious song with which Moses addresses the congregation, he invites the people to think of the Torah – their covenant with God – as if it were like the rain that waters the ground so that it brings forth its produce:

> Let my teaching drop as rain,
> My words descend like dew,
> Like showers on new grass,
> Like abundant rain on tender plants. (Deut. 32:2)

God's word is like rain in a dry land. It brings life. It makes things grow. There is much we can do of our own accord: we can plough the earth and plant the seeds. But in the end our success depends on something beyond our control. If no rain falls, there will be no harvest, whatever preparations we make. So it is with Israel. It must never be tempted into the hubris of saying: "My power and the strength of my hands have produced this wealth for me" (Deut. 8:17).

The sages, however, sensed something more in the analogy. This is how Sifrei (a compendium of commentaries on Numbers and Deuteronomy dating back to the Mishnaic period) puts it:

> Let my teaching drop as rain: Just as the rain is one thing, yet it falls on trees, enabling each to produce tasty fruit according to the kind of tree it is – the vine in its way, the olive tree in its way, and the date palm in its way – so the Torah is one, yet its words yield Scripture, Mishna, laws, and lore. Like showers on new grass: Just as showers fall upon plants and make them grow, some green, some red, some black, some white, so the words of Torah produce teachers, worthy individuals, sages, the righteous, and the pious.[1]

There is only one Torah, yet it has multiple effects. It gives rise to different kinds of teaching, different sorts of virtue. Torah is sometimes seen by its critics as overly prescriptive, as if it sought to make everyone the same. The midrash argues otherwise. The Torah is compared to rain precisely to emphasise that its most important effect is to make each of us grow into what we could become. We are *not* all the same, nor does Torah seek uniformity. As a famous mishna puts it: "When a human being makes many coins from the same mint, they are all the same. God makes everyone in the same image – His image – yet none is the same as another" (Mishna Sanhedrin 4:5).

This emphasis on difference is a recurring theme in Judaism. For example, when Moses asks God to appoint his successor, he uses an unusual phrase: "May the Lord, *God of the spirits of all mankind*, appoint a man over the community" (Num. 27:16). On this, Rashi comments:

> Why is this expression ("God of the spirits of all mankind") used? [Moses] said to him: Lord of the universe, You know each person's character, and that no two people are alike. Therefore, appoint a leader for them who will bear with each person according to his disposition.

1. Sifrei, *Haazinu* 306.

One of the fundamental requirements of a leader in Judaism is that he or she is able to *respect the differences* between human beings. This is a point emphasised by Maimonides in *Guide for the Perplexed*:

> Man is, as you know, the highest form in creation, and he therefore includes the largest number of constituent elements. This is why the human race contains so great a variety of individuals that we cannot discover two persons exactly alike in any moral quality or in external appearance.... This great variety and the necessity of social life are essential elements in man's nature. But the well-being of society demands that there should be a leader able to regulate the actions of man. He must complete every shortcoming, remove every excess, and prescribe for the conduct of all, so that the natural variety should be counterbalanced by the uniformity of legislation, so that social order be well established.[2]

The political problem as Maimonides sees it is how to regulate the affairs of human beings in such a way as to respect their individuality while not creating chaos. A similar point emerges from a surprising rabbinic teaching: "Our rabbis taught: If one sees a crowd of Israelites, one says: Blessed Be He who discerns secrets – because the mind of each is different from that of another, just as the face of each is different from another" (Berakhot 58a).

We would have expected a blessing over a crowd to emphasise its size, its mass: human beings in their collectivity.[3] A crowd is a group large enough for the individuality of the faces to be lost. Yet the blessing stresses the opposite – that each member of a crowd is still an individual with distinctive thoughts, hopes, fears, and aspirations.

The same was true for the relationship between the sages. A mishna states:

> When R. Meir died, the composers of fables ceased. When Ben Azzai died, assiduous students ceased. When Ben Zoma died, the

2. Maimonides, *Guide for the Perplexed*, II:40.
3. See Elias Canetti, *Crowds and Power* (Harmondsworth: Penguin, 1973).

> expositors ceased. When R. Akiva died, the glory of the Torah ceased. When R. Ḥanina died, men of deed ceased. When R. Yose Ketanta died, the pious men ceased. When R. Yoḥanan b. Zakkai died, the lustre of wisdom ceased.... When Rabbi died, humility and the fear of sin ceased. (Mishna Sota 9:15)

There was no single template of the sage. Each had his own distinctive merits, his unique contribution to the collective heritage. In this respect, the sages were merely continuing the tradition of the Torah itself. There is no single role model of the religious hero or heroine in Tanakh. The patriarchs and matriarchs each had their own unmistakable character. Moses, Aaron, and Miriam emerge as different personality types. Kings, priests, and prophets had different roles to play in Israelite society. Even among the prophets, "No two prophesy in the same style," said the sages (Sanhedrin 89a). Elijah was zealous, Elisha gentle. Hosea speaks of love, Amos speaks of justice. Isaiah's visions are simpler and less opaque than those of Ezekiel.

The same applies to even to the revelation at Sinai itself. Each individual heard, in the same words, a different inflection:

> The voice of the Lord is with power (Ps. 29:4): that is, according to the power of each individual, the young, the old, and the very small ones, each according to their power [of understanding]. God said to Israel, "Do not believe that there are many gods in heaven because you heard many voices. Know that I alone am the Lord your God."[4]

According to Maharsha, there are 600,000 interpretations of Torah. Each individual is theoretically capable of a unique insight into its meaning. The French philosopher Emmanuel Levinas commented:

> The Revelation has a particular way of producing meaning, which lies in its calling upon the unique within me. It is as if a multiplicity of persons...were the condition for the plenitude of "absolute

4. Exodus Rabba 29:1.

> truth," as if each person, by virtue of his own uniqueness, were able to guarantee the revelation of one unique aspect of the truth, so that some of its facets would never have been revealed if certain people had been absent from mankind.[5]

Judaism, in short, emphasises the other side of the maxim *E pluribus unum* ("Out of the many, one"). It says: "Out of the One, many."

The miracle of creation is that unity in heaven produces diversity on earth. Torah is the rain that feeds this diversity, allowing each of us to become what only we can be.

5. Emmanuel Levinas, "Revelation in the Jewish Tradition," in *The Levinas Reader*, ed. Sean Hand (Oxford: Wiley-Blackwell, 2001), 190–210.

The Faith of God

After the introduction to his song in *Haazinu,* Moses turns to his central theme, the acts of God in history, beginning with a poetic declaration:

> The Rock, His work is perfect,
> For all His ways are just;
> A God of faith without iniquity
> Righteous and upright is He. (Deut. 32:4)

This is an axiom of prophetic faith. God is just. It is human beings who act unjustly. To this day, this verse is part of *tzidduk hadin,* "accepting the justice" of the bad things that happen to us. It is a central part of the funeral service. Despite our sense of loss, we forgo our anger at what may seem like the cruelty of fate.

There is, however, one ancient rabbinic interpretation of part of this verse that deserves reflection in its own right. It opens the way to one of the most far-reaching and revolutionary of all Jewish ideas. On the phrase "a God of faith," Sifrei states: "'A God of faith' – He who had *faith in the universe* and created it."[1] Creation was an act of faith on the part of God.

When we use the word "faith" in a religious context we naturally assume that the word refers to our faith in God. Understandably so, for it is we who are finite in our understanding, whether of the universe or the full perspective of history. It is we who must make the leap from the known to the unknowable, from the visible to the invisible, from what we see and infer to what lies beyond.

Using the philosophical categories of the West, which come to us from ancient Greece, it makes no sense at all to speak of an act of faith on the part of God. God is, in terms of these categories, omniscient and omnipotent, all-knowing and all-powerful. He is the unmoved mover, the first cause, the necessary being, the unchanging essence of reality.

These propositions are surely true. Yet this is not God as we meet Him in the pages of Tanakh. Instead this is God as a philosophical abstraction, detached from the human drama. If the Torah teaches us anything it is that God is *not* detached from the human drama. He is intimately, even passionately, involved in it. There is a difference between the God of the philosophers and the God of the prophets; between – as Judah Halevi put it – the God of Aristotle and the God of Abraham, even though they are the same God, whose parallel lines meet in infinity.[2]

God as we encounter Him in the Torah takes a risk, monumental in its implications. He creates one being, Homo sapiens, capable of being itself creative; He creates, that is to say, a being in His own image. This one act alters the whole nature of the universe. For there is now a being capable of language, thought, reflection, imagination, and choice: the one being capable of conceiving the idea of God, but also, given the very nature of freedom and the human imagination, the one being capable of rebelling against God. The implication is the most far-reaching in all of creation, for it means that there is now one form of life that can choose between obedience and disobedience, good and evil, turning nature to good ends or, God forbid, destroying it altogether.

1. Sifrei, *Haazinu* 307.
2. *Kuzari*, IV:16; this point was later made by Blaise Pascal in his *Pensées* (trans. A. J. Krailsheimer [Harmondsworth: Penguin, 1966], 309).

Human freedom, the result of language and self-consciousness, is the great unknown and unknowable within the otherwise orderly processes of nature mapped by science. There can never be a science of freedom, for the very concept is a contradiction in terms. Science is about causes, freedom about purposes. Science explains phenomena in terms of other phenomena that preceded them. Free action, by contrast, is explicable only in terms of the future we intend to bring about, not any past event, historical, biochemical, or neurophysiological. To be sure, there are many influences on human behaviour, some genetic, others cultural, environmental, social, economic, and political. But they are *influences*, not *causes* in the sense in which that term is used in the natural sciences.

For almost every act we do, we could have chosen otherwise (the qualification "almost" is necessary, for there are some acts – from reflex movements to unwilling behaviour under threat of death – that are not free in such a way as to render their agent responsible for them; Jewish law calls such behaviour *ones*, i.e., action under coercion). Time and again in the course of civilisation, human freedom has been called into question. There were some who believed in astrology: the fault lay not in us but in our stars. Philosophers like Spinoza and scientists like Comte believed that since we are physical beings in the material world, we are a form of matter, and all matter is governed by laws of cause and effect. The most recent form of determinism comes from neo-Darwinians. Human action is genetically determined. As one of the most extreme proponents of this view puts it, human beings are a gene's way of producing another gene.[3] There were even figures within Judaism itself – the medieval philosopher Hasdai Crescas is the most famous example – who held that free will was an illusion and that the only operative principle in human affairs is divine providence (this view was, according to Josephus, held by the sectarians of the Second Temple period known as the Essenes). Maimonides, however, was emphatic in ruling out these views:

3. This, roughly speaking, is the argument of Richard Dawkins, *The Selfish Gene* (Oxford: Oxford University Press, 1989).

> Free will is bestowed on every human being. If one desires to turn towards the good way and be righteous, he has the power to do so. If one wishes to turn towards the evil way and be wicked, he is at liberty to do so.... Every human being may become righteous like Moses our teacher, or wicked like Jeroboam; wise or foolish, merciful or cruel, niggardly or generous, and so with all other qualities.... This doctrine is an important principle, the pillar of the law and the commandments, as it is said, "See I have set before you today life and good, death and evil" (Deut. 30:15), and again it is written, "See, I am setting before you today a blessing and a curse" (Deut. 11:26). This means that the power is in your hands, and whatever a man desires to do among the things that human beings do, he can do, whether they are good or evil.... If God had decreed that a person should be either righteous or wicked, or if there were some force inherent in his nature which irresistibly drew him to a particular course... what room would there be for the whole of the Torah? By what right or justice could God punish the wicked or reward the righteous? "Shall not the Judge of all the earth deal justly?" (Gen. 18:25).[4]

Some consequences of this view are obvious. It means that we are responsible for what we do. Judaism is an ethic of responsibility. It also means that we are capable of recognising and acknowledging our mistakes and choosing to act differently in the future. Hence the concept of *teshuva*. This is turn entails that the future need not be like the past. With this realisation a new concept was born: history as the arena of human development and growth. As the late John H. Plumb pointed out, Jews were the first people to attach significance to, and see meaning in, history.[5]

But there is another far more paradoxical consequence. God, by entering the human situation, enters time, and thus uncertainty, and thus risk. The grant of freedom to humanity was an immense act of self-limitation on the part of God – what the exponents of Lurianic kabbala

4. Maimonides, *Mishneh Torah, Hilkhot Teshuva* 5:1–4.
5. John H. Plumb, *The Death of the Past* (London: Pelican, 1973), 56–57.

called *tzimtzum*. The nature of this drama is made clear at almost the beginning of biblical time:

> Then the Lord said to Cain, "Why are you angry? Why is your face downcast? If you do what is right, will you not be accepted? But if you do not do what is right, sin is crouching at your door; it desires to have you, but you must master it." Now Cain said to his brother – and while they were in the field, Cain attacked his brother Abel and killed him. (Gen. 4:8)

Here the entire paradox of the divine-human encounter is present in its pristine form. God knows that Cain is jealous of Abel and plans to kill him. That is why He speaks to him and warns him. Yet Cain does not listen. The murder takes place. How did God let it happen? The answer can only be: a grant of freedom to X by a superior power, which is suspended every time X acts in a way of which the superior power disapproves, is not a grant of freedom. This is a logical proposition true in all possible worlds. God does not abandon the world. He speaks to mankind; He teaches us how to behave; He instructs us in the ways of justice and equity, mercy, and compassion. But if mankind closes its ears and refuses to listen, there is nothing God can do, short of taking away its freedom, the very thing He granted in creating mankind.

Hence creation involves risk. For us that is true of *all* acts of creation. Every technology can be misused. Every form of art can become idolatry. For God it is true of only *one* act of creation, namely, the making of humanity. That is why here alone in the Torah's account of creation, we find not a simple "Let there be" but a deliberative prologue, "Let us make man in our image after our own likeness" (Gen. 1:26).

The creation of mankind was anything but straightforward. Homo sapiens (neo-Darwinism notwithstanding) is *not* simply an evolutionary variant of other forms of life. The use of language, the future tense, an ability to recall the remote past, self-consciousness and deliberative rationality – the things that make Homo sapiens unique – are qualitative leaps, not quantitative developments. A lump of metal and a car may be composed of the same elements but they are not the same thing, or the same kind of thing. That we share many elements of our

DNA with the primates does not mean that man is simply a "naked ape" or a "gene-producing machine." This is a fallacy – intelligible, even at a superficial level plausible, but a fallacy nonetheless. Because we can conceive intentions and act on them, no purely causal explanation of human behaviour will ever be adequate. We are dust of the earth, but there is within us the breath of God.

In creating mankind God was therefore taking the risk that one of His creations might turn against its Creator. Faith means the courage to take a risk. An extraordinary passage in the Babylonian Talmud explains this precisely:

> R. Yehuda said in the name of Rav: When the Holy One, Blessed Be He, wished to create man, He first created a company of ministering angels and said to them, Is it your desire that we make man in our image? They answered, Sovereign of the universe, what will be his deeds? Such and such will be his deeds, He replied [He showed them the course of human history]. They thereupon exclaimed, Sovereign of the universe, "what is man that you are mindful of him and the son of man that you think of him?" (Ps. 8:5). At this, He stretched out His finger and consumed them with fire. The same thing happened with a second company of angels. The third company said to him, Sovereign of the universe, what did it avail the former angels when they spoke to You? The whole world is Yours; do whatever You wish. God then created mankind. When it came to the age of the Flood and of the division [of tongues, i.e., the Tower of Babel] whose deeds were corrupt they said to Him, Sovereign of the universe, did not the first angels speak correctly? God replied: "Even to old age I am the same, and even to grey hairs I will forbear" (Is. 46:4). (Sanhedrin 38b)

The central question of faith is not "Does God exist?" but "Given that God exists, how does man exist?" The angels had reason on their side. Knowing in advance the course of human history, the predominance of war over peace, corruption over justice, cruelty over compassion, what reason could there be for introducing so wayward a creature as man into the universe?

To this, Judaism proposes a surpassingly beautiful answer. God has faith in man. To be sure, that faith is often abused, not to say betrayed. Yet God has infinite patience. "Even to grey hairs I will forbear." Though human beings inflict suffering on one another, God does not give up on His creation. We are here because of an act of supreme love on the part of the author of being. However corrupt we are, He does not relinquish the faith that we will change. However lost, He does not cease to believe that one day we will find our way back to Him. For in His Torah, He has given us the map, the code, the guide, the way. Even a handful of righteous individuals justifies His faith in humanity.

One of the cruellest of all misrepresentations of Judaism is the claim that it is not a religion of love. Judaism is a faith suffused with love: love of God, love of neighbour, and, repeatedly, love of the stranger. But infinitely transcending man's love of God is *God's love of mankind,* for which (in the necessarily human language, the only language we can know) He suffers every time human beings wrong one another, and yet He is prepared to suffer rather than take from mankind the unique gift of freedom He bestowed on them, which is necessarily freedom to do wrong as well as freedom to do right.

According to Judaism, the classic questions of Western theology are precisely wrong, upside down – for the Torah is not a human book of God, but God's book of humankind. *More than we search for God, God searches for us,* asking us, as He did to Adam and Eve, "Where are you?" In its simple way, the comment of the Sifrei is as profound as theology gets. Creation, even God's creation when it involves endowing a creature with the capacity to act in freedom, involves risk and therefore faith. "God of faith" means, "He who had *faith in the universe* and created it." I know of no lovelier account of the (often unlovely) human condition.

We are here because someone wanted us to be. We are free because the Master of all made space for our freedom. We are at home in the universe to the extent that we make of our universe a home for God.

A Warped and Twisted Generation

In his great concluding song, Moses delivers a visionary overview of Jewish history. God as we encounter Him in the Hebrew Bible is not a theoretical construct, a First Cause who sets the universe in motion and then retires from the affairs of mankind. To the contrary, He is involved in history. He is a God of engagement in the arena of mankind.

History to the eye of faith is not what Joseph Heller once called it: "A trash bag of random coincidences torn open in a wind."[1] It is instead a drama, a narrative, the story of the covenant, the mutual commitment on the part of Israel to be loyal to God, and of God to be a guardian of Israel, leading it, in the words of the psalm, "in the paths of righteousness for His name's sake" (Ps. 23:3). Hence reflection on history is fundamental to the Judaic vision. As Moses himself puts it in the song:

> Remember the days of old,
> Consider the years of many generations.
> Ask your father and he will declare to you,
> Your elders and they will tell you. (Deut. 32:7)

1. *Good as Gold* (New York: Simon & Schuster, 1997), 72.

There will, says Moses to future generations, be times when you feel deserted by God. It is then that you must reflect, not on God but on humanity. God is just, but human beings are not:

> The Rock, His work is perfect,
> For all His ways are just;
> A God of faith without iniquity
> Righteous and upright is He.
> Is destruction His?
> No: the blemish belongs to His children,
> A warped and twisted generation. (Deut. 32:4–5)

One commentary to these words deserves close attention. It comes from the Netziv. In 1854, he became head of the Volozhin yeshiva which, under his leadership, became a centre of Jewish learning in Russia, attracting many outstanding students, among them Rabbi Avraham Kook, first Ashkenazic chief rabbi of pre-state Israel, and the Hebrew poet Hayim Nahman Bialik.

The Netziv was a man of immense scholarship and broad horizons. He wrote a commentary to the Sifrei (*Emek HaNetziv*), another to the geonic work *She'iltot* (*Haamek She'ala*), and an important collection of responsa, *Meshiv Davar*. As a teacher, he was devoted to his students, who equally revered him. An early supporter of the proto-Zionist movement Hibat Zion, he encouraged Orthodox Jews to settle in Israel. His son, Rabbi Meir Bar-Ilan, became a leading Religious Zionist, after whom Bar-Ilan University is named. The Netziv was greatly opposed to the establishment of separatist Orthodox communities, and believed that the task of Orthodox Jews was to be an influence in the Jewish world as a whole through teaching Torah. His commentary to the Torah, *Haamek Davar*, is a magnificent work, reflecting both his erudition and originality.

Central to his understanding of the two verses above is that they relate to the two great tragedies of ancient Israel, the destruction of the First and Second Temples. In each case, the first half of the verse refers to the former, the second to the latter. There was, however, a massive difference between the two events. Following rabbinic tradition and the plain sense of the prophetic books, the Netziv holds that the Israelites of the First Temple period were guilty of cardinal sins: idolatry, murder, and forbidden sexual relations. They had drifted tragically far from the life of Torah. By the time of the Second Temple, however, many of these faults had been overcome.

The Babylonian Talmud attributes the destruction at the hands of the Romans to *sinat ḥinam*, internal animosities between Jews, "baseless hatred." The Netziv says candidly that at that time Jews were "occupied with Torah and the service of God." However, that led, he says, to "bloodshed for the sake of heaven." How so? "Because they judged anyone who transgressed in any respect to be a Sadducee or traitor or heretic, and as a result their conduct became corrupt, despite the fact that it was for the sake of heaven." That is why they are called a "warped and twisted generation," because good and evil were so interwoven in their conduct, and "it is difficult to separate good and evil when evil is done in a holy cause."

In the following verse, Moses uses the phrase "you foolish people [*am naval*] and unwise" (Deut. 32:6). This too, says the Netziv, refers to the men of the Second Temple. He cites the *Targum*, which translates the phrase *am naval* not as "a foolish people" but as "the people who received the Torah." This is a strange translation. The Netziv explains that the word *naval* comes from the same root as *novelet*, which means "unripe fruit" or "the incomplete or lesser substitute for something else." There is a midrashic tradition that the Torah is *novelet ḥokhma shel maala*, "a substitute for, an incomplete version of the divine wisdom."[2] In other words, God's wisdom as it is in itself is infinitely greater than that part of it – the Torah – which He has communicated to human beings. According to the *Targum*, therefore, the phrase in *Haazinu* should be read as "the people which, though it received the Torah, remained unwise."

This, says the Netziv, was the situation during the last days of the Second Temple. We have no problem in understanding why the people of the First Temple suffered defeat. They were far removed from the Torah, guilty of cardinal sins. However, the men of the late Second Temple "studied and laboured in the Torah, which prepares us to be righteous and upright." That is why Moses is so caustic about them, for

2. Genesis Rabba 17:5.

they "remained unwise, and were not careful to avoid bad conduct." The tragedy of the Second Temple period is that "some of the worst behaviour came from those who were outstanding Torah scholars [*ba hakilkul al yedei gedolei Torah*]."

This is no stray comment on the part of the Netziv. He makes it in several other places in his Torah commentary.[3] However, his clearest exposition comes in his preface to the book of Genesis. Genesis, he notes, is called by the sages *Sefer HaYashar*, "The Book of the Upright." Why so? asks the Netziv. Once again he turns to the phrase in *Parashat Haazinu*, "a warped and twisted generation," which again he applies to the people of the Second Temple:

> Our explanation [of this phrase] is that they were righteous and pious [*tzaddikim veḥasidim*] and laboured in the Torah. But they were not upright in their dealings with the world. Thus, as a result of the baseless hatred in their hearts, they suspected anyone who did not act in accordance with their opinions of being a Sadducee and a heretic. As a result they descended to murder and other evils, until eventually the Temple was destroyed. It is about this that Moses vindicates divine justice, for the Holy One, Blessed Be He, is upright [*yashar*] and does not tolerate righteous people such as these unless they act uprightly in their dealings with the world rather than in a twisted manner even though their intention is for the sake of heaven, for this causes the ruination of the world and the destruction of society [*ḥurban habriya veharisut yishuv haaretz*].
>
> This therefore was the merit of the patriarchs, that beside the fact that they were righteous and pious and loved God to the utmost extent, they were also *upright*. In their relations with gentiles – even the worst idolaters – they acted out of love, and sought their good, for this is what allows the world to endure. Thus we find that Abraham, though he hated their wickedness, prostrated himself in prayer for the people of Sodom, for he wanted them to survive. On this the Midrash Rabba says, "'You

3. See *Haamek Davar* to Deut. 4:14 and Num. 35:34.

> love righteousness and hate wickedness' (Ps. 45:8) – this is what God said to Abraham, namely: You love to justify your fellow human beings and hate to condemn them as wicked…" Similarly we see how readily Isaac let himself be placated by his enemies, and on the basis of a few apologetic words from Avimelekh and his companions, he made his peace with them. So too we find with Jacob who, though he knew that Laban sought to destroy him, spoke to him gently, on which the Midrash says, "Better the anger of the patriarchs than the meekness of their children."[4] Thus we learn much from the way the patriarchs conducted themselves with civility [*derekh eretz*].

The Netziv's comments are not in themselves exceptional. We find many such remarks by the sages in their reflections on the tragedies that befell them at the hands of the Romans. One such passage – used by the Netziv as a prooftext – is to be found in the Tosefta:

> Why was Jerusalem at the time of the First Temple destroyed? Because of the idolatry, forbidden sexual relationships, and bloodshed that were to be found therein. But as for the Second Temple, we recognise that its inhabitants laboured in the Torah and were scrupulous in giving tithes. Why then were they exiled? Because they loved money and hated one another – which teaches us that God hates hatred between people, and Scripture reckons it as equal to idolatry, forbidden sex, and bloodshed combined.[5]

The Netziv is unusual only in the degree to which he saw the problem as fundamental. He returned to it time and again. It is possible, in his words, to be "righteous and pious and to labour in the Torah" and yet nonetheless to be guilty of "twistedness" (*akmumiyut*) in one's dealings with others – indeed to be part of what the Torah itself calls "a warped and twisted generation." This is no minor

4. Genesis Rabba 74:10.
5. Tosefta, Menaḥot 13:4.

matter. Because of it, the Second Temple was destroyed, Jerusalem was reduced to rubble, and the Jewish people were condemned to the longest exile in history.

We recognise in the Netziv's words a theme set out with great passion and depth by the prophets. There are failings to which intensely religious people are sometimes prone, namely, indifference to the injustices of society, a willingness to overlook corruption within their own ranks, and a tendency to believe that attachment to God relieves one of the duty to be upright, civil, and gracious in one's dealings with human beings.

Two phenomena are often confused: righteousness and *self*-righteousness. Outwardly they appear similar but between them is all the difference in the world. The righteous see the good in people, the self-righteous see the bad. The righteous have a high opinion of others, the self-righteous a high opinion of themselves. The righteous leave us feeling enlarged, the self-righteous leave us feeling diminished. The righteous lift us up, the self-righteous put us down.

The Netziv could not have set out the alternatives more starkly. The patriarchs of Genesis were generous in their behaviour even to idolaters. The Torah scholars of the Second Temple – at least some of them – were vicious in their conduct even towards other religious Jews if they acted in any way differently from them, treating them as if they were heretics or sectarians.

That, suggests the Netziv, is why we must return time and again to Tanakh, especially to Genesis, for though it contains narrative rather than law, it teaches something that cannot be taught by law alone, namely, how to behave uprightly in one's dealings with others.

Law alone is no defence against self-righteousness. Indeed law alone can *lead* to self-righteousness, for it can convince those who study it that the law is on their side. It may be on their side, but what the law, in and of itself, cannot teach us is that the other person is also a human being, with feelings that can be injured and with merits that may not be apparent to those who view humanity in black-and-white terms, dividing it, as did the Second Temple sectarians, into the "children of light" and the "children of darkness."

Narrative teaches us the complexity of the moral life and the light-and-shade to be found in any human personality. Without this, self-righteousness can destroy the very perceptions and nuances, the tolerance and generosity of spirit on which society depends.

Vengeance

One of the most tragic moments in Western civilisation came when Christians began distinguishing between what they called "the Old Testament God of vengeance" and the "New Testament God of love." This was not a small error. One trembles to think how many Jews lost their lives because of it. It survives today, even among good and sensitive people. There is hardly a week when I do not see some reference to it in the national press. It is one of those taken-for-granted assumptions that lie buried so deep within a culture that rarely if ever are they examined in the clear light of day.

Let us state a proposition so obvious that it should go without saying. According to Christianity, the God of the Old Testament and the God of the New Testament is the same God. If He were not, the whole structure of Christianity would crumble and fall. There was one thinker – Marcion in the second century – who reached the alternative conclusion, namely, that the values of Judaism and Christianity are so different that they cannot be seen as worship of the same God. Therefore Christianity would have to stand on the New Testament alone. The Old Testament could not be, for Christians, sacred scripture. The Marcionite option was rejected and branded a heresy.

It follows therefore that if vengeance is wrong, it could not have been commanded by God – not to Christians, and not to Jews. If it were commanded, we must be able to make moral sense of it, whether we are Jews or Christians. The idea that God can change His mind on something as fundamental as this must undermine all faith. For if we believe we are commanded anything at all by God, we must believe that God, a decade or a century from now, will not change His mind and permit what He had previously forbidden or forbid what He had previously permitted. And if we believe we are beloved of God, we must believe that this love, too, will last – that God will not cast us off in favour of someone else, at sometime else. For God is faithful; He does not go back on His word. A god who is faithless would not be a god worthy of worship.

In fact, God forbids vengeance (Lev. 19:18). He commands forgiveness, as Joseph forgave his brothers who sought to kill him – and as we, on Judaism's holiest day, ask Him to forgive us. To quote Maimonides:

> As long as one nurses a grievance and keeps it in mind, one may come to take revenge. The Torah therefore emphatically warns us not to bear a grudge, so that the impression of the wrong shall be wholly obliterated and no longer remembered. This is the right principle. It alone makes society and human interaction possible.[1]

Note that Maimonides talks about human interaction, not Jewish interaction. He means this as a general rule for all humanity.

However, *Parashat Haazinu* contains lines (and there are many others elsewhere, in both the Hebrew Bible and the New Testament) that are difficult to reconcile with an ethic of non-revenge:

> "I lift My hand to heaven and declare:
> As surely as I live forever,
> When I sharpen My flashing sword
> And My hand grasps it in judgement,
> I will take vengeance on My adversaries

1. Maimonides, *Mishneh Torah, Hilkhot Deot* 7:8.

> And repay those who hate Me..."
> Rejoice, O nations, with His people,
> For He will avenge the blood of His servants;
> He will take vengeance on His enemies
> And make atonement for His land and people. (Deut. 32:40–43)

Three thinkers, Jan Assmann, the Jewish scholar Henri Atlan, and the Christian theologian Miroslav Volf, have something deeply insightful to say about divine vengeance. Assmann points out a fundamental difference between the civilisation described in the Hebrew Bible and other ancient civilisations. In the others, the human king takes on the attributes of a god. The anger of the king is the anger of the god; the latter legitimates the former. In avenging himself against his enemies, the king is doing god's work. Violence receives religious sanction. In the Hebrew Bible, by contrast, there is a profound and unbridgeable distance between the human king and God. Anger is "theologised" and thus "transferred...from earth to heaven."[2]

Atlan argues likewise, suggesting that "the best way to rid the world of the violent sacred is to reject it onto a transcendence." The "transcendence of violence" results in "its being expelled from the normal horizon of things." In other words – vengeance is removed from human calculation. It is God, not man, who is entitled to exercise it.[3] To be sure, there are times when God commands human beings to act on His behalf – the battles against the Midianites and the Amalekites are two obvious examples. But once prophecy ceases, as it has done since late Second Temple times, so too does violence in the name of God.

Volf agrees with this analysis, and adds that "in a world of violence we are faced with an inescapable alternative: either God's violence or human violence." He adds:

> Most people who insist on God's "nonviolence" cannot resist using violence themselves (or tacitly sanctioning its use by others). They deem the talk of God's judgment irreverent, but

2. Quoted in Miroslav Volf, *Exclusion and Embrace* (Nashville: Abingdon, 1996), 297.
3. Quoted in ibid., 302–3.

> think nothing of entrusting judgment into human hands.... And so violence thrives, secretly nourished by belief in a God who refuses to wield the sword.[4]

Volf, who won the 2002 Grawemeyer Award for his book *Exclusion and Embrace,* from which these words are taken, is a native Croatian whose theology was shaped by the experience of living and teaching in the former Yugoslavia throughout the ethnic wars of the 1990s. Real confrontation with violence makes one think differently about biblical texts. What Volf goes on to say next is remarkable for its brutal candour:

> My thesis that the practice of nonviolence requires a belief in divine vengeance will be unpopular with many Christians, especially theologians in the West. To the person who is inclined to dismiss it, I suggest imagining that you are delivering a lecture in a war zone.... Among your listeners are people whose cities and villages have been first plundered, then burned and leveled to the ground, whose daughters and sisters have been raped, whose fathers and brothers have had their throats slit. The topic of the lecture: a Christian attitude to violence. The thesis: we should not retaliate since God is perfect noncoercive love. Soon you would discover that it takes the quiet of a suburban home for the birth of the thesis that human nonviolence corresponds to God's refusal to judge. In a scorched land, soaked in blood of the innocent, it will invariably die. And as one watches it die, one will do well to reflect about many other pleasant captivities of the liberal mind.[5]

These are words that, to me, have the ring of truth as well as honesty. I think of the Jews of the Middle Ages, who saw their fellow Jews accused of killing Christian children to drink their blood, of poisoning wells, desecrating the host, and spreading the plague (the classic work is Joshua

4. Ibid., 303.
5. Ibid., 304.

Trachtenberg's *The Devil and the Jews*[6]), and then murdered en masse in the name of the God of love. We can still hear their responses: they are recorded for us in many of the lamentations, *kinot*, we say on Tisha B'Av.

Yes, they appeal to God's vengeance, which is to say, to God's justice. But Jews do not seek to take vengeance. That is something you leave to God. There is a justice we will not see this side of the end of days. In the meantime, it is sufficient to live, and affirm life, and seek no more than the right to be true to your faith without fear – no more than the right to live and defend that selfsame right for your children. The search for perfect justice is not for us, here, now.[7] It is – as Moses taught the Israelites in the great song he sang at the end of his life – something that faith demands we leave to God, who alone knows the human heart, who alone knows what is just in a world of conflicting claims, and who will establish perfect justice at a time, and in a way, of His choosing, not ours.[8]

In a world of ethnic conflict, fuelled by sometimes deadly religious fervour, that is a truth in need of reinstatement. There are things we must leave to God. Otherwise we will find ourselves in the condition of humanity before the Flood, when the world was "filled with violence" and God "regretted that He had made man on earth, and His heart was filled with pain" (Gen. 6:6). Vengeance belongs to God. It must not be practised by human beings in the name of God.

---

6. Joshua Trachtenberg, *The Devil and the Jews* (Philadelphia: Jewish Publication Society of America, 1983).
7. Thomas Sowell, *The Quest for Cosmic Justice* (New York: Free Press, 2002).
8. More recently, remarkable empirical evidence has emerged, confirming the argument presented here. In his book, *Big Gods: How Religion Transformed Cooperation and Conflict* (Princeton, NJ: Princeton University Press, 2013), 33–54, Ara Norenzayan assembles research data that show overwhelmingly that people and cultures that believe in a punishing God are nicer, kinder, more law-abiding, and more forgiving than those who believe in a non-punishing, systematically forgiving God. See also Dominic Johnson, *God Is Watching You: How Fear of God Makes Us Human* (New York: Oxford University Press, 2015).

Vezot Haberakha
וזאת הברכה

Vezot Haberakha is Moses' blessing, delivered in the last day of his life, to the Israelites, tribe by tribe. It concludes poignantly with Moses' death and his burial, seemingly by the hand of God, in the land of Moab, so that "to this day no one knows his burial place" (Deut. 34:6). The closing verses of the Torah are a tribute to the greatest leader and prophet the Israelites ever had, yet the ultimate accolade the Torah gives him is touching in its simplicity. He was "the man Moses" (Num. 12:3), "the servant of the Lord" (Deut. 34:5). The *parasha*, read not as an ordinary Shabbat portion, but on the festival of Simḥat Torah, is a profound commentary on mortality and the human condition. The Moses we encounter in the Torah is simply a human being made great by the task he was set and by the humility that made him supremely one through whom the word and power of God flowed.

The first two essays are about the preamble to the blessings, which talk of "the love of nations" (Deut. 33:3) and speak of the Torah as "an inheritance of the congregation of Jacob" (33:4). The next three are about what Moses' life teaches us, about service as greatness, about the human condition, and about mortality. The last essay is about the extraordinary structure of the Mosaic books, and of the Hebrew Bible as a whole, in that they end without an ending. What does this tell us about the message the Torah seeks to convey?

The Love of Nations

Like Jacob at the end of his life, Moses at the end of his blesses the next generation. There is something particularly beautiful about this. Having been relentless in his criticism of the people throughout the book of Deuteronomy, Moses softens, and lets them know in his final words how much God loves them: "Happy are you, Israel. Who is like you, a people saved by the Lord?" (Deut. 33:29).

Just as he handed on his role to his successor, Joshua, with a full heart,[1] so here he blesses them with a full heart, giving each tribe[2] the words that would encourage them to fulfil their destiny. On the opening words of the *parasha*, "This is the blessing with which Moses, the man of God, blessed the Israelites before his death" (Deut. 33:1), there is a beautiful midrash: "Moses was not called 'the man of God' until he

1. God had told Moses to "lay his hand on him," ordaining him to be his successor, but the text says that Moses laid "his hands on him," in the plural – signalling, said the sages, that he did so with magnanimity (Num. 27:18, 23; see Rashi ad loc.).
2. Except the tribe of Simeon. It seems that Moses foresaw that Simeon's descendants would be scattered among the tribes, as Jacob had indicated in his deathbed words, and thus did not merit a blessing of their own.

blessed the Israelites."[3] You do not need to be Godly to criticise. Anyone can do that. Godliness lies with those who praise, defend, and bless.

I want in this essay to focus on one verse near the beginning of Moses' speech, whose meaning is obscure but whose importance is great. Moses begins with a reference to the giving of the Torah at Mount Sinai: "The Lord came from Sinai and dawned over them from Seir; He shone forth from Mount Paran. He came with myriads of holy ones and with His right hand gave them a law of fire" (Deut. 33:2). Two verses on, he returns to the theme: "Moses commanded us the Torah, an inheritance of the congregation of Jacob" (33:4).

Both of these verses became important texts in the history of Judaism. The first, with its vivid description of the revelation at Sinai, gave rise to the image of Torah as written "with black fire on white fire" (Y. Shekalim 6:1). The second became – along with the *Shema* – among the first words that a Jewish parent is to teach his or her child.[4] Its significance is the subject of the next essay.

It is the verse between these two (33:3) that is difficult at every level. The text is cryptic and obscure, and many translators admit that its precise meaning is unrecoverable. Here are four recent translations:

> Lover, indeed, of the people/Their hallowed are all in Your hand.
> They followed in Your steps/Accepting Your pronouncements. (Jewish Publication Society)[5]

> Although there is love for nations/All Your holy ones are in Your hand.
> They follow Your footsteps/And uphold Your word. (Aryeh Kaplan)[6]

3. *Pesikta DeRav Kahana, Vezot Haberakha.*
4. Maimonides, *Mishneh Torah, Hilkhot Talmud Torah* 1:6.
5. *The Holy Scriptures: The New JPS Translation According to the Traditional Hebrew Text* (Philadelphia: Jewish Publication Society, 1985).
6. *The Living Torah: The Five Books of Moses and the Haftarot* (Brooklyn, NY: Moznaim, 1981).

> Yes, lover of peoples is He/All His holy ones in Your hand,
> And they are flung down at Your feet/He bears Your utterances. (Robert Alter)[7]
>
> Though He has-affection-for the peoples/All His holy-ones (are) in Your hand,
> They place themselves at Your feet/Bearing Your words. (Everett Fox)[8]

A key difficulty lies in knowing what the first phrase – in Hebrew, *Af ḥovev amim* – means, especially the word *amim*, "peoples." Moses is blessing the Israelites and talking to them. Does "peoples" refer to the nations of the world? Or is it a reference to the tribes, each of which has become, as it were, a people in its own right? Aryeh Kaplan lists some of the interpretations:

- Although beloved by nations (*Targum Yonatan*, Hizkuni)
- Although He loves gentiles (who become proselytes; Rashbam)
- He also loves them above all nations (Sifrei, Rabbenu Baḥya)
- He also loves the tribes of Israel (*Targum*, Saadia Gaon)
- Although He loves the tribes, all Your holy ones (Levi) are in Your hand (Ibn Ezra)
- Although He shelters the tribes (Nahmanides, Gersonides)
- He spared His people, [and] all His holy ones are in His hands (Septuagint)
- Also to take nations to duty, You take all Your holy ones in Your hand (Samson Raphael Hirsch)

The list shows that many, even most, commentators understand "peoples" to refer to the tribes of Israel – a natural reading, given that the chapter

7. *The Five Books of Moses: A Translation with Commentary* (New York: W. W. Norton, 2008).
8. *The Five Books of Moses: Genesis, Exodus, Leviticus, Numbers, Deuteronomy* (New York: Schocken, 2000).

is about Moses blessing each of the tribes. Rashbam's suggestion is fascinating: before turning to the tribes, Moses specifically includes converts – signalling that the children of Israel are not a race or ethnicity but a religious community defined by their covenant with God. Whoever wishes to join and undertake the responsibilities of that covenant may do so. Rashbam is here echoing the sentiment of Maimonides' famous letter to Obadiah the Proselyte, written at about the same time, in which he explains that converts are the spiritual children of Abraham, and should not think of themselves as inferior to the biological children of Abraham.

Several commentaries reflect the particular concerns of the commentators. Hizkuni, for example, reads the verse as: "Even though God may [temporarily] favour the nations by handing the Israelites over to them, nonetheless Your holy ones remain in Your hands. They are beaten and crushed because of [their faith in] You, but they continue to uphold Your word." It is widely believed that his father was tortured at a time of religious persecution, and his interpretation here bears the mark of suffering and grief.

Samson Raphael Hirsch reads it to mean, "You guide the nations towards a consciousness of moral duty [reading the root letters of *ḥovev*, Ḥ-V-V, as an intensive form of Ḥ-V, 'obligation'] by taking Your holy ones [i.e., Israel] in Your hand [i.e., as Your channel of communication to the world]." Hirsch here is expressing his characteristic sense of the "mission of Israel" as the teachers of monotheism and ethics to humanity.

Sforno understands it thus:

> Even though You love all peoples, as it is said, "You shall be beloved to Me more than other peoples" (Ex. 19:5), implying that God loves all peoples, though not all in the same way, as it is said, "Precious is humankind because it was created in the image" of God (Mishna Avot 3:14), still all Your holy ones, i.e., Israel, are in Your hands, as it is said, "You shall be to Me a kingdom of priests and a holy nation" (Ex. 19:6) and "Beloved are Israel for they are called the children of God" (Mishna Avot 3:14).

Sforno is writing against the backdrop of the Italian Renaissance, its universalism, and humanism. For him, the relationship between Israel and the nations is the same as that between priest and people. God loves all humanity and has chosen Israel to bring all people to the recognition of His existence and sovereignty.[9]

A fascinating reading is given in a manuscript published for the first time relatively recently, *Pitron Torah*.[10] The unknown author, whom Urbach conjectures to have been among the circle of Rabbi Hai Gaon (Sura, late ninth century), quotes the interpretation of the Karaite scholar Benjamin ben Moses Nahawendi (Nehavend, Persia, c. 830–860):

> The peoples of the world – all the holy ones thereof – they too love the Torah, that which is in Your hand, for the scriptures of the Edomites and Ishmaelites [i.e., Christians and Muslims], they took from the words written in the Torah. They follow in Your footsteps, meaning: they, the peoples, have become beloved to the One who leads. They carry Your utterances – this means that they carry, take, and accept some of the words of the Torah – and thus people say, "Moses commanded us the Torah." However the congregation of Jacob [i.e., the Jews] have received it as a heritage.

This is a remarkable reading, all the more so given that it comes from more than a thousand years ago. Nahawendi is emphasising the commonalities of the three Abrahamic monotheisms and the indebtedness of Christianity and Islam to Judaism. Whether we follow Hirsch or Sforno or the Karaite Nahawendi (recalling Maimonides' rule: accept the truth from whatever source it comes[11]), there is a note of universalism in Moses' final words that we need to hear again in this tense and troubled age. God loves not one nation but all, for they are all the work of His hands.

---

9. See also his commentary to Ex. 19:5.
10. Ephraim Urbach, ed., *Pitron Torah* (Jerusalem: Magnes, 1978).
11. Maimonides, *Shemona Perakim*, introduction.

The Inheritance That Belongs to All

Commenting on a key verse from *Parashat Vezot Haberakha*, a midrash tells a pointed story:

> Once R. Yannai was walking along the way when he met a man who was elegantly dressed. He said to him, "Will the master be my guest?" He replied, "As you please."
>
> R. Yannai then took him home and questioned him on Bible, but he knew nothing; on Talmud, but he knew nothing; on Aggada, but he knew nothing. Finally, he asked him to say Grace. The man, however, replied, "Let Yannai say grace in his house."
>
> R. Yannai then said to him, "Can you repeat what I tell you?" The man answered, "Yes." R. Yannai then said: "Say a dog has eaten Yannai's bread."
>
> The guest then rose up and seized R. Yannai, demanding, "Where is my inheritance that you have and are keeping from me?"
>
> "What inheritance of yours do I have?"

> He replied, "The children recite, 'Moses commanded us the Torah, an inheritance of the congregation of Jacob' (Deut. 33:4). It is not written, 'congregation of Yannai,' but 'congregation of Jacob.'"[1]

It is a powerful story. R. Yannai sees an elegantly dressed stranger and assumes that he must be well educated. He takes him home and discovers the man has had no Jewish education whatsoever. He knows nothing of the rabbinic literature. He cannot even say Grace after Meals.

R. Yannai, a Torah scholar, looks down at the guest with contempt. But the stranger, with great dignity, says to him in effect: "The Torah is my inheritance as well as yours. Since you have much, and I have none, share a little of what you have with me. Instead of dismissing me, teach me."

Few ideas in the history of Judaism have greater power than this: the idea that Torah knowledge belongs to everyone; that everyone should have the chance to learn; that education should be universal; that everyone should be, if possible, literate in the laws, the history, and the faith of Judaism; that education is the highest form of dignity and should be accessible to all.

This idea goes so far back and so deep in Judaism that we can easily forget how radical it is. Knowledge – in the phrase commonly attributed to Sir Francis Bacon – is power. Those who have it are usually reluctant to share it with others. Most societies have had literate elites who controlled the administration of government. To this day, many professions use a technical vocabulary intelligible only to insiders, so that their knowledge is impenetrable to outsiders. [2]

Judaism was different, profoundly so. I have speculated that this is connected with the fact that the birth of Judaism happened at roughly the same time as the birth of the Proto-Semitic alphabet, appearing in the age of the patriarchs, and whose earliest traces have been discovered in the Sinai desert in areas where slaves worked. The alphabet, with its

---

1. Leviticus Rabba 9.
2. See Amos Funkenstein and Adin Steinsaltz, *The Sociology of Ignorance* [Hebrew] (Tel Aviv: Ministry of Defence, 1988).

mere twenty-two symbols, for the first time opened up the possibility of a society of universal literacy. Judaism, as we saw earlier, bears the mark of this throughout. Abraham was chosen to be a teacher: "For I have chosen him so that he will instruct his children and his household after him to keep the way of the Lord" (Gen. 18:19). Moses repeatedly speaks about education: "Teach them to your children, speaking of them when you sit at home and when you travel on the way, when you lie down and when you rise" (Deut. 11:19).

Above all is the personal example of Moses himself. At a critical moment, when Eldad and Medad were prophesying in the camp and Joshua felt that Moses' authority was being challenged, Moses replied: "Are you jealous on my behalf? Would that all the Lord's people were prophets and that the Lord would put His Spirit on them!" (Num. 11:29). Moses wished that everyone shared his access to the Divine.

The distinctive character of the covenant-making ceremony at Mount Sinai lay in the fact that it was, uniquely in the religious history of humankind, a revelation of God not to a prophet or an elite but to *the entire people*, a point the Torah stresses repeatedly: "The people all responded together" (Ex. 19:8); "Then he took the Book of the Covenant and read it to the people" (Ex. 24:7).

The septennial covenant renewal ceremony, *hak'hel*, was to include everyone: "Assemble the people – men, women, and children, and the strangers living in your towns – so they can listen and learn to fear the Lord your God and follow carefully all the words of this law" (Deut. 31:12). It was not that everyone *may* have knowledge of the laws and traditions of the people; it was that they *must*. This was a path-breaking form of egalitarianism: not equality of power or wealth but equality of access to education.

The speeches that constitute the book of Deuteronomy were in themselves the record of a pioneering adult education experience in which the master-prophet took the entire people as his disciples, teaching them both the law – the commands, statutes, and judgements – and no less importantly, the history that lay behind the law. Hence the prologue to the "song" of *Haazinu*: "Moses recited the words of this song from beginning to end in the hearing of the whole assembly of Israel" (Deut. 31:30).

Hence, likewise, the prologue to Moses' blessing in *Parashat Vezot Haberakha*: "This is the blessing with which Moses, the man of God, blessed the Israelites before his death.... Moses commanded us the Torah, an inheritance of the congregation of Jacob" (Deut. 33:1, 4). This is the verse quoted by R. Yannai's guest as proof that Torah belongs to everyone. It is the possession not of the learned, the elect, the specially gifted, not of a class or caste. It is the inheritance of the entire congregation of Jacob.

The impact of this radical democratisation of knowledge can be seen in a remarkable detail in the book of Judges. The context is this: Gideon (c. 1169 BCE) had been waging war against the Midianites. He asks the people of the town of Sukkoth to give his troops food. They are famished and exhausted. The people refuse. First, they say, win the war, and then we will give you food. Gideon is angry, but goes on to win the war. On his return, we read: "He caught a young man of Sukkoth and questioned him, and the young man wrote down for him the names of the seventy-seven officials of Sukkoth, the elders of the town" (Judges 8:14). The rest of the story does not concern us here. What is extraordinary is that, more than three thousand years ago, an Israelite leader took it for granted that a young man, chosen at random, could read and write! What is more impressive is that this is an incidental detail rather than something to which the narrator wishes to draw attention.

Nor was the lesson forgotten. In the fifth century BCE, seeking to restore coherence to a nation that had suffered defeat and exile by the Babylonians, Ezra convened the people in Jerusalem, giving them what in essence was an adult education seminar in Jewish literacy:

> So on the first day of the seventh month Ezra the priest brought the Law before the assembly, which was made up of men and women and all who were able to understand. He read it aloud from daybreak till noon as he faced the square before the Water Gate in the presence of the men, women, and others who could understand. And all the people listened attentively to the Book of the Law. (Neh. 8:2–3)

He and Nehemiah had positioned Levites throughout the crowd so that they could explain to everyone what was being said and what it meant

(Neh. 8:8). This went on for many days. Ezra became, as was Moses, an exemplar of a new kind of leadership, born in biblical Israel: *the teacher as hero*. Eventually this became the basis of the Judaism that survived the cultural challenge of Greece and the military might of Rome: not the Judaism of kings, priests, palaces, and Temple but the Judaism of the school, the synagogue, and the house of study. By the first century, a complete system of universal, compulsory education was in place, an achievement the Talmud attributes to Yehoshua b. Gamla (Bava Batra 21a), the first of its kind anywhere in the world.

Not until modern times did this idea of universal education spread beyond Judaism. It did not exist even in England, then the premier world power, until the Education Act of 1870. It has taken the internet revolution – Google and the rest – to make it a reality throughout the world. Even today, some fifty million children are still deprived of education, in countries like Somalia, Eritrea, Haiti, Comoros, and Ethiopia.

That education is the key to human dignity and should be equally available to all is one of the most profound ideas in all of history. It was born in those powerful words of *Parashat Vezot Haberakha*: "Moses commanded us the Torah, an inheritance of the congregation of Jacob."

Moses the Man

"And Moses the servant of the Lord died there in Moab as the Lord had said. He buried him in Moab, in the valley opposite Beth Peor, but to this day no one knows his burial place" (Deut. 34:5–6). With these words the life of the greatest leader Israel ever had draws to a close.

The Torah ends as it began, with an act of tenderness on the part of God. Just as, at the beginning, He had breathed the breath of life into the first man, so now at the close of the Mosaic books He buries the greatest of men as the breath of life departs from him. There is a kind of closure, a redemption, a *tikkun*: Adam and Eve had been prevented from eating from the Tree of Life, but Moses gave the Torah – "a tree of life to all who hold fast to it" (Prov. 3:18) – to Israel, granting them their taste of eternity. But there is also a sense of exile and incompletion: just as Adam and Eve had been forced to leave Eden, so Moses was prevented from entering the Promised Land.

Both stories are essentially about what it is to be human. The name *Adam* itself comes from the word *adama*, "the earth." The same play on words appears in both cases. In that of Adam, "the Lord God formed the man [*haadam*] from the dust of the ground [*haadama*] and breathed into his nostrils the breath of life" (Gen. 2:7). In the case of Moses, "the man Moses was very humble, more humble than any man [*haadam*] on the face of the earth [*haadama*]" (Num. 12:3).

The parallel is striking. Though we are each in the "image and likeness" of God, we are also "dust of the earth," embodied souls, part of the natural universe with its inexorable laws of growth, decay, and decline. We cannot live forever, and neither the first man, fashioned by God Himself, nor the greatest man, who saw God "face-to-face," is an exception to the rule. For each of us there is a Jordan we will not cross, a journey we will not finish, a paradise we will not reach this side of the grave.

Each age has had its own image of Moses. For the more mystically inclined sages Moses was the man who ascended to heaven at the time of the giving of the Torah, where he had to contend with the angels who opposed the idea that this precious gift be given to mere mortals. God told Moses to answer them, which he did decisively: "Do angels work that they need a day of rest? Do they have parents that they need to be commanded to honour them? Do they have an evil inclination that they need to be told, 'Do not commit adultery'?" (Shabbat 88a). This is the Moses who out-argues angels.

Other sages saw Moses as *Rabbenu*, "our teacher" – a scholar and master of the law, a role which they invested with astonishing authority. They went so far as to say that when Moses prayed for God to forgive the people for the Golden Calf, God replied, "I cannot, for I have already vowed, 'One who sacrifices to any god shall be destroyed' (Ex. 22:19), and I cannot revoke My vow." Moses replied, "Master of the universe, have You not taught me the laws of annulling vows? One may not annul his own vow, but a sage may do so." Moses thereupon annulled God's vow.[1]

For Philo, the first-century Jewish philosopher from Alexandria, Moses was a philosopher-king of the type depicted in Plato's *Republic*.[2] He governs the nation, organises its laws, institutes its rites, and conducts himself with dignity and honour. He is wise, stoical, and

1. Exodus Rabba 43:4.
2. Philo, *The Life of Moses*.

self-controlled. This is the Greek Moses, looking not unlike Michelangelo's famous sculpture.

Yet what is so moving about the portrayal of Moses in the Torah is none of these. Rather, it is that he appears before us as quintessentially human. No religion has more deeply and systemically insisted on the absolute otherness of God and man, heaven and earth, the Infinite and finite. Other cultures have blurred the boundary, making some human beings seem godlike, perfect, infallible. There is such a tendency – marginal to be sure, but never entirely absent – within Jewish life itself: to see sages as saints, great scholars as angels, to gloss over their doubts and shortcomings and turn them into superhuman emblems of perfection. Tanakh, however, is greater than that. It tells us that God, who is never less than God, never asks us to be more than simply human.

Moses is a human being. We see him despair and want to die. We see him lose his temper. We see him on the brink of losing his faith in the people he has been called on to lead. We see him beg to be allowed to cross the Jordan and enter the land. Moses is the hero of those who wrestle with the world as it is and with people as they are, knowing that "it is not for you to complete the task, but neither are you free to desist from it" (Mishna Avot 2:16).

The Torah insists that "to this day no one knows his burial place" (Deut. 34:6), to avoid his grave being made a place of pilgrimage or worship. It is all too easy to turn human beings, after their death, into saints and demigods. Moses does not exist in Judaism as an object of worship but as a role model for each of us to aspire to. He is the eternal symbol of a human being made great by what he strove for, not by what he actually achieved. The titles conferred by him in the Torah – "the man Moses" (Num. 12:3), "servant of the Lord" (Deut. 34:6), "a man of God" (Deut. 33:1) – are all the more impressive for their modesty. Moses continues to inspire.

The power of Moses' story is precisely that it affirms our mortality. There are many explanations of why Moses was not allowed to enter the Promised Land, but one of the most persuasive is that of Franz Kafka:

> He is on the track of Canaan all his life; it is incredible that he should see the land only when on the verge of death. This dying

> vision of it can only be intended to illustrate how incomplete a moment is human life; incomplete because a life like this could last for ever and still be nothing but a moment. Moses fails to enter Canaan not because his life was too short but because it is a human life.[3]

Moses was not Abraham, irenic, serene, composed, a man who lived far from the clamour of politics, private in his relationship with God. He belonged to a later stage of history, when Israel was no longer a family clan but a people, with all that implies in terms of potential conflict and strife. He was a man poised between earth and heaven, bringing God's word to the people and the people's word to God, often wrestling with both, trying to persuade the people to obey and God to forgive.

Not only did Moses encounter God in a burning bush; he *was* a burning bush, aflame with a passion for justice, who (unlike Aaron, his brother) preferred principle to compromise. Rashi notes that the mourning for Aaron was more widespread than for Moses (of Aaron it says, "The entire house of Israel grieved" [Num. 20:29]; in the case of Moses the word "entire" is missing [Deut. 34:8]). The reason is that Aaron was a man of peace; Moses was a man of truth. We love peace, but truth is sometimes hard to bear. People of truth have enemies as well as friends.

Five times, the Torah refers to Moses as *ish*, "man."[4] Moses was the greatest Jew who ever lived, but he was and remained a human being. This is an unmistakable theme of these closing chapters. The Torah is intimating an axiom fundamental to its vision: *if God is God then humanity can become humanity*. Never may the boundaries be blurred. The heroes of Judaism are not gods in human form. To the contrary, *the absolute transcendence of God means the absolute responsibility of mankind.*

In Judaism more than any other faith in history, the human person reaches its full stature, dignity, and freedom. We are not tainted with original sin. We are not bidden to total submission. These are honourable ways of seeing the human condition, but *they are not the Jewish way.*

3. Franz Kafka, *Diaries 1914–1923*, ed. Max Brod, trans. Martin Greenberg and Hannah Arendt (New York: Schocken, 1965), 195–96.
4. Ex. 11:3, 32:1, 23; Num. 12:3; Deut. 33:1.

That is why Judaism was and always will be a distinctive voice in the conversation of mankind.

Ha'ish Moshe: Moses, mortal, fallible, full of doubts about himself, often frustrated, occasionally angry, once falling into an abyss of despair – that is the Moses who set his seal on the people he led to freedom, permanently enlarging their horizons of aspiration. The Moses we meet in the Torah is not a mythical figure, an epic hero, an archetype, his blemishes airbrushed away to turn him into an object of adoration. He is human – gloriously human.

Maimonides writes, in his great declaration of human free will: "Every human being [note: not just "every Jew"] may become *righteous like Moses our teacher* or wicked like Jeroboam" (emphasis added).[5] Such an assertion, made of any other founder of any other faith, would sound absurd, but of Moses it does not sound absurd. His very humanity brings him close and summons us to greatness. The clear, absolute, ontological boundary between heaven and earth means that God never asks humanity to be more or less than human.

This is an austere view of the world but it is also the most lucid I know, and ultimately the most humane. It is the most lucid because it insists on a radical distinction between the infinite and finite, the eternal and ephemeral, God and us. It is the most humane because it invests each of us, equally, with dignity sub specie aeternitatis. We are, all of us, the image and likeness of God. We need no intermediary to speak to God. We need no priest or divine intercessor to be forgiven by God. We are each the son or daughter of God.

The distance between us and God may be infinite, but there is a bridge across the abyss, namely, *language*, words, communication. In revelation God speaks to us. In prayer we speak to God. It is that shared conversation that allows an Abraham, who calls himself "dust and ashes" (Gen. 18:27), to say to God, "Shall not the Judge of all the earth deal justly?" (18:25). It is that possibility of dialogue that allows Moses to say, "But now, please forgive their sin – but if not, then blot me out of the book You have written" (Ex. 32:32). It is that ongoing dialectic of Written and Oral Torah – divine word and human interpretation – that

5. Maimonides, *Mishneh Torah, Hilkhot Teshuva* 5:2.

has embraced patriarchs and prophets, sages and scribes, poets and philosophers, commentators and codifiers, and has not ceased from Moses' day to ours.

Not wrongly, therefore, did Jewish tradition, when it sought to accord Moses the highest honour, call him not Moses the liberator, the lawgiver, architect of a nation, military hero, or even greatest of the prophets, but simply *Moshe Rabbenu*, Moses our teacher. "Moses commanded us the Torah, an inheritance of the congregation of Jacob" (Deut. 33:4). Those words – no mere words but the covenantal text shaping the pattern of Jewish life and the structure of Jewish history – are in every generation the link between us and heaven: never broken, never annulled, never lost, never old. God may "hide His face" but He never withdraws His word.

As we take our leave of Moses, and he of us, the picture we have is indelible: it is a picture of the man who came close to despair yet left an immortal legacy of hope, who died without finishing his journey yet who has been with the Jewish people on its journeys ever since. It is his very humanity that shines forth from the pages of the Torah, sometimes with such radiance that we are afraid to look, but always and only a mortal and fallible human being, a medium through whom God spoke, an emissary through whom God acted, reminding us eternally that though we too are only mortal, we too can achieve greatness to the extent that we allow the presence of God to flow through us, His word guiding us, His breath giving us life.

To Live Is to Serve

What choice would you have made in the circumstances? There are three options. You have the chance to live the life of an adopted son of a princess in the greatest empire of the ancient world at the summit of its achievements. It would have been an existence of almost unimaginable wealth and power. The tomb of Tutankhamun, discovered in 1922 by the English archaeologist Howard Carter, still staggers the imagination by what it contained: the gold, the jewels, the artistry, the veneration to the point of deification. To be part of the inner circle of the court of the pharaohs at around that time would have made you a member of a gilded elite such as has existed only rarely in human history.

Alternatively, you could spend your days as a shepherd in Midian, with a loyal wife, an influential father-in-law, and two sons, tending your flock in the quiet and peace, far from the struggles of the world, alone with the landscape and the wind and the sky, at one with God who lets you lie down in green pastures, leading you by the still waters, restoring your soul. This is not a life of wealth and power but it is one in gentle harmony with the universe, a pastoral symphony.

Or, third, you could take on the leadership of a notoriously fractious nation of slaves, tasked with leading them to freedom. This will force you into repeated confrontations with Pharaoh and the Egyptians, with your own people, and often enough with God Himself. Why would anyone take this third option? Small wonder that, when God called him to undertake the mission, Moses kept saying no until at last God became angry and refused to take no for an answer.

The result was forty tempestuous years in which there was little tranquillity, still less appreciation on the part of those he led, and a succession of moments of frustration, anger, and disappointment. On one occasion Moses fell into a pit of despair so intense that he asked God to kill him rather than force him to continue: "If this is how You are going to treat me, kill me now, if I have found favour in Your sight, and let me not see my misery" (Num. 11:15).

There never was nor ever will be another Moses, but his life overturned all conventional wisdom about leadership. We judge leaders by their success. Moses failed at almost every stage. When he first tried to secure freedom for the Israelites, Pharaoh responded by making their burdens worse. The Israelites complained. They continued to complain through the long years of wandering. They had no food; they had no water; the food was boring; the water was bitter; they wanted to go back. Three days after the miracle of the division of the Red Sea, the people were again complaining. Forty days after the greatest revelation in history, at Mount Sinai, the people made a Golden Calf. On the brink of entry into the land, the spies brought back a demoralising report, delaying their arrival by forty years.

Korah challenged Moses' leadership. His own brother and sister spoke negatively about him. He himself, for a momentary lapse in striking the rock, was forbidden to enter the Promised Land, and all his prayers to have the decree lifted were refused. His own sons failed to follow in his footsteps; neither became his successor. He was devastated at how little his impact was on the people. Despite all they had experienced, they did not change. Nor did he hold out any great hope for the future. As he told the next generation, "I know how rebellious and stiff-necked you are! See, even while I am still alive with you today, you have rebelled against the Lord. How much more will you do so after my death?" (Deut. 31:27).

Can a life of failures be a success? In worldly terms, no. In spiritual terms, emphatically yes. His obituary in *Parashat Vezot Haberakha* may begin in an exceptionally low-key way: "And Moses the servant of the Lord died there in Moab as the Lord had said" (Deut. 34:5). But the Torah does not leave it that way. It adds, in its closing words:

> Since then, no prophet has risen in Israel like Moses, whom the Lord knew face-to-face, who did all those signs and wonders the Lord sent him to do in Egypt – to Pharaoh and to all his officials and to his whole land. For no one has ever shown the mighty power or performed the awesome deeds that Moses did in the sight of all Israel. (Deut. 34:10–12)

The sages debated who wrote those words. Was it Moses himself, at God's dictation, writing with tears in his eyes, or was it his faithful disciple Joshua (Bava Batra 15a)? I like to think it was the second, because it was the verdict of history, and we never get to see the verdict of history in our lifetime, not even Moses. He was one of the first of that long list of people who did not live to see their fame.

Jeremiah was mocked and abused for his prophetic warnings. At one time he was imprisoned, at another he narrowly escaped death. His prophecies were ignored. He lived to see his nation conquered, the Temple destroyed, and the people taken into captivity. R. Akiva believed that Bar Kokhba was a messianic figure destined to restore freedom to his people. Instead the rebellion was suppressed by the Romans and Akiva himself put to an agonising death. In more recent times, the great rabbi and diplomat from Amsterdam, Menasseh ben Israel, petitioned Cromwell in 1655 to readmit Jews to England. In the end, Cromwell issued no formal declaration, having been advised by his own counsellors that none was necessary. Menasseh returned home in 1657, a disappointed man convinced, wrongly, that he had failed. Yet each of these in different ways was a hero of their time, their achievements celebrated by posterity.

This applies not only to religious leaders but to many others. During his lifetime, Johann Sebastian Bach was not considered the greatest composer of his day – not even of his own family. Van Gogh sold only one painting. Emily Dickinson had only ten poems published. Not until many years after his death did people realise the significance of Gregor Mendel's discovery of the principles of genetics. Not only did Franz Kafka have no idea of the fame he would posthumously achieve, but he had instructed his friend Max Brod to destroy his unpublished manuscripts after he died. Only because Brod decided not to do we have such masterpieces as *The Trial* and *The Castle*. We never know what will happen to what we leave behind, including our place in people's hearts.

But there are certain things we can know. I discovered this as soon as I became a rabbi and had to officiate at funerals. Because I was new to the community, for the first few years I did not always know the deceased, and had to ask family and friends what they most respected and admired about those they had lost. That was when I discovered the difference between what David Brooks calls *résumé virtues* and *eulogy virtues*.[1]

Résumé virtues are what we write on job applications: our qualifications, skills, achievements, and worldly successes. Not surprisingly I discovered that these were not the things people were remembered for. They were remembered for their steadfastness as marriage partners, parents, and friends; for the acts of kindness they performed; for the way they supported the community and their favourite charities; for the willingness with which they gave their time when help was needed. These are the quiet virtues but they are our greatest legacy to the future. Comforting mourners, and being comforted, I discovered how deeply acts of kindness engrave themselves in people's memories and live on as they inspire their recipients to "pay it forward" and do acts of *ḥesed* to others as a way of acknowledging the *ḥesed* that was done to them. Good deeds as well as bad are contagious. Live in the company of altruistic people and you will become more altruistic.

In the end what made Moses so compelling a role model is not that he performed wonders nor that he spoke God's word and taught His laws. The wonders and the words were not his. They were God's. Moses' greatness lay in the fact that he was a "servant of the Lord." That is the accolade the Torah gives him: "And Moses the servant of the Lord

1. I make the point in my book *Celebrating Life* (New York: Continuum, 2012), 50–52; David Brooks makes it much more eloquently in *The Road to Character* (London: Allen Lane, 2015).

died there in Moab." He is called this eighteen times in Tanakh. The only other person to win this accolade was Joshua, who is called this twice. Moses went where God sent him, never claimed credit for himself, and he, the humblest of men, was never guilty of hubris. He simply served.

Moses defended the people to God even when they were guilty, because he knew that God had appointed him their defender. He thought of himself as an ordinary person through whom extraordinary things happened. Surely, he eventually understood that the things he thought disqualified him from leading turned out to be his most important strengths. For instance, the fact that he could not speak, was not a man of words, and was, as he put it, a man of uncircumcised lips, meant that when the words flowed from his mouth, people knew they were God's, not his.

What Moses taught us is that we are as big as the space we create within ourselves for people other than us, causes bigger than us, ideals that make the world a more just and gentle place; what makes us great are the principles by which, and the causes for which, we live.

Clever, gifted people sometimes fail to see this. I have known successful business people who ruined their reputation and ended their days in shame for the sake of a deal, a deception, a cover-up, they should not have made, for a financial gain they did not need. I have seen successful people take advantage of their position to perform acts that abused others, thinking that their power made them immune from prosecution. I have seen politicians betray their colleagues out of frustrated ambition or spite or revenge, heedless of the fact that they were thereby ending their careers, because no one with sense would ever respect or trust them again. I have seen people harm others and destroy themselves because they tried to be clever and failed to be wise. Thinking they could deceive others, they forgot that we cannot deceive God, and the only person we ever really deceive is ourselves. Moses is a standing refutation of shallowness in the course of a life.

In one of the more extraordinary moments of modern times, on April 3, 1968, Martin Luther King Jr. delivered a sermon in a church in Memphis, Tennessee. At the end of his address, he turned to the last day of Moses' life, when the man who had led his people to freedom was taken by God to a mountaintop from which he could see in the distance the land he was not destined to enter. That, said King, was how he felt that night:

> I just want to do God's will. And He's allowed me to go up to the mountain. And I've looked over. And I've seen the promised land. I may not get there with you. But I want you to know tonight that we, as a people, will get to the promised land.[2]

That night was the last of his life. The next day he was assassinated. At the end, the still young Christian preacher – he was not yet forty – who had led the civil rights movement in the United States identified not with a Christian figure but with Moses.

He learned from Moses' life that "it is not for you to complete the task" (Mishna Avot 2:16). He learned something more: "Everybody can be great," he said, "because anybody can serve. You do not have to have a college degree to serve. You do not have to make your subject and verb agree to serve. You only need a heart full of grace. A soul generated by love."[3]

What then does the story of Moses tell us? That it is right to fight for justice even against regimes that seem indestructible. That God is with us when we take our stand against oppression. That we must have faith in those we lead, even if they lack faith in us. That change, though slow, is real. That people are eventually transformed by high ideals even though it may take centuries. That we rarely live to see the full impact of our lives. What matters is to do right because it is right, to be honourable, do our duty, accept responsibility, and blame no one but ourselves for our failures. Nor do we need seek recognition for our success. If we have earned it, it will come, even if we do not live to see it. That is the way of Moses.

In one of its most powerful statements about him, the Torah states that he was "a hundred and twenty years old when he died, yet his eyes

2. Martin Luther King Jr., *I've Been to the Mountaintop* (San Francisco: HarperCollins, 1994), 34.
3. Martin Luther King Jr., "The Drum Major Instinct" speech (Ebenezer Baptist Church, Atlanta, GA, February 4, 1968).

were undimmed and his strength unabated" (Deut. 34:7). I used to think that "his eyes were undimmed" and "his strength unabated" were merely two sequential phrases, until I realised that the first was the explanation for the second. Why was Moses' strength unabated? Because his eyes were undimmed – because he never lost the ideals of his youth. Though he sometimes lost faith in himself and his ability to lead, he never lost faith in the cause: in God, service, freedom, the right, the good, and the holy. His words at the end of his life were as impassioned as they had been at the beginning.

That is Moses, the eternal symbol of how a human being, without ever ceasing to be human, can become a giant of the moral life by being "a servant of God." Life is the opportunity to serve. The rest is commentary. Go and do. Go and teach. Go and heal. Go and be a blessing. That is Jewish spirituality, standing on one leg.

Mortality

In the whole of Midrash there is nothing to match, for drama and tragic depth, the extraordinary cycle of rabbinic comments on the death of Moses. Here, as nowhere else, rabbinic Judaism comes close to the great tragedies of ancient Greece, or the powerful prose of the book of Job.

In the Torah itself, the account of Moses' death is marked more by what is left unsaid than by what is said. Early in the book of Deuteronomy there is a brief reference to Moses' anguish that he would not be allowed to enter the land:

> I pleaded with the Lord at that time, saying, "O Lord God…let me, I pray, cross over and see the good land on the other side of the Jordan…." But the Lord was angry with me on your account and would not listen to me. The Lord said to me, "Enough! Never speak to Me of this matter again." (Deut. 3:23–26)

So Moses inducted Joshua as his successor. Then came his final moments, as God showed him the land across the Jordan while he stood on Mount Nebo, close yet heartbreakingly distant. Finally we read his obituary:

"So Moses the servant of the Lord died there in Moab as the Lord had said. He buried him ... in the valley... to this day no one knows his burial place" (Deut. 34:5–6).

The poignancy is almost unbearable, all the more so for being so understated. Even the greatest of human beings is mortal. All people have a Jordan they will not cross, a future they may glimpse from afar but will not live to see. Moses does not, like Abraham, grow old gracefully. He is still full of energy, his "strength unabated" (Deut. 34:7). God Himself attends to the funeral. We see God here as we saw Him at the beginning of the human story – tender, close, intimate, gentle. Yet the decree is inexorable. To be human is one day to die. Eternity belongs to God alone.

This simple narrative became high drama in the rabbinic literature. It is impossible here to give more than a taste of the long narrative told by the sages in various midrashim, eventually turned into an entire book known as *Petirat Moshe*, "The Death of Moses." Here, though, are some fragments from Deuteronomy Rabba:

> Ten times it was decreed that Moses should not enter the land of Israel.... Moses, however, made light of this, saying: "Israel committed great sins many times, but whenever I prayed for them, God immediately answered my prayer...seeing that I have not sinned from my youth, does it not stand to reason that when I pray on my own behalf, God should answer my prayer?"
>
> When God saw that Moses was making light of the matter...He swore by His great name that Moses should not enter the land of Israel...
>
> When Moses saw that the decree against him had been sealed, he began to fast and drew a circle and stood within it and said, "I will not move from here until You annul the decree ..."
>
> What did God do? At that moment He had it proclaimed in every gate of every heaven and in every court that they should not receive Moses' prayer, nor bring it before Him, because the decree against him had been sealed...
>
> Moses said to God, "Master of the universe, You know the labour and the pains I devoted to making Israel believe Your name..." [but his prayer was not answered]...

> Then Moses said to God, "Master of the universe, if You will not bring me into the land of Israel, leave me in this world so that I may live and not die." God replied to Moses, "If I do not make you die in this world, how can I bring you back to life in the World to Come?"...
>
> At that hour God said to [the angel] Gabriel, "Gabriel, go forth and bring Moses' soul." Gabriel however replied, "Master of the universe, how can I witness the death of him who is equal to sixty myriads, and how can I behave harshly to one who possesses such qualities?"
>
> Then God said to [the angel] Michael, "Go forth and bring Moses' soul." Michael however replied, "Master of the universe, I was his teacher and he was my pupil, and I cannot therefore witness his death..."
>
> Then God kissed Moses and took away his soul with a kiss of the mouth, and God (as it were) wept, saying, "Who will rise up for Me against the evildoers? Who will stand up for Me against the workers of iniquity?"... The heavens wept, saying, "The godly man is perished out of the earth."[1]

These are fragments of an anguished drama. Moses begs to be allowed to live – if not across the Jordan, then in the desert; if not as a teacher, then as a disciple; if not as a human being then "as one of the beasts of the field." The heavens shake and the earth trembles with the force of his prayer, but to no avail. Moses is human, and even the greatest human must die. Yet the very angels refuse God's request that they bring Him Moses' soul. Eventually God knows that it must be He who does it – and He does it "with a kiss," the rabbinic phrase for a serene death. Even God weeps that such a man must die, yet such is the condition of life under the heavens. All that is physical must decline and decay; life on earth is transitory. To wish it otherwise is to will the impossible.

1. An extensive selection and translation can be found in Hayim Nahman Bialik and Yehoshua Ravnitzky, *The Book of Legends*, trans. William Braude (New York: Schocken, 1992), 101–5.

The midrash does not underplay the tragedy of death, despite the eternity of the soul and its life in the World to Come. The sages knew that death is part of life and what makes us human.

If we lived forever, life itself would have no shape, no edge, no urgency, no compelling purpose. We would not act. For anything we wished to do, there would always be time in the future. We would leave our children, and be left by our parents, no space to be ourselves, to write our own chapter in the human story. The very fact of our mortality means that we have our moment on the stage of history, when everything depends on us. Our parents are already old or middle-aged; our children are too young. That is when we give to both, our parents by our care, our children by our nurture, for it is our turn to achieve full strength, to exercise the range and scope of our powers and make our unique contribution. Space is what our parents give us and what we give our children – and space is a product of time. If we did not vacate our place, what would we confer on our children but an endless sense of belatedness, of arriving on the scene too late?

If we lived forever, would we not know love, for the very power of love – like a tree in blossom, a flower in bloom – is tied to the knowledge that its moment is all too brief and that soon it too will perish. Love lives in its vulnerability. It is our deepest longing for timelessness in the midst of time. It transfigures us precisely because we know we cannot hold on to it. Lover and beloved will age; first one then the other will die. So we hold on to one another, hoping that the intensity of our longing and belonging will still the moment, knowing that even if it does not, at least we will have known that "love is as strong as death" (Song 8:6).

If we lived forever, we would not create – for the deepest source of the creative urge is the desire to make something that will live on after us, that will have the immortality we lack. Hence those great lines of Shakespeare where he speaks of the power of poetry to defeat death and the loss of beauty and love:

> But thy eternal Summer shall not fade
> Nor lose possession of that fair thou owest;
> Nor shall Death brag thou wanderest in his shade,

When in eternal lines to time thou growest:
So long as men can breathe, or eyes can see,
So long lives this, and this gives life to thee.[2]

Death gives meaning to life as a frame gives shape to a picture, as the last page gives structure to a story, as the closing chord gives form to the symphony. The very knowledge that we will not live forever, that we are here for all too short a time, that the world will continue after us, charges us with our most compelling energies. We have dreams but we know they will not all be fulfilled. Therefore we must choose and plan and act. We become creators of the single most consequential work of art we will ever execute – our life itself. We are the co-author and central character of our story – and because it is finite, life is capable of having a story-like structure. A novel that never ends is not a story. The ending itself – happy, tragic, serene, unfulfilled – is what gives the whole its colour and tone. That is why we read stories, watch films and plays. They allow us momentarily to experience life as art, to step out of time the better to understand time.

We are mortal. But we have immortal longings. That is the tension resolved by R. Tarfon's great imperative: "It is not for you to complete the task, but neither are you free to desist from it" (Mishna Avot 2:16).

We live on because the story of which we are a part is itself immortal. The world did not begin with us, nor will it end with our departure. We belong to a larger narrative, the story of a people who, long ago in the days of Abraham and Sarah, set out on a journey to a land of promise and a distantly glimpsed, not-yet-reached, vision of redemption.

The Argentinean writer Jorge Luis Borges has a poem, "Limits," in which he reflects on the poignancy of finitude, of the knowledge that we do not know when our life will end:

Of all the streets that blur in to the sunset,
there must be one (which, I am not sure)
that I by now have walked for the last time
without guessing it, the pawn of that Someone

2. Shakespeare, *Sonnet* 18.

who fixes in advance omnipotent laws,
sets up a secret and unwavering scale
for all the shadows, dreams, and forms
woven into the texture of this life.

If there is a limit to all things and a measure
and a last time and nothing more and forgetfulness,
who will tell us to whom in this house
we without knowing it have said farewell?[3]

All this is by way of prelude to one of the most paradoxical statements about death, given by the early-second-century sage R. Meir. To understand it, we must recall that in ancient Hebrew, *dalet* [=d] and *tav* [=t] were not hard consonants as they are for most speakers today. They were soft sounds – something like *th*. Hence the words *me'od* ("very") and *mavet* ("death") sounded far more alike than they do now. Playing on this similarity, R. Meir made a wordplay of far-reaching significance: "And God saw all that He had made, and behold it was very good [*tov me'od*]. This means, 'And behold *death* was good [*tov mavet*].'"[4]

This brief comment transforms our understanding of the Torah's account of humanity. Death was not a *punishment* brought about by the sin of the first human beings. It is, as Maimonides says in *Guide for the Perplexed*, the very condition of our existence as physical beings in a material world. To be physical *means* to be subject to decay and eventual oblivion.

To be sure, death is not the end. Something of us – the soul – endures. There is eternal life. But life in the World to Come, without a body, without wants, needs, desires, dreams, hopes, fears, is so unlike the one we experience here on earth that we cannot imagine it, nor even in any straightforward sense look forward to it. Though we know all the pain of bodily existence and though we know that one day our souls will be "bound in the bond of eternal life," yet we cling to this life as if it

3. Jorge Luis Borges, "Limits" (trans. Alastair Reid; see *The Oxford Book of Latin American Poetry: A Bilingual Anthology*, ed. Cecilia Vicuña and Ernesto Livon-Grosman [Oxford: Oxford University Press, 2009], 205).
4. Genesis Rabba 9:5.

were all, and we are not wrong to do so. Eternity, serenity, being bathed in the radiance of God transcend all we know or can ever know this side of the grave. Yet we sense that the very transience of this life gives it its vividness, the fragility of beauty which is the beauty of fragility.

So the Torah begins and ends with death. It begins with the decree of death when, in the Garden of Eden, Adam and Eve chose the pleasures of sight and touch and taste over those of the soul. It ends with the actuality of death when Moses, the hero of the Torah's central narrative, dies without crossing the Jordan and setting foot in the land to which he spent his life as a leader leading others.

In both cases we are conscious of *the beyond*: the beyond of Eden, paradise lost, and the beyond of the Promised Land, paradise not yet reached. These two define the human condition for us as individuals, and for Homo sapiens as a species. We live in *the between,* the liminal space between two eternities, the world of harmony that once was and the age of harmony that will be but is not yet. The world we inhabit is fissured and fractured by pain, conflict, violence, evil, hopes dashed, dreams unfulfilled, ideals disappointed, desires unsatisfied. Yet it remains glorious because it is never uneventful or predictable, transfiguring because of the power of love and art and goodness to capture within its finite frame signals of transcendence. No theistic religion has argued as consistently as Judaism for the presence of God and truth and beauty *here,* in this world, not just the next; in time, not just eternity; in life, not death and the World to Come.

That is why Moses *must* fight death and prefer life on earth to life among the ministering angels amid the deathless glory of heaven. The Moses we know – the man who fought injustice and slavery, who stood up against the most powerful empire of the ancient world, who more than any other "wrestled with God and with men" (Gen. 32:29) – was the figure who gave ultimate dignity to this world, not the next. Moses was not a man prepared to make his peace with the wrongs of his time in the knowledge that somewhere else, in some other order of existence, there is a world of perfect justice. "Do not go gentle into that dark night," wrote Dylan Thomas. "Rage, rage against the dying of the light."[5] Those

5. "Do Not Go Gentle into That Good Night," in *The Poems of Dylan Thomas,* ed. John Goodby (New York: New Directions, 2003), 239.

words could not have been said of Abraham or Isaac or Jacob. But they epitomise Moses. And to be a Jew is to be a disciple of Moses.

Yet Moses must lose the fight, his life an unfinished symphony. For R. Tarfon was right – "It is not for you to complete the task." Just as we did not begin the story we inherit, so we will leave it in God's time to those who are our heirs. To have had a part in it, to spend our hour on the stage, faithful to those who came before us and preparing those who will follow us to play their role in moving humanity one more step closer to redemption – that is life at its highest, knowing that we will not see the full fruits of our labours but knowing that what we have planted, others will reap, and what we have begun others will complete.

That bond of the generations we call covenant – the ethical connection between past and future – is what rescues life from tragedy, death from having the final word.

End Without an Ending

What an extraordinary way to end a book: not just *a* book but *the* Book of books – with Moses seeing the Promised Land from Mount Nebo, tantalisingly near yet so far away that he knows he will never reach it in his lifetime. This is an ending to defy all narrative expectations. A story about a journey should end at journey's end, with arrival at the destination. But the Torah terminates before the terminus. It concludes in medias res. It ends in the middle. It is constructed as an unfinished symphony.

We, the readers and listeners, feel Moses' personal sense of incompletion. He had dedicated a lifetime to leading the people out of Egypt to the Promised Land. Yet he was not granted his request to complete the task and reach the place to which he had spent his life as a leader leading the people. When he prayed, "Let me...cross over and see the good land on the other side of the Jordan," God replied, "Enough! Never speak to Me of this matter again" (Deut. 3:25–26).

Moses – the man who stood before Pharaoh demanding his people's freedom, who was unafraid even to challenge God Himself, who when he came down the mountain and saw the people dancing around the Golden Calf smashed the divinely hewn tablets, the holiest object ever to be held by human hands – pleaded for the one small mercy that would give completion to his life's work, but it was not to be. When he prayed for others he succeeded. When he prayed for himself, he failed. That in itself is strange.

Yet the sense of incompleteness is not merely personal, not just a detail in the life of Moses. It applies to the entire narrative as it has unfolded from the beginning of the book of Exodus. The Israelites are in exile. God charges Moses with the task of leading the people out of Egypt and bringing them to the land flowing with milk and honey, the country He had promised to Abraham, Isaac, and Jacob. It seems simple enough. Already in Exodus 13, the people have left, sent on their way by a Pharaoh and an Egypt ravaged by plagues. Within days, they hit an obstacle. Ahead of them is the Red Sea. Behind them are the rapidly approaching chariots of Pharaoh's army. A miracle happens. The sea divides. They pass over on dry land. Pharaoh's troops, their chariot wheels caught in the mud, drown. Now all that stands between them and their destination is the wilderness. Every problem they face – a lack of food, water, direction, protection – is solved by divine intervention mediated by Moses. What is left to tell, if not their arrival?

Yet *it does not happen*. Spies are sent to determine the best way of entering and conquering the land, a relatively straightforward task. They come back, unexpectedly, with a demoralising report. The people lose heart and say they want to go back to Egypt. The result is that God decrees that they will have to wait a full generation, forty years, before entering the land. It is not only Moses who does not cross the Jordan. The entire people have not done so by the time the Torah ends. That must await a new book, Joshua, not itself part of the Torah but rather of the *Nevi'im*, the later prophetic and historical texts.

This, from a literary point of view, is odd. But it is not accidental. In the Torah, style mirrors substance. The text is telling us something profound. The Jewish story ends without an ending. It closes without closure. There is in Judaism no equivalent of "and they all lived happily ever after" (the closest the Bible comes to this is the book of Esther). Biblical narrative lacks what Frank Kermode called "the sense of an ending."[1]

1. Frank Kermode, *The Sense of an Ending* (New York: Oxford University Press, 1967).

Jewish time is open time – open to a denouement not yet realised, a destination not yet reached.

This is not simply because the Torah records history, and history has no end. The Torah is telling us something quite different from history in the way the Greeks, Herodotus and Thucydides, wrote it. Secular history has no meaning. It simply tells us what happened. Biblical history, by contrast, is saturated with meaning. Nothing merely happens *bemikreh*, by chance.

This becomes clearer and clearer as we look, for example, at Genesis. God summons Abraham to leave his land, his birthplace, and his father's house and go "to the land I will show you" (Gen. 12:1). Abraham does so, and by verse 5, he has arrived. This sounds like the end of the story, but it turns out to be hardly the beginning. Almost immediately, there is a famine in the land and he has to leave. The same thing happens to Isaac, and eventually to Jacob and his children. The story that began with a journey to the land ends with the main characters outside the land, with both Jacob (49:29) and Joseph (50:25) asking their descendants to bring them back to the land to be buried.

Seven times, God promises Abraham the land – "Look around from where you are, to the north and south, to the east and west. All the land that you see I will give to you and your offspring forever" (Gen. 13:14–15). Yet when Sarah his wife dies, he has not a single plot of land in which to bury her, and has to buy one at an inflated price. Something similar happens to Isaac and Jacob. Genesis ends as Deuteronomy ends – with the promise but not yet the fulfilment, the hope but not yet the realisation.

So does Tanakh as a whole. The second book of Chronicles ends with the Israelites in exile. In its closing verse, the last line of Tanakh, Cyrus king of Persia gives permission for the exiles to return to their land: "Anyone of His people among you – may the Lord his God be with him, and let him go up" (II Chr. 36:23). Again, anticipation but not yet reality.

There is something significant here – though it lies so deep it is hard to explain. The Bible is a battle against myth. In myth, time is as it is in nature. It is cyclical. It goes through phases – spring, summer, autumn, winter; birth, growth, decline, death – but it always returns to where it began. The standard plot of myth is that order is threatened by the forces of chaos. In ancient times these were the gods of destruction. In modern times they are the dark forces of *Star Wars* and *Lord of the Rings*. The hero battles against them. He slips, falls, almost dies, but ultimately succeeds. Order is restored. The world is once again as it was. Hence "they all lived happily ever after." The future is the restoration of the past. There is a return to order, to the way things were before the threat, but there is no history, no progress, no development, no unanticipated outcome.

Judaism is a radical break with this way of seeing things. Instead, time becomes the arena of human growth. The future is not like the past. Nor can it be predicted, foreseen, the way the end of any myth can be foreseen. Jacob, at the end of his life, told his children, "Gather round, and I will tell you what will happen to you at the end of days" (Gen. 49:1). Rashi, quoting the Talmud, says: "Jacob sought to reveal the end, *but the Divine Presence departed from him.*" We cannot foretell the future, because *it depends on us* – how we act, how we choose, how we respond.

The future cannot be predicted, because we have free will. Even we ourselves do not know how we will respond to crisis until it happens. Only in retrospect do we discover ourselves. *We face an open future.* Only God, who is beyond time, can transcend time. Biblical narrative has no sense of an ending because it constantly seeks to tell us that we have not yet completed the task. That remains to be achieved in a future we believe in but will not live to see. We glimpse it from afar, the way Moses saw the holy land from the far side of the Jordan, but like him, we know we have not yet arrived. Judaism is the supreme expression of *faith as the future tense.*

The nineteenth-century Jewish philosopher Hermann Cohen put it this way:

> What Greek intellectualism could not create, prophetic monotheism succeeded in creating.... For the Greek, history is oriented solely toward the past. The prophet, however, is a seer, not a scholar.... The prophets are the idealists of history. Their seerdom created the concept of history as *the being of the future.* (Emphasis added.)[2]

2. Quoted in Ernst Cassirer, *The Philosophy of Symbolic Forms*, vol. 2, *Mythical Thought* (New Haven: Yale University Press, 1953), 120.

Harold Fisch, the literary scholar, summarised this in a hauntingly beautiful phrase: "the unappeased memory of a future still to be fulfilled."[3]

Judaism is the only civilisation to have set its golden age not in the past but in the future. We hear this at the beginning of the Moses story, although not until the end do we realise its significance. Moses asks God: What is Your name? God replies: *Ehyeh asher Ehyeh*, literally, "I will be what I will be" (Ex. 3:14). We assume this means something like "I am what I am – unlimited, indescribable, beyond the reach of a name." That may be part of the meaning. But the fundamental point is: *My name is the future.* "I am what will be." God is in the call from the future to the present, from the destination to us who are still on the journey. What distinguishes Judaism from Christianity is that in answer to the question "Has the Messiah come?" the Jewish answer is always: Not yet. Moses' death, his unfinished life, his glimpse of the land of the future, is the supreme symbol of the not-yet.

"It is not for you to complete the task, but neither are you free to desist from it" (Mishna Avot 2:16). The challenges we face as human beings are never resolved simply, quickly, completely. The task takes many lifetimes. It is beyond the reach of a single individual, even the greatest; it is beyond the scope of a single generation, even the most epic. Deuteronomy ends by telling us: "Never again has there arisen in Israel a prophet like Moses" (Deut. 34:10). But even his life was, necessarily, incomplete.

As we see him, on Mount Nebo, looking across the Jordan to Israel in the distance, we sense the vast, challenging truth that confronts us all. Each person has a promised land he or she will not reach, a horizon beyond the limits of his or her vision. What makes this bearable is our intense existential bond between the generations – between parent and child, teacher and disciple, leader and follower. The task is bigger than us, but it will live on after us, as something of us will live on in those we have influenced.

The greatest mistake we can make is to do nothing because we cannot do everything. Even Moses discovered that it was not for him to

3. Harold Fisch, *A Remembered Future* (Bloomington, IN: Indiana University Press, 1984), 19.

complete the task. That would only be achieved by Joshua, and even then the story of the Israelites was only just beginning. Moses' death tells us something fundamental about mortality. Life is not robbed of meaning because one day it will end. For in truth – even in this world, before we turn our thoughts to eternal life in the World to Come – we become part of eternity when we write our chapter in the book of the story of our people and hand it on to those who will come after us.

The task – building a society of justice and compassion, an oasis in a desert of violence and corruption – is greater than any one lifetime. The Jewish people have returned to the land, but the vision is not yet complete. This is still a violent, aggressive world. Peace still eludes us, as does much else. We have not yet reached the destination, though we see it in the distance, as did Moses.

The Torah ends without an ending to tell us that we too are part of the story; we too are still on the journey. And as we reach the Torah's closing lines we know, as did Robert Frost in his famous poem, that

> I have promises to keep,
> And miles to go before I sleep.[4]

4. Robert Frost, "Stopping by Woods on a Snowy Evening," from *The Poetry of Robert Frost,* ed. Edward Connery Lathem (New York: Holt, Rinehart and Winston, 1969), 224.

The fonts used in this book are from the Arno family

The Covenant & Conversation Series:

Genesis: The Book of Beginnings
Exodus: The Book of Redemption
Leviticus: The Book of Holiness
Numbers: The Wilderness Years
Deuteronomy: Renewal of the Sinai Covenant

Ceremony and Celebration
Lessons in Leadership
Essays on Ethics

Maggid Books
The best of contemporary Jewish thought from
Koren Publishers Jerusalem Ltd.